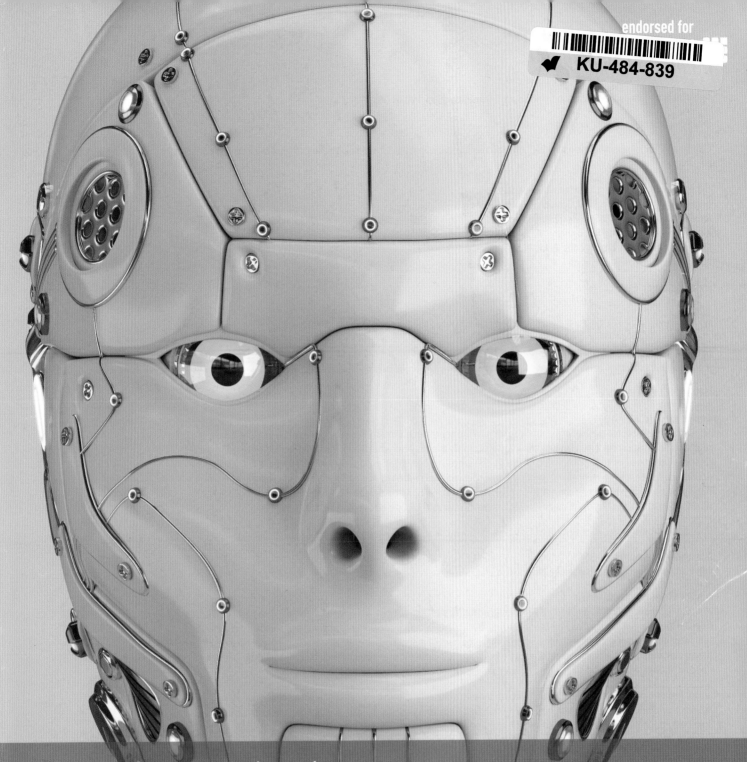

# Edexcel GCSE (9-1)
# Computer Science

Series Editor: Ann Weidmann

Authors: Chris Charles   Alex Hadwen-Bennett   David Waller   Jason Welch   Shaun Whorton

ALWAYS LEARNING

**PEARSON**

Published by Pearson Education Limited, 80 Strand, London, WC2R 0RL.

www.pearsonschoolsandfecolleges.co.uk

Copies of official specifications for all Edexcel qualifications may be found on the website: www.edexcel.com

Text © Pearson Education.
Typeset by Tek-Art, East Grinstead, West Sussex
Illustrations by Tek-Art, East Grinstead, West Sussex
Original illustrations © Pearson Education
Designed by Colin Tilley Loughrey
Cover photo: Shutterstock.com: Deniseus, Ociacia
Indexed by Sharon Redmayne

First published 2016

19 18 17 16
10 9 8 7 6 5 4 3 2 1

**British Library Cataloguing in Publication Data**
A catalogue record for this book is available from the British Library

**ISBN** 978 1 292 12588 6

Printed and bound in Great Britain at Bell & Bain, Glasgow

**Acknowledgements**
For acknowledgements please see page viii.

**A note from the publisher**
In order to ensure that this resource offers high-quality support for the associated Pearson qualification, it has been through a review process by the awarding body. This process confirms that this resource fully covers the teaching and learning content of the specification or part of a specification at which it is aimed. It also confirms that it demonstrates an appropriate balance between the development of subject skills, knowledge and understanding, in addition to preparation for assessment.

Endorsement does not cover any guidance on assessment activities or processes (e.g. practice questions or advice on how to answer assessment questions), included in the resource nor does it prescribe any particular approach to the teaching or delivery of a related course.

While the publishers have made every attempt to ensure that advice on the qualification and its assessment is accurate, the official specification and associated assessment guidance materials are the only authoritative source of information and should always be referred to for definitive guidance.

Pearson examiners have not contributed to any sections in this resource relevant to examination papers for which they have responsibility.

Examiners will not use endorsed resources as a source of material for any assessment set by Pearson.

Endorsement of a resource does not mean that the resource is required to achieve this Pearson qualification, nor does it mean that it is the only suitable material available to support the qualification, and any resource lists produced by the awarding body shall include this and other appropriate resources.

# Contents

ALFRED GEMBEH MSC MPhil PGCE

# Welcome to Edexcel GCSE (9-1) Computer Science

## Computational thinking in context

This course is designed to help you develop your knowledge and understanding of computer science through studying the importance of computation in the world and how it will evolve in the future. Through practical involvement in a range of activities you will apply this knowledge and develop the skills to help you succeed in your chosen pathway.

There are many benefits to taking the Edexcel GCSE Computer Science course:

- It has a **real applied focus**. You will be encouraged to put the theory you are learning into context and apply what you have learned to your own practical activities. This makes it much more fun.

- It reflects **today's world** – the issues and topics you will learn about are up to date and will help you to understand how technology can be used to tackle current issues that impact on modern society.

- You will gain a **well-rounded understanding of computer science**. Through an engaging introduction to the core principles, you will develop skills in problem solving and computational thinking. You will learn how to decompose and model aspects of real-world situations, and as a result be able to design, build and test a fully programmed solution to a problem.

- You will also have the opportunity to improve your **transferable skills**, developing 'underpinning' concepts that are useful in many subjects and careers, such as mathematics, science and engineering.

- If you do well in this course you will be in a good position to **progress to the next level of study** – whether this is an A level or a vocational qualification, such as a BTEC National. The content of this GCSE is ideal grounding for other qualifications; it has been designed using a similar approach to make the experience of moving on a smooth one.

## How you will be assessed

The GCSE course consists of three separate components:

Component 1: Principles of Computer Science

Component 2: Application of Computational Thinking

Component 3: Project

Components 1 and 2 are assessed by written examinations, each accounting for 40 per cent of the total mark. Component 3 is worth 20 per cent of the total mark and is internally assessed by your school. For more information about how you will be assessed, see the 'Preparing for your exam' section on page 226.

# How to use this book

This book is organised in the same way as the Edexcel GCSE specification, with six main chapters plus an additional section that supports you in preparing for examinations.

Each chapter gives you all the information you need to know and guides you through the content of the course in a practical and engaging way, making it clear what you will cover and giving you useful activities and questions to help you practise what you have learned.

In this student book there are lots of different features. They are there to help you learn about the content in your course in different ways, understand it from multiple perspectives and get the most from your learning.

- **Learning outcomes** – these are listed at the beginning of each chapter so you know exactly what you are going to learn and understand the related success criteria.

## Learning outcomes

By the end of this section you should be able to:

- describe what an algorithm is.
- explain what algorithms are used for.
- express algorithms as flowcharts, pseudo-code and written descriptions.
- use and describe the purpose of arithmetic operators.

- **Key terms** – there are certain terms that you will need to know and be able to explain. These boxes explain what the words mean. The words themselves are also highlighted in the main text, and you will find all the key terms in the Glossary at the end of the book.

## Key terms

**Sequence**: an ordered set of instructions.

**Algorithm**: a precise method for solving a problem. It consists of a sequence of step-by-step instructions.

- **Activities** – these are designed to build your knowledge and understanding and develop your computational and problem-solving skills.

## Activity 1 ?

Produce a written description of an algorithm for getting to school. It should start with leaving home and end with arriving at school. For example, the algorithm could start with 'Walk to bus stop'.

- **Worked example** – this feature has been included to help you understand how to carry out practical skills before you try an activity yourself.

## Worked example

```
SET correct TO 'LetMeIn'          #The variable 'correct' is assigned
                                   the value of the password stored in
                                   the system.

FOR index FROM 1 TO 3 DO
   SEND 'Please enter your password.' TO DISPLAY
   RECEIVE password FROM KEYBOARD
   IF password = correct THEN
      SEND 'You entered the correct password.' TO DISPLAY
   END IF
END FOR
```

# Introduction

- **Exam tip** – hints and tips to aid your learning and help you in the exam.

## Exam tip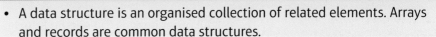

This question is testing your ability to select and design data structures. Make sure you have:

- identified a suitable data structure to store the data and justified your choice;
- provided the sample data requested (i.e. sales figures for two products for the first three months of the year).

Row and column headings can be included as long as they are clearly distinguishable from the data.

- **Summary** – a handy revision checklist of key points you will need to remember about the chapter.

## Summary

- A data structure is an organised collection of related elements. Arrays and records are common data structures.
- A one-dimensional array is a list of elements, each of which has a unique index value representing its position in the list.
- A two-dimensional array is a matrix of rows and columns. Each element in the array has a unique pair of indices, one to identify the row and one the column in which it is located.
- All the elements in an array have the same data type.
- A record consists of a collection of fields. The values stored in a record can be of different data types.

## Preparing for your exams

At the end of Chapter 6 there is an exam preparation section with tips and guidance for achieving success in your written exams. You will find example questions and answers, together with detailed notes and explanations about the quality of the answers shown. This will help you build your understanding of how to write better answers and achieve more marks.

# Acknowledgements

The publisher would like to thank the following for their kind permission to reproduce their photographs:

(Key: b-bottom; c-centre; l-left; r-right; t-top)

**123RF.com:** 123rf.com 140bc, blueximages 1, stockyimages 66; **Alamy Images:** Agencja Fotograficzna Caro 139, Andrew Aitchison 219, hugh nutt 206, Ian Dagnall 2, imageBROKER 211, Jan Miks 45, Jonathan Ball 145r, Paul Broadbent 145l, Richard Levine 55; **Photolibrary.com:** Image Source 75; **Shutterstock.com:** Adisa 140tl, Baloncici 56b, bloomua 140br, Burlingham 46, DavidTB 41, Dja65 140tc, Gaby Kooijman 56t, K. Miri Photography 140bl, kavione 140tr, Monkey Business Images 84, Pakhnyushcha 140c, Petros Tsonis 91, Platslee 110l, 123l, 123r, 110R, vectorfusionart 171, wavebreakmedia 74

**Cover images:** *Front:* **Shutterstock.com:** Deniseus, Ociacia

All other images © Pearson Education

The publisher would also like to thank the Python Software Foundation (www.python.org) for their kind permission to reproduce screenshots.

| | | | | 544,00 | | |
|---|---|---|---|---|---|---|
| ,00 | - | 36,29 % | | | 6.401,00 | - |
| 7,00 | + | 31,74 % | | 6.422,00 | | |
| 3,00 | + | 229,81 % | | 65.646,00 | 64.922,00 | + |
| 42,00 | + | 52,61 % | | 6.546,00 | 6.693,00 | - |
| 431,00 | + | 7,10 % | | 6.422,00 | 3.572,00 | + |
| .244,00 | + | 60,80 % | | 654,00 | 745,00 | - |
| .927,00 | + | 24,46 % | | 65.642,00 | 63.090,00 | |
| 1.498,00 | - | 29,53 % | | 64.565,00 | 55.245,00 | + |
| 45.229,00 | | 23,24 % | | 5.424,00 | 5.636,00 | + |
| 997,00 | + | 36,43 % | | 642,00 | 734,00 | - |
| 528,00 | + | 38,92 % | | 56.257,00 | 54.732,00 | + |
| 6.928,00 | + | | | 6.796,00 | 6.798,00 | + |
| | | | | 643,00 | 834,00 | - |

Problem solving

| | | | | 48.447,00 | 39.643,00 | - |
|---|---|---|---|---|---|---|
| 00 | 8.864,00 | 61,66 % | | 87.995,00 | 80.354,00 | + |
| ,00 | 1.282,00 | 3,36 % | | 7.653,00 | 7.934,00 | + |
| 1,00 | 4.920,00 | 7,19 % | | 73,00 | 127,00 | + |
| 39,00 | 129,00 | 23,35 % | | 1.223,00 | 1.583,00 | - |
| 36,00 | 6.582,00 | 18,68 % | | 32.124,00 | 31.844,00 | |
| 938,00 | 5.642,00 | 6,26 % | | 7.665,00 | 6.255,00 | + |
| .611,00 | 11.822,00 | 6,51 % | | 674,00 | 1.073,00 | + |
| 5.911,00 | 6.296,00 | 5,07 % | | 17.442,00 | 18.456,00 | - |
| 3.792,00 | 26,10 % | | | 6.378,00 | 5.724,00 | + |

(right column percentages: 44, 13,9, 3,8, 14,44, 3,91, 14,33 %, 2,71 %, 0,03 %, 29,70 %, 18,17 %, 8,68 %, 3,67 %, 73,97 %, 29,44 %, 0,87 %, 18,40 %, 59,20 %, 5,81 %, 10,25 %, 4,03 %)

# Problem solving

The route on this interactive map has been calculated using an algorithm

## 1.1 Algorithms

### Understanding algorithms

**Learning outcomes**

By the end of this section you should be able to:

- describe what an algorithm is.
- explain what algorithms are used for.
- express algorithms as flowcharts, pseudo-code and written descriptions.
- use and describe the purpose of arithmetic operators.

### An example of an algorithm

An interactive map is a useful way to find a route between two locations. This image shows a route between two cities that was calculated by a mapping program.

- It is **unambiguous** in telling the driver exactly what to do, like 'turn left', 'turn right' or 'continue straight'.
- It is a **sequence** of steps.
- It can be used again and will always provide the same result.
- It provides a solution to a problem, in this case how to get from London to Glasgow.

A solution to a problem with these characteristics is called an **algorithm**. Most problems have more than one solution, so different algorithms can be created for the same problem.

**Key terms**

**Unambiguous**: this means that the instructions cannot be misunderstood. Simply saying 'turn' would be ambiguous because you could turn left or right.

All instructions given to a computer must be unambiguous or it won't know what to do.

**Sequence**: an ordered set of instructions.

**Algorithm**: a precise method for solving a problem.

**Did you know?**

The computer program that created the algorithm to travel from London to Glasgow was following an algorithm of its own – an algorithm instructing it how to create another algorithm.

### Successful algorithms

There are three criteria for deciding whether an algorithm is successful.

- **Accuracy** – it must lead to the expected outcome (e.g. create a route from London to Glasgow).
- **Consistency** – it must produce the same result each time it is run.
- **Efficiency** – it must solve the problem in the shortest possible time using as few computer resources as possible. In this example the mapping software is replacing a manual method, and if it were no faster than looking in an atlas then it would not be an improvement on the older method. Later in the chapter there is a section on algorithms used to sort and search data. Some of these algorithms are more efficient than others and will sort the data far more quickly.

### The relationship between algorithms and programs

Algorithms and programs are closely related, but they are not the same. An algorithm is a detailed design for a solution; a program is the implementation of that design.

This chapter is all about algorithms. We look at how algorithms are implemented in **high-level programming languages** in Chapter 2. It's up to you whether you study these two chapters sequentially or in parallel. So you could either study Chapter 1 followed by Chapter 2, or learn about algorithms and how to create them in this chapter and at the same time consult Chapter 2 to find out how to translate algorithms into programs.

## Displaying an algorithm

We carry out many everyday tasks using algorithms because we are following a set of instructions to achieve an expected result, for example making a cup of coffee. If we have performed the task many times before, we usually carry out the instructions without thinking, but if we are doing something unfamiliar, such as putting together a flat-pack chest of drawers, then we follow the instructions very carefully.

An algorithm can be expressed in different ways.

### Written descriptions

A written description is the simplest way of expressing an algorithm. Here is an algorithm describing the everyday task of making a cup of instant coffee.

| Algorithm for making a cup of instant coffee |
|---|
| Fill kettle with water. |
| Turn on kettle. |
| Place coffee in cup. |
| Wait for water to boil. |
| Pour water into cup. |
| Add milk and sugar. |
| Stir. |

### Flowcharts

**Flowcharts** can be used to represent an algorithm graphically. They provide a more visual display.

There are formal symbols that have to be used in a flowchart – you can't just make up your own because nobody else would be able to follow your algorithm.

Figure 1.1 shows the flowchart symbols that should be used.

---

**Activity 1** ?

Produce a written description of an algorithm for getting to school. It should start with leaving home and end with arriving at school. For example, the algorithm could start with 'Walk to bus stop'.

 Indicates the start or end of an algorithm.

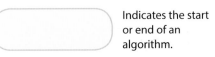 Indicates a process to be carried out.

 Indicates a decision to be made.

 Indicates an input or output.

Shows the logical flow of the algorithm.

**Figure 1.1** Flowchart symbols

# Problem solving

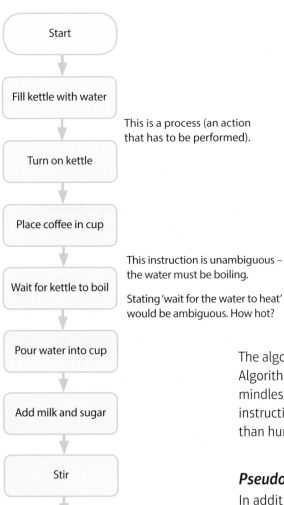

This is a process (an action that has to be performed).

This instruction is unambiguous – the water must be boiling.

Stating 'wait for the water to heat' would be ambiguous. How hot?

**Figure 1.2** Flowchart of an algorithm to make a cup of coffee

### Key term

**Pseudo-code**: a structured, code-like language that can be used to describe an algorithm.

### Activity 4 ?

There are many different versions of pseudo-code and often they are unique to a particular organisation or examination board. Investigate the Edexcel pseudo-code that you will need for your GCSE course and which will be used in this book.

The flowchart in Figure 1.2 is an alternative way of depicting the algorithm expressed above as a written description.

### Activity 2 ?

Display the 'journey to school' algorithm, which you created in the previous activity, as a flowchart.

### Activity 3 ?

A student has created a written algorithm for preparing a bath. Display the following as a flowchart – you may need to change the order or add actions.

- Put in the plug.
- Fill bath to the correct level.
- Check temperature is OK.

The algorithms you have looked at so far are designed for humans to follow. Algorithms also form the basis of computer programs. A computer is a mindless machine that simply does exactly what it is told and follows a set of instructions, but computers can carry out these instructions far more quickly than humans. That is why they are so useful.

## Pseudo-code

In addition to flowcharts and written descriptions, algorithms can also be expressed in **pseudo-code**. The pseudo-code can then be used to code the solution in an actual programming language.

It allows the developer to concentrate on the logic and efficiency of the algorithm without having to bother about the rules of any particular programming language. It is relatively straightforward to translate an algorithm written in pseudo-code into any high-level programming language.

## Example of a simple algorithm

To introduce the Edexcel pseudo-code, here is a simple algorithm that asks the user to input two numbers and then outputs the result of adding them together.

## Written description

### Algorithm for adding two numbers

Enter first number.
Enter second number.
Calculate total by adding first and second numbers.
Output total.

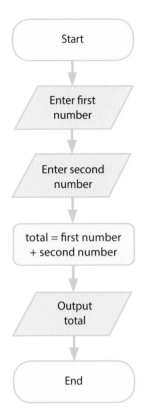

**Figure 1.3** Flowchart showing the adding of two numbers

*Pseudo-code*

### Algorithm for adding two numbers

```
SEND 'Please enter the first number.' TO DISPLAY
RECEIVE firstNumber FROM KEYBOARD
SEND 'Please enter the second number.' TO DISPLAY
RECEIVE secondNumber FROM KEYBOARD
SET total TO firstNumber + secondNumber
SEND total TO DISPLAY
```

The pseudo-code spells out the step-by-step instructions that the computer will be expected to carry out. It also introduces some important programming concepts.

- The numbers entered by the user are stored in two **variables** with the **identifiers** 'firstNumber' and 'secondNumber'.
- The result of adding the numbers together is stored in the variable 'total'.
- When some text is to be displayed, for example 'Please enter the first number.', it has to be enclosed in quotation marks, either single or double.
- When a variable is to be displayed, the quotation marks are not used. If they were, then, in the last instruction, the word 'total' would be displayed and not the number it represents.
- **Arithmetic operators** are used to perform calculations. This box shows the arithmetic operators.

### Key terms

**Variable**: a 'container' used to store data. The data stored in a variable is referred to as a value. The value stored in a variable is not fixed. The same variable can store different values during the course of a program and each time a program is run.

**Identifier**: a unique name given to a variable or a constant. Using descriptive names for variables makes code much easier to read.

**Arithmetic operator**: an operator that performs a calculation on two numbers.

### Arithmetic operators

| Operator | Function | Example |
|---|---|---|
| + | Addition: add the values together. | 8 + 5 = 13<br>myScore1 + myScore2 |
| - | Subtraction: subtract the second value from the first. | 17 - 4 = 13<br>myScore1 - myScore2 |
| * | Multiplication: multiply the values together. | 6 * 9 = 54<br>numberBought * price |
| / | Real division: divide the first value by the second value and return the result including decimal places. | 13/4 = 3.25<br>totalMarks/numberTests |
| DIV | Quotient: like division, but it only returns the whole number or *integer*. | 13 DIV 4 = 3<br>totalMarks DIV numberTests |
| MOD | Modulus/modulo: this will return the remainder of a division. | 13/4 = 3 remainder 1<br>Therefore 13 MOD 4 = 1 |
| ^ | Exponentiation: this is for 'to the power of'. | 3^3 = 27<br>It is the same as writing $3^3$ |

5

# Problem solving

## Variables and constants

Variables play an important role in algorithms and programming. The value stored by a variable can change as a program is running. Variables are extremely useful in programming because they make it possible for the same program to process different sets of data.

A **constant** is the opposite of a variable. It is a 'container' that holds a value that always stays the same. Constants are useful for storing fixed information, such as the value of pi, the number of litres in a gallon or the number of months in a year.

Each variable and constant in an algorithm has to have a unique identifier. It is important to choose descriptive names for identifiers. This will make your code much easier to read. For example, a variable to hold a user's first name could be given the identifier 'firstName' so that it is indicative of the data it contains. If it were given the identifier 'X' then it would be ambiguous what data it contained.

## Naming conventions for variables and constants

It is good practice to adopt a consistent way of writing identifiers throughout an algorithm.

A common convention is to use *camel case* for compound words (e.g. firstName, secondName) with no space between words and the second word starting with a capital letter. Alternatives are to capitalise the first letter of both words, e.g. FirstName, SecondName, or to separate the words with an underscore, e.g. first_name, second_name, known as snake case.

### Activity 5

Here is a written description of an algorithm.

Enter the first number.
Enter the second number.
The third number is equal to the first number multiplied by the second number.
Display the third number.

Express this algorithm in pseudo-code.

## Activity 6 ?

This algorithm is displayed as a flowchart.

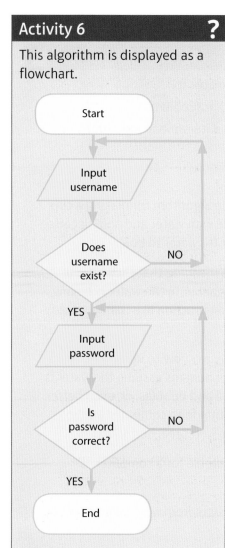

**Figure 1.4** Flowchart of an algorithm

Produce a written description of this algorithm.

## Extend your knowledge

When you enter a search term into Google®, a list of links to websites is returned. But why are they presented in that particular order? Research the PageRank algorithm that Google® uses to rate the importance of websites and write a short report about your findings that explains how the order is determined.

## Summary

- An algorithm is a precise method for solving a problem.
- Algorithms can be displayed as written descriptions, flowcharts and in pseudo-code.
- Pseudo-code is a structured, code-like language.
- Pseudo-code is translated into program code.
- Arithmetic operators are used in calculations.
- Variables and constants are 'containers' for storing data. The value stored in a variable can change, whereas the value of a constant never changes.
- Selecting descriptive names for identifiers makes code easier to read.

## Checkpoint

### Strengthen

**S1** Produce a written description of an algorithm for borrowing a book from the library.

**S2** Describe what each of the seven arithmetic operators does.

**S3** Describe what a variable is and explain why variables are useful.

**S4** Explain the difference between a variable and a constant.

### Challenge

**C1** Produce a flowchart describing an algorithm for making a cheese sandwich.

**C2** Write an algorithm expressed in pseudo-code that receives three numbers from the keyboard, calculates and displays the average.

How confident do you feel about your answers to these questions? If you're not sure you answered them well, try the following.

- For S1 reread page 3.
- For S2 study the table on page 5.
- For S3 and S4 look again at page 6.

# Problem solving

## Key terms

**Construct**: a component from which something is built. Letters and numbers (i.e. a to z and 0 to 9) are the constructs we use to build our language and convey meaning. Bricks and cement are the basic constructs of a building.

**Selection**: a construct that allows a choice to be made between different alternatives.

**Iteration**: a construct that means the repetition of a process. An action is repeated until there is a desired outcome or a condition is met. It is often referred to as a loop.

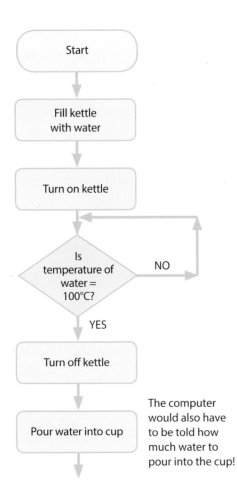

**Figure 1.5** Part of an algorithm suitable for a computer for making coffee

## Creating algorithms

### Learning outcomes

By the end of this section you should be able to:

- create an algorithm to solve a particular problem.
- use command sequence, selection and iteration in algorithms.

### Algorithms for computers

There was an ambiguous statement in the algorithm for making a cup of coffee on page 3. After filling the kettle with water and adding coffee to the cup, the next instruction was 'Wait for water to boil'.

A human can interpret this instruction as meaning that they have to keep checking the kettle over and over again until the water is boiling. But a computer is unable to interpret an instruction like that. It would just wait. And wait. Forever.

Even worse, the algorithm didn't explicitly say how to determine if the water was boiling. Through experience we humans assume the water is boiling when there is lots of steam, sound and bubbles; or, even better, when the kettle turns itself off. An algorithm for a computer would have to state that it was waiting until the water reached 100°C.

A version of this part of the algorithm, suitable for a computer, is shown in Figure 1.5.

This example introduces two new **constructs** from which algorithms are created.

We have already met the construct *command sequence* – step-by-step instructions in the correct order. To add to this we now have **selection** and **iteration**.

### Did you know?

We use iteration in our daily lives whenever we carry out an action over and over again. For example, at mealtimes we keep on eating until our plate is empty or we have had enough to eat.

When we're travelling by car and the traffic lights are red we have to keep waiting until they change to green.

An actor repeats their lines over and over again until they are word perfect.

## Representing selection and iteration in a flowchart

Selection and iteration are represented in a flowchart as shown in Figure 1.6.

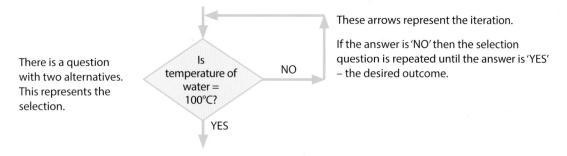

There is a question with two alternatives. This represents the selection.

These arrows represent the iteration.

If the answer is 'NO' then the selection question is repeated until the answer is 'YES' – the desired outcome.

**Figure 1.6** Selection and iteration in a flowchart

## Representing selection and iteration in pseudo-code

### Selection

Selection in pseudo-code is represented exactly as we would say it using an **IF...THEN...ELSE statement**.

### IF...THEN...ELSE statement

```
IF Temperature = 100°C THEN
     Switch off kettle
ELSE
     Keep waiting
END IF
```

This is an oversimplification as the commands 'Switch off kettle' and 'Keep waiting' mean nothing to a computer.

An IF...THEN statement can be used without an ELSE if there is only one course of action to be taken, providing the condition in the IF statement is met.

### IF...THEN statement

```
IF score >= 90 THEN
   SEND 'Excellent' TO DISPLAY
END IF
```

For selection, **relational operators** are used to compare the values.

---

**Key terms**

**IF...THEN...ELSE statement**: the IF...THEN...ELSE statement allows a choice to be made between two alternatives based on whether or not a condition is met (e.g. IF it is cold THEN wear a jumper ELSE wear a T-shirt).

**Relational operator**: an operator that compares two values.

---

# Problem solving

Relational operators are used to compare two values. The operators that you will be using are:

| | |
|---|---|
| = | equal to |
| > | greater than |
| >= | greater than or equal to |
| < | less than |
| <= | less than or equal to |
| <> | not equal to |

## Using relational operators

```
SET passMark TO 75
RECEIVE mark FROM KEYBOARD
IF mark >= passMark THEN
    SEND 'Well done. You've passed.' TO DISPLAY
ELSE
    SEND 'Bad luck. You've failed.' TO DISPLAY
END IF
```

Notice the use of indentation in an IF…THEN…ELSE statement. In this example there is only one statement for each alternative, but imagine if there were many. The indentation makes it easier to see which statement(s) belong to each alternative. Indentation is a useful technique for improving the readability of algorithms expressed in pseudo-code. You should get into the habit of using it. When you move on to implementing your algorithms in a high-level programming language you might find that the computer won't be able to execute your programs unless you have used indentation correctly.

## Activity 7

```
IF score <= highScore THEN
    SEND 'You haven't beaten your high score.' TO DISPLAY
ELSE
    SEND 'You've exceeded your high score!' TO DISPLAY
END IF
```

State the output of the algorithm when
- score = 5 and highScore = 10
- score = 20 and highScore = 10
- score = 15 and highScore = 15

## Activity 8　?

A driving school uses this rule to estimate how many lessons a learner will require.

- Every learner requires at least 20 lessons.
- Learners over the age of 18 require more lessons (two additional lessons for each year over 18).

Create an algorithm expressed in pseudo-code that inputs a learner's age and calculates the number of driving lessons they will need.

### Nested selection

The IF…THEN…ELSE statement allows a choice to be made between two possible alternatives. However, sometimes there are more than two possibilities. This is where a **nested IF statement** comes in useful.

## Worked example

A learner handed in three homework assignments, which were each given a mark out of 10. All the marks were different. Write an algorithm that would print out the highest mark.

Figure 1.7 shows the algorithm expressed as a flowchart:

## Key term

**Nested IF statement**: a nested IF statement consists of one or more IF statements placed inside each other. A nested IF is used where there are more than two possible courses of action.

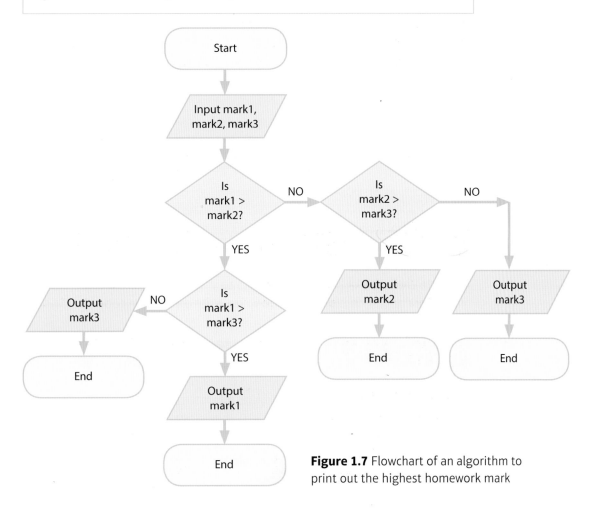

**Figure 1.7** Flowchart of an algorithm to print out the highest homework mark

# Problem solving

The variables mark1 and mark2 are compared using a relational operator. If mark1 is greater than (>) mark2 then it is compared with mark3. If it is not greater than mark2, then mark2 must be greater than mark1 and it is then compared with mark3.

This algorithm can also be expressed in pseudo-code:

```
RECEIVE mark1 FROM KEYBOARD
RECEIVE mark2 FROM KEYBOARD
RECEIVE mark3 FROM KEYBOARD
IF mark1 > mark2 THEN
        IF mark1 > mark3 THEN        #This is an IF statement
                                     within another IF statement.
                                     It is called a nested IF.

                SEND mark1 TO DISPLAY
        ELSE
                SEND mark3 TO DISPLAY
        END IF
ELSE
        IF mark2 > mark3 THEN        #This is another nested IF
                                     statement.
                SEND mark2 TO DISPLAY
        ELSE
                SEND mark3 TO DISPLAY
        END IF
END IF
```

In this algorithm there are three IF...THEN...ELSE statements. Two of them are completely nested within the outer one.

## Top tip

When you are creating nested IF statements you have to ensure that each one is completed with an END IF statement at the correct indentation level. Some programming languages do not need an END IF statement and just use the indentation levels to indicate when statements are grouped.

## Top tip

The # symbol indicates a comment. This is some text used to explain the code and the # symbol shows that it is not to be executed. It can be on a line of its own or at the end of the line to which it applies. You should get into the habit of adding comments to your algorithms to explain how they work and should do the same when writing program code.

## Activity 9

A learner is creating a guessing game. A player has to enter a number no greater than 10. If it is too high, they are informed that they have made an error, but if it is within the range 1 to 10, they are told whether or not they have guessed the correct number. (Assume that the correct number is 3.)

Create an algorithm to solve this problem and express it as a flowchart and in pseudo-code.

## Activity 10 ?

A school uses this algorithm to calculate the grade learners achieve in end-of-topic tests.

```
RECEIVE testScore FROM KEYBOARD
IF testScore >= 80 THEN
     SEND 'A' TO DISPLAY
ELSE
     IF testScore >= 70 THEN
          SEND 'B' TO DISPLAY
     ELSE
          IF testScore >= 60 THEN
               SEND 'C' TO DISPLAY
          ELSE
               IF testScore > 0 THEN
                    SEND 'D' TO DISPLAY
               ELSE
                    SEND 'FAIL' TO DISPLAY
               END IF
          END IF
     END IF
END IF
```

What would be the output of this algorithm for these test scores: 91, 56 and 78?

### Iteration

When writing programs it is often necessary to repeat the same set of statements several times. Rather than simply making multiple copies of the statements you can use iteration to repeat them. The algorithm for making a cup of coffee includes an instruction to keep waiting until the water in the kettle boils.

## Waiting for the kettle to boil

```
IF temperature = 100°C THEN
     Switch off kettle
ELSE
     Keep waiting
END IF
```

Selection would be useless without iteration. The question would be asked once and then the program would move on or just stop. There has to be a method for repeating the question until there is a desired outcome. In a flowchart this is easy to implement – you just have to draw some arrows.

In both pseudo-code and program code you have to construct a loop, or iteration. There are two types of iteration: **indefinite iteration** and **definite iteration**.

## Key terms

**Indefinite iteration**: this is used when the number of iterations is not known before the loop is started. The iterations stop when a specified condition is met. This sort of loop is said to be condition controlled.

**Definite iteration**: this is used when the number of iterations, or turns of the loop, is known in advance. It can be set to as many turns as you want. This sort of loop is said to be count controlled.

# Problem solving

## Indefinite iteration

Obviously in this example it is not known how many times the program will have to check until the water temperature reaches 100°C.

Therefore we have to use indefinite iteration. There are two ways of doing this in pseudo-code: you can use a REPEAT…UNTIL loop or a WHILE…DO loop.

A REPEAT…UNTIL loop checks the condition when it gets to the end of the loop. This means that the statements contained within the loop will be executed at least once. A WHILE…DO loop checks the condition at the start of the loop so in some circumstances the statements contained within the loop will not be executed.

### Using REPEAT…UNTIL

| | |
|---|---|
| `REPEAT` | #This starts the REPEAT…UNTIL loop. |
| `   RECEIVE temp FROM SENSOR` | #The temperature of the water is input from a temperature sensor. |
| `UNTIL temp = 100` | #This sets the condition for the loop to stop. When 'temp' is equal to 100 the loop will stop. |
| `Switch off kettle` | #This is the next command to be executed when the loop has finished. |

Using a WHILE…DO loop the algorithm shown above would be

### Using WHILE…DO

```
RECEIVE temp FROM SENSOR
WHILE temp < 100 DO
.  RECEIVE temp FROM SENSOR
END WHILE
Switch off kettle
```

### Activity 11

1  Write an algorithm expressed in pseudo-code that asks the user to enter a number between 1 and 6. If the number entered matches the value stored in the variable diceRoll the message 'Well done you guessed correctly.' is displayed. Otherwise the user is invited to guess again.

Use a WHILE…DO loop and include comments to explain what each line of code does.

2  Produce a second version of the algorithm using a REPEAT…UNTIL loop.

## Definite iteration

This is used when the number of iterations, or turns of the loop, is known in advance.

One method is to use a REPEAT…TIMES loop.

## Using REPEAT… TIMES

```
REPEAT 50 TIMES
    SEND '*' TO DISPLAY
END REPEAT
```

A FOR loop is another method of repeating a sequence of instructions a fixed number of times.

## Worked example

A learner is designing a program to help younger children with their times tables. When a user enters a number the program will output the times table up to 12.

```
RECEIVE number FROM KEYBOARD        #The number entered is assigned
                                     to the variable 'number'.

FOR index FROM 1 TO 12 DO           #The loop is set up using the
                                     variable 'index' which will
                                     change from 1 to 12 at each
                                     turn of the loop.

    SEND number * index TO DISPLAY  #The value of 'number' is
                                     multiplied by the value of 'index'
                                     at each turn of the loop.

END FOR                             #This command is used to close
                                     the loop.
```

This loop will be repeated 12 times. At each turn of the loop the variable 'index' is incremented by one.

## Top tip

Variables in a FOR loop can be used to indicate the start and end values of the loop, for example

```
start = 25
finish = 50
FOR index FROM start TO finish DO
    SEND 'Congratulations' TO DISPLAY
END FOR
```

## Activity 12

Create an algorithm expressed in pseudo-code that asks a user to enter a start number and an end number and then outputs the total of all the numbers in the range. For example, if the start number was 1 and the end number was 10, the total would be 55 (1 + 2 + 3 + 4 + 5 + 6 + 7 + 8 + 9 + 10).

**Tip**:
You should initialise the variable total to zero before the start of the loop.

# Problem solving

Another example of a fixed number of iterations is when you have to enter a password and you only get three attempts. It could be implemented in the following way.

## Worked example

```
SET correct TO 'LetMeIn'          #The variable 'correct' is assigned
                                   the value of the password stored in
                                   the system.

FOR index FROM 1 TO 3 DO
   SEND 'Please enter your password.' TO DISPLAY
   RECEIVE password FROM KEYBOARD
   IF password = correct THEN
      SEND 'You entered the correct password.' TO DISPLAY
   END IF
END FOR
```

The loop will ask for the password to be input three times, but what if the user gets the password correct on the first attempt? They do not want to have to enter it twice more.

Another solution would be to use indefinite iteration and keep count of the number of iterations.

## Worked example

```
SET count TO 0                    #The variable 'count' is assigned
                                   the value 0.

SET correct TO 'LetMeIn'          #The variable 'correct' is assigned
                                   the value of the password stored
                                   in the system.

REPEAT
   SET count to count + 1         #The variable 'count' is
                                   incremented by 1 on each turn.
   SEND 'Please enter your password.' TO DISPLAY
   RECEIVE password FROM KEYBOARD
   IF password = correct THEN
      SEND 'Correct password.' TO DISPLAY
   ELSE
      SEND 'Incorrect password.' TO DISPLAY
   END IF
UNTIL password = correct OR count = 3
```

The loop will end if either of the conditions is met – if the password is correct or the number of attempts is equal to 3.

We have used a compound comparison by joining two conditions together using an 'OR', which is a **logical operator**.

## Key term

**Logical operator**: a Boolean operator using AND, OR and NOT.

## Logical operators

AND     If two conditions are joined by the 'AND' operator, then they must both be true for the whole statement to be true.

OR     If two conditions are joined by the 'OR' operator, then either one must be true for the whole statement to be true.

NOT     The NOT operator reverses the logic of the AND and OR statements. The statement 'IF A = 3 AND B = 6' will be true only if the conditions are met, i.e. A and B are both equal to the values stated.

The statement IF NOT (A = 3 AND B = 6) will be true whenever both A and B are NOT equal to the values stated i.e. either or both are not equal to those values.

The NOT operator is often used when setting a selection criterion, for example IF NOT LENGTH(password) > 8 THEN to ensure a minimum password length.

## Activity 13     ?

In Activity 9 you had to create an algorithm for a guessing game. This game is more difficult. It should generate a **random number** between 1 and 20.

- Ask the user to guess the number.
- Allow the user three attempts.
- Display a message if the attempt is correct.
- Display a message if the attempt is incorrect and inform the player if their attempt is too high or too low.
- Display a message to the player after three incorrect attempts informing them of the correct number.

### Nested loops

A **nested loop** comprises a loop within a loop. When one loop is nested within another, each iteration of the outer loop causes the inner loop to be executed until completion.

In this example a nested loop is used to calculate and display the average mark achieved by each student in a group of twenty for a series of five tests.

The outer loop iterates through each student in turn. The inner loop receives each set of five marks and adds them together. The outer loop calculates and displays the average mark before moving on to the next student.

## Worked example

```
FOR student = 1 TO 20
    SET sum = 0
    FOR mark = 1 TO 5
        RECEIVE nextMark FROM KEYBOARD
        SET sum TO sum + nextMark
    END FOR
    SET averageMark TO sum/5
    SEND averageMark TO DISPLAY
END FOR
```

## Key terms

**Random number**: a number within a given range of numbers that is generated in such a way that each number in the range has an equal chance of occurring.

There are many devices for generating random numbers. A die is used in games to get a random number from 1 to 6. Computer programming languages have a function for generating random numbers across variable ranges.

In the Edexcel pseudo-code there is a useful built-in RANDOM command.

```
RANDOM(upperLimit)
```

For example, number = RANDOM(6) would generate a random number from the numbers 1 to 6.

**Nested loop**: a loop that runs inside another loop. The inner one executes all of its instructions for each turn of the outer loop.

# Problem solving

A learner has a Saturday job selling cups of tea and coffee. The tea is £1.20 per cup and the coffee is £1.90. He is supposed to keep a record of the number of cups of each he sells.

Unfortunately he has been so busy that he has lost count but he knows that he did not sell more than 100 of each.

He has collected £285.

Write a program that will calculate how many cups of tea and coffee he sold.

```
SET teaCost TO 1.2
SET coffeeCost TO 1.9
FOR numCoffees FROM 1 TO 100 DO
      FOR numTeas FROM 1 TO 100 DO        #This loop for the teas is
                                           nested inside the loop for
                                           coffees.

            SET total TO (numCoffees * coffeeCost) +
            (numTeas * teaCost)
            IF total = 285 THEN
                  SET teas TO numTeas      #These 'teas' and 'coffees'
                                            variables are needed as
                                            the loops will continue and
                                            'numCoffees' and 'numTeas'
                                            will change.
                  SET coffees TO numCoffees
            END IF
      END FOR
END FOR
SEND 'The number of teas is' & teas & 'and the number of
coffees is' & coffees TO DISPLAY
```

## Key term

**Concatenation**: the linking together of two or more items of information.

## Did you know?

Different symbols are used in other pseudo-codes and programming languages, with the '+' symbol being the most popular.

In this SEND command, four items of information are displayed. First there is some literal text enclosed in quotation marks – 'The number of teas is' – followed by the value of the variable teas, followed by some more literal text – 'and the number of coffees is' – followed by the value of the variable coffees. The four are joined by an '&' symbol – known as the append operator. Joining items of information in this way is called **concatenation**.

If this algorithm was converted into program code and executed this sentence would be displayed on the screen:

'The number of teas is 95 and the number of coffees is 90'

## Activity 14

Create an algorithm that will print out the times tables (up to 12 times) for the numbers 2 to 12. You should use concatenation so that the printouts state "2 x 2 = 4", "2 x 3 = 6", "9 x 8 = 72", etc.

## Summary

- The constructs command sequence, selection and iteration are the basic building blocks of algorithms.
- Nested IF statements allow for more than two alternatives.
- There are two types of iteration – definite and indefinite.
- Another name for iteration is loop. Loops can be nested.
- Comments make algorithms easier to understand. The # symbol indicates a comment in pseudo-code.
- Concatenation is the linking together of two or more items of information.

## Checkpoint

### Strengthen

**S1** Explain, using examples, how command sequence, selection and iteration are used in algorithms.

**S2** Explain what each of the six relational operators does.

### Challenge

**C1** Design an algorithm in pseudo-code that asks the user to enter their height (in metres) and weight (in kilograms) and displays their body mass index (BMI). The formula for calculating BMI is weight / height$^2$.

**C2** Design an algorithm expressed as a flowchart to control the heating in a house. A thermostat monitors the temperature within the house. During the week the temperature should be 20°C between 6.00 and 8.30 in the morning and between 17.30 and 22.00 at night. At weekends it should be 22°C between 8.00 and 23.00. If the temperature in the house falls below 10°C at any time the boiler is switched on.

How confident do you feel about your answers to these questions? If you're not sure you answered them well, try the following activities again.

- For S1 have a look at the key terms on pages 2 and 8.
- For S2 have a look at the table on page 10.

# Problem solving

## Working with algorithms

### Learning outcomes

By the end of this section you should be able to:

- describe the purpose of a given algorithm and explain how it works.
- determine the correct output of an algorithm for a given set of data.
- identify and correct errors in algorithms.

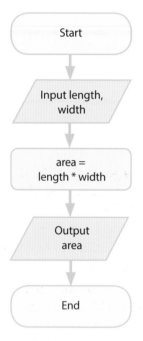

**Figure 1.8** Flowchart of an algorithm showing area of a rectangle

### The purpose of an algorithm

When you look at an algorithm, expressed either in pseudo-code or as a flowchart, it is sometimes easy to see its purpose.

Have a look at the algorithm in Figure 1.8.

The purpose of this algorithm is to find the area of a rectangle. It works like this.

- The length of the rectangle is input and is stored in the variable 'length'.
- The width of the rectangle is input and is stored in the variable 'width'.
- The variable 'length' is multiplied by the variable 'width' to find the area of the rectangle, which is stored in the variable 'area'.
- The value of the variable 'area' is output.

Here is another algorithm, this time displayed in pseudo-code.

```
SET totalFor TO 0
SET totalAgainst TO 0    #These variables hold the running totals
                          and are initialised to 0 at the start of the
                          algorithm.
SET win TO 0
SET loss TO 0
SET draw TO 0
SET anotherEntry TO 'Y'

WHILE anotherEntry = 'Y' DO
    SEND 'Enter goals for:' TO DISPLAY
    RECEIVE goalsFor FROM KEYBOARD
    SEND 'Enter goals against:' TO DISPLAY
    RECEIVE goalsAgainst FROM KEYBOARD
    SET totalFor TO totalFor + goalsFOR
    SET totalAgainst TO totalAgainst + goalsAgainst
    IF goalsFor > goalsAgainst THEN
        SET win TO win + 1
```

```
      ELSE
          IF goalsFOR < goalsAgainst THEN
              SET loss TO loss + 1
          ELSE
              SET draw TO draw + 1
          END IF
      END IF
      SEND 'Press 'Y' to enter another result.' TO DISPLAY
      RECEIVE anotherEntry from KEYBOARD
  END WHILE
  SEND 'Total wins: ' & win TO DISPLAY
  SEND 'Total losses: ' & loss TO DISPLAY
  SEND 'Total draws: ' & draw TO DISPLAY
```

So what can we say about this algorithm?

- Its purpose is to allow a user to enter match scores for a particular team and sport. It could be something like football or hockey.
- It calculates the total goals that were scored for and against the team.
- It calculates the number of matches that were won, lost and drawn.
- It displays the number of wins, losses and draws to the user.
- The variables to hold these values are initialised – declared and assigned a start value at the beginning of the algorithm.
- The algorithm uses indefinite iteration. It loops until the user presses any key other than the 'Y' key.

### Checking the output

A good way to follow the reasoning behind an algorithm, and also to find any **logic errors**, is to use some sample data and check if the output is what you expect.

---

**Activity 15**   ?

Use the following scores as test data.

1–0

3–2

0–2

1–1

Calculate the expected end states of the variables from these results.

Track the entry of each score through the algorithm and see if they are the same as your expected results.

---

### Trace tables

The formal way of checking the logic of an algorithm is to use a **trace table**.

---

**Top tip**

In the algorithm the SEND statement at the end of the loop uses double quotation marks. This is because the text to be displayed includes the letter 'Y' in single quotes.

You can use double quotation marks in a SEND statement where the text includes single quotes or an apostrophe. Pseudo-code is very forgiving, so it doesn't matter if you don't do this, but it does matter when the algorithm is converted into program code.

---

**Key terms**

**Logic error**: an error in an algorithm that results in incorrect or unexpected behaviour.

**Trace table**: a technique used to identify any logic errors in algorithms. Each column represents a variable or output and each row a value of that variable.

# Problem solving

## Activity 16

Complete a trace table for this algorithm.

```
SET number1 TO 2
SET number2 TO 3
FOR index FROM 1 TO 5 DO
   SET number1 TO number1 * index
   SET number2 TO number2 + number1
END FOR
```

## Exam-style question

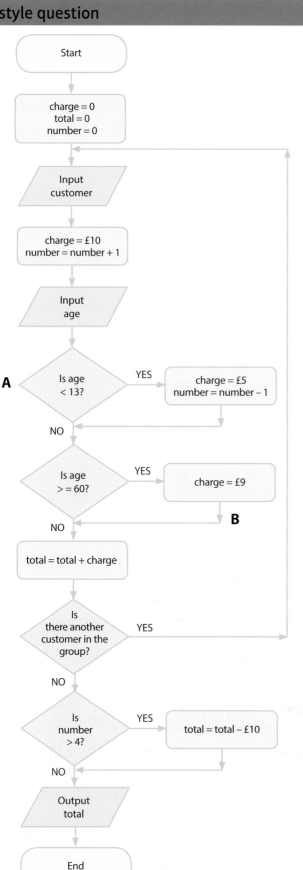

This flowchart displays an algorithm used by Holiday Theme Parks Limited.

1   Describe how the algorithm calculates the total amount that should be paid.

2   Give **two** variables that are used in the algorithm.

3   In the flowchart, two of the constructs are labelled A and B. State the type of each construct.

4   The Smith family is visiting the park. The family consists of two children, one aged 8 and one aged 10, their two parents and their grandfather, who is aged 65. Use the algorithm to calculate how much the family should have to pay for entry.

**Figure 1.9** Flowchart of an algorithm showing charges in a theme park

# Problem solving

## Key term

**Simulation**: a representation of a real-world process or system.

## Activity 17

Here is part of a **simulation** for a payment system at a car park.

```
SET parkCharge to RANDOM(20)   #As this is a simulation, a parking
                                charge is generated as a random
                                number between 1 and 20, i.e. £1
                                and £20.
SET payment TO 0

WHILE payment < parkCharge OR payment > 20 DO
   SEND 'The charge is ' & parkCharge TO DISPLAY
   SEND 'Enter payment up to £20 maximum.' TO DISPLAY
   RECEIVE payment FROM KEYBOARD
   SET changeDue TO payment - parkCharge
   WHILE changeDue >= 10 DO
      SEND '£10 note' TO DISPLAY
      SET changeDue TO changeDue - 10
   END WHILE
   WHILE changeDue >= 5 DO
      SEND '£5 note' TO DISPLAY
      SET changeDue TO changeDue - 5
   END WHILE
   WHILE changeDue >= 2 DO
      SEND '£2 coin' TO DISPLAY
      SET changeDue TO changeDue - 2
   END WHILE
END WHILE
```

What is the maximum charge at the car park?

Explain how the algorithm calculates the change due and decides how many notes or coins should be given. Complete the algorithm so that it includes the payment of £1, 50p, 20p, 10p, 5p, 2p and 1p coins and add comments to show how the code works. If the charge is £6.90 and the person pays with a £20 note, use the completed algorithm to determine how many of each type of denomination (£20, £10 and £5 notes and £2, £1, 50p, 20p, 10p, 5p, 2p and 1p coins) will be issued.

### Identifying errors

There are three types of error in computer programs.

- Syntax errors occur when algorithms are being converted into program code.
- Runtime errors occur when the program is executed.
- Logic errors are errors in the design of algorithms.

Syntax and runtime errors will be covered in Chapter 2. Pseudo-code purposefully doesn't really have any syntax so that the developer can concentrate on noting down the logic without having to be bothered with the rules of syntax. Obviously, you won't have syntax or runtime errors in pseudo-code.

## Worked example

Here is an algorithm to find the average of two numbers.

```
RECEIVE number1 FROM KEYBOARD
RECEIVE number2 FROM KEYBOARD
SET average TO number1 + number2 / 2
SEND average TO DISPLAY
```

This seems logical. Two numbers are input, they are added together and then they are divided by 2.

However, if this algorithm was given 12 and 6 as the two numbers it would return 15 as the average instead of 9. There is a logic error.

Instead of adding the two numbers and then dividing by two, as the developer intended, it is dividing the second number by 2 and then adding the result to the first number.

The developer should have written the third line as

```
SET average TO (number1 + number2) / 2
```

## Did you know?

So far you have been using the Edexcel pseudo-code that is provided in the specification. In the examination, questions will be asked using this version, but if you have to answer a question by writing pseudo-code, you do not have to use Edexcel's version. As long as your answer is logical and can be understood by a competent person, then it will be accepted.

## Did you know?

In computer programming the order of precedence (the order in which you do each calculation) is the same as in mathematics and science – BIDMAS.

This is how $3^2 \times 9 + (5 - 2)$ would be evaluated.

| **B**rackets | $3^2 \times 9 + (3)$ |
| **I**ndices | $9 \times 9 + (3)$ |
| **D**ivision | |
| **M**ultiplication | $81 + (3)$ |
| **A**ddition | $84$ |
| **S**ubtraction | |

To calculate $24/3 - 2$, the division would be calculated before the subtraction.

$24/3 = 8$

$8 - 2 = 6$

The best way to find logic errors is to use the technique in the section above – use sample data and check if the actual output from the algorithm is as expected. You'll learn more about this in Chapter 2.

# Problem solving

This is part of a larger algorithm designed to ensure that input data falls within a certain range. It is part of a school management system and checks that the 'year group' entry is acceptable. It has learners aged 11 to 18 years with year groups of 7 to 13.

The staff using the system congratulated themselves on never making an error when entering the year group, but when learner lists were printed out they immediately received complaints.

What is the logic error in the algorithm?

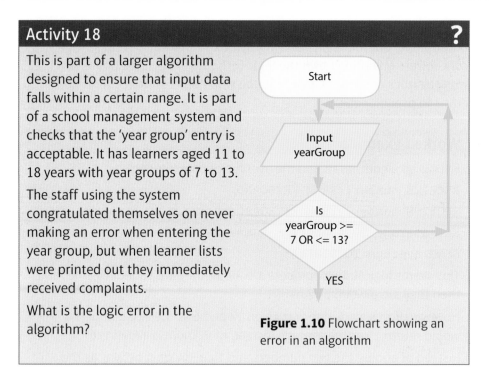

**Figure 1.10** Flowchart showing an error in an algorithm

Often logic errors occur when designing loops.

## Worked example

Study this algorithm.

```
WHILE index < 10 DO
    SET index TO 1
    SEND index TO DISPLAY
    SET index TO index + 1
END WHILE
```

The expected output is 1, 2, 3, 4, 5, 6, 7, 8, 9.

But there is a logic error. The variable 'index' is initialised in the wrong place. It should be done before the start of the WHILE loop.

This algorithm would loop forever because at each turn in the loop the variable index is set to 1. It will never reach 10. This is an example of an '**infinite loop**'. The algorithm should have been written as shown below.

```
SET index TO 1
WHILE index < 10
    SEND index TO DISPLAY
    SET index TO index + 1
END WHILE
```

## Key term

**Infinite loop**: a loop that is never-ending since the condition required to terminate the loop is never reached.

## Activity 19   ?

Find and correct the errors in these algorithms.

- Example 1

```
SET index TO 1
WHILE index < 10
   SEND index TO DISPLAY
END WHILE
```

- Example 2

```
SET index TO 1
WHILE index < 10
   SEND index TO DISPLAY
   SET index TO index - 1
END WHILE
```

- Example 3

```
SET index TO 1
WHILE index < 1
   SEND index TO DISPLAY
   SET index TO index + 1
END WHILE
```

## Summary

- A logic error in an algorithm will produce an incorrect result.
- Tracing the value of variables in an algorithm helps to identify logic errors.
- Understanding the order of precedence of arithmetic operators and the significance of brackets will help you to avoid making logic errors.

## Checkpoint

### Strengthen

**S1** Describe the purpose of an algorithm and explain how it works.

**S2** Explain, using examples, what a logic error is.

**S3** Use a trace table to check the output of an algorithm and identify any logic errors. Explain what BIDMAS means and demonstrate how this expression would be evaluated.
$4^3 \times 10 / 2 + (8 - 3)$

# Problem solving

**C1** State the purpose of this algorithm and explain the rules behind the calculation.

```
SEND 'Enter the weight of your parcel in kilograms'
TO DISPLAY
RECEIVE parcelWeight FROM KEYBOARD
IF parcelWeight <= 2 THEN
     postage = 8
ELSE
     IF parcelWeight <= 10 THEN
          postage = 8 + ((parcelWeight - 2) * 2.5)
     ELSE
          postage = 8 + (8 * 2.5) + ((parcelWeight - 10) *
          3.5)
     IF END
IF END

SEND 'The cost of posting your parcel is ' & postage
TO DISPLAY
```

**C2** People often want to know the human-equivalent age of their dog or cat. The rules for calculating this are:
A 1-year-old cat is equivalent in age to a 15-year-old human, a 2-year-old cat is equivalent in age to a 24-year-old human. Add four years for every year after that.
A 1-year-old dog is equivalent in age to a 12-year-old human, a 2-year-old dog is equivalent in age to a 24-year-old human. Add four years for every year after that.
Design an algorithm expressed in pseudo-code that allows the user to input the age of their dog or cat and outputs its equivalent human age. It should allow the user to have another go.
Use a trace table and test data to check the logic of your algorithm.

How confident do you feel about your answers to these questions? If you're not sure you answered them well, try the following activities again.

- For S1 reread pages 20–21 and have another go at all the activities.
- For S2 and S3 reread the section on trace tables on pages 21–22 and the section on identifying errors on pages 24–25.

# Sorting and searching algorithms

Two of the most common tasks in computer programs are sorting data into a particular order and searching for particular items of information.

There might be millions of items of stored data and searching for information would be very inefficient if the data was not sorted. Imagine the confusion and difficulty of having to find something in a dictionary that wasn't in alphabetical order or planning a trip with train timetables that weren't sorted into time order. Even small lists such as football league tables or the top-20 music charts are much more useful if they are sorted into order.

## Arrays

All sorting and searching algorithms work on lists of data. As you already know, a variable stores just a single value (e.g. SET age TO 15 or SET firstName TO 'David').

But what if a programmer wants to store lots of related values, such as the names of a group of friends? A tedious way of doing it might look something like this.

```
SET friend1 TO 'Alice'
SET friend2 TO 'Barry'
SET friend3 TO 'Catherine'
```

It would be much easier if all the names could be stored in one list to which the names of new friends can be added. That's exactly what an **array** allows you to do.

An array with the identifier 'arrayFriends' would store the data items like this.

```
arrayFriends = ['Alice', 'Barry', 'Catherine']
```

This array has three elements.

## Key term

**Array**: an organised collection of related values that share a single identifier.

# Problem solving

## Array indexes

Each element in an array has an index number. In the example above the index number for 'Alice' is 0 and the index number for 'Catherine' is 2. (Index numbering starts at 0.)

A new element can be inserted into an array like this.

```
SET arrayFriends[3] TO 'David'
SET arrayFriends[4] TO 'Eva'
```

This would insert the name 'David' at index position 3 and the name 'Eva' at index position 4 – the fourth and fifth positions in the array.

> **Worked example**
>
> This code will traverse an array named 'arrayFriends' and print out each element of the array.
>
> ```
> FOR index FROM 0 TO LENGTH(arrayFriends) - 1 DO
>                              #The loop has to run to the length of
>                              the array minus 1 as indexing starts at
>                              0. For example, if there are 10 items
>                              then they will be indexed as 0 to 9
>                              (10 -1).
>     SEND arrayFriends[index] TO DISPLAY
> END FOR
> ```

> **Activity 20** ?
>
> An array named 'arrayScores' contains a set of marks that a learner has obtained during her computer science course.
>
> Create an algorithm expressed in pseudo-code to find and display her highest mark and her average mark.

Activity 19 would have been a whole lot easier if the elements of the array had been sorted into order. We will next be looking at two ways this can be done.

## Sorting algorithms

As sorting is such a widely used procedure, many algorithms have been created to carry it out. As with all algorithms, some are more efficient than others.

### Bubble sort

When data is sorted, different items must be compared with each other and moved so that they are in either **ascending order** or **descending order**.

The bubble sort algorithm starts at one end of the list and compares pairs of data items. If they are in the wrong order, they are swapped. The comparison of pairs continues to the end of the list, each complete **traversal** of the list being called a pass. This process is repeated until there have been no swaps during a pass, indicating that the items must all be in the correct order.

The algorithm can be described as follows.

## Bubble sort (ascending order)

1 Start at the beginning of the list.
2 Compare the values in position 1 and position 2 in the list – if they are not in ascending order then swap them.
3 Compare the values in position 2 and position 3 in the list and swap if necessary.
4 Continue to the end of the list.
5 If there have been any swaps, repeat steps 1 to 4.

## Worked example

Here is an example of a bubble sort in action.

**Pass 1**

| | | | | | |
|---|---|---|---|---|---|
| 4 | 2 | 6 | 1 | 3 | Items 1 and 2 must be swapped. |
| 2 | 4 | 6 | 1 | 3 | Items 1 and 2 are swapped. |
| 2 | 4 | 6 | 1 | 3 | Items 2 and 3 are already in ascending order. |
| 2 | 4 | 6 | 1 | 3 | Items 3 and 4 must be swapped. |
| 2 | 4 | 1 | 6 | 3 | Items 3 and 4 have been swapped. |
| 2 | 4 | 1 | 6 | 3 | Items 4 and 5 must now be swapped. |
| 2 | 4 | 1 | 3 | 6 | Items 4 and 5 have been swapped. |

**Pass 2**

| | | | | | |
|---|---|---|---|---|---|
| 2 | 4 | 1 | 3 | 6 | Items 1 and 2 are in correct order. |
| 2 | 4 | 1 | 3 | 6 | Items 2 and 3 must be swapped. |
| 2 | 1 | 4 | 3 | 6 | Items 2 and 3 have been swapped. |
| 2 | 1 | 4 | 3 | 6 | Items 3 and 4 must be swapped. |
| 2 | 1 | 3 | 4 | 6 | Items 3 and 4 have been swapped. |
| 2 | 1 | 3 | 4 | 6 | Items 4 and 5 do not need to be swapped. |

**Pass 3**

| | | | | | |
|---|---|---|---|---|---|
| 2 | 1 | 3 | 4 | 6 | Items 1 and 2 must be swapped. |
| 1 | 2 | 3 | 4 | 6 | Items 1 and 2 have been swapped. |
| 1 | 2 | 3 | 4 | 6 | All items are now in the correct order. |

**Figure 1.11** A bubble sort

It would take a human three passes to carry out this bubble sort, but a computer would need four passes because it must continue until there have been no swaps. A computer cannot just look at all of the numbers at once and see that they are all in order.

## Did you know?

Do you know why it is called 'bubble sort'? If you look carefully, you can see that gradually the largest items move to the end, like bubbles rising in water. After the first pass, the largest number is in its correct position. Then after the second pass, the next largest is in its correct position. This happens on each pass and so if the algorithm is to be made more efficient the last set of comparisons can be omitted.

# Problem solving

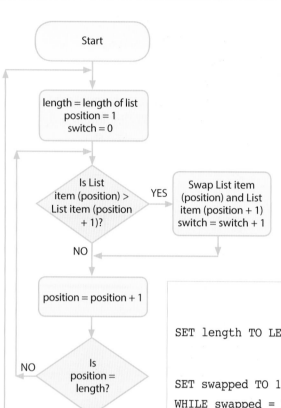

**Figure 1.12** Bubble sort algorithm written as a flowchart

The bubble sort algorithm can be represented as a flowchart as shown in Figure 1.12.

## Activity 21    ?

Study the flowchart of the bubble sort algorithm.

Using the variables declared, explain the logic behind the algorithm – explain how it functions to sort a list.

The bubble sort algorithm can also be expressed in pseudo-code. It assumes that the items to be sorted are stored in an array.

|  |  |
|---|---|
| | #The items to be sorted are in an array with the identifier 'items'. |
| `SET length TO LENGTH(items) - 1` | #The variable 'length' is set to the length of the array minus one to represent the last index position. |
| `SET swapped TO 1` | #The variable 'swapped' is assigned the value of 1. |
| `WHILE swapped = 1 DO` | #The loop will run while the value of 'swapped' is equal to 1. |
| `    swapped = 0` | #The variable 'swapped' is changed to 0. It will be changed back to 1 if a swap occurs. |
| `    FOR index FROM 1 TO length DO` | #This will set up a loop from 1 to the value of 'length' which is the length of the array minus one. |
| `      IF items[index-1] > items[index] THEN` | #On the first loop this will compare the value of the item at index 1 with that at index 0. |
| `        SET temp TO items[index-1]` | #This block of code will swap the two items if the first is larger than the second. |
| `        SET items[index-1] TO items[index]` | |
| `        SET items[index] TO temp` | |
| `        SET swapped TO 1` | #Swapped is set to 1 to indicate that a swap has occurred and so the 'WHILE' loop will turn again. |
| `      END IF` | |
| `    END FOR` | #This ends the 'FOR' loop and so the variable 'index' will be incremented by 1 for the next iteration. When it is greater than the 'length' variable the 'FOR' loop will stop. |
| `END WHILE` | |

## Activity 22    ?

A tutor has stored a set of class examination results in an array named 'exam1'. Write an algorithm expressed in pseudo-code to sort the results into descending order and then output the highest and lowest result.

## Merge sort

Merge sort is a sorting algorithm that divides a list into two smaller lists and then divides these until the size of each list is one. Repeatedly applying a method to the results of a previous application of the method is called **recursion**.

In computing a problem is solved by repeatedly solving smaller parts of the problem. A part of a program can be run and rerun on the results of the previous run (e.g. repeatedly dividing a number by 2).

## Worked example

Here is an example of a merge sort which will sort the following list into ascending order.

| 8 | 4 | 2 | 6 | 1 | 3 | 5 | 7 |

The list is recursively split into half to produce a left list and a right list each time.

| 8 | 4 | 2 | 6 | 1 | 3 | 5 | 7 |

| 8 | 4 | 2 | 6 | 1 | 3 | 5 | 7 |

This continues until there is only one item in each list. Therefore each list is sorted into order.

| 8 | 4 | 2 | 6 | 1 | 3 | 5 | 7 |

The left and right lists are now recursively merged with the items in the correct order.

| 4 | 8 | 2 | 6 | 1 | 3 | 5 | 7 |

The leftmost items in each list are the lowest items of those lists and the algorithm compares them – in this case 4 with 2. The 2 is inserted in the new list and the 4 is then compared with the second number of the right list – 6. The 4 is inserted and the 6 is compared with the second number of the left list.

| 2 | 4 | 6 | 8 | 1 | 3 | 5 | 7 |

The algorithm now merges these two lists in the same way to produce the final sorted list. 1 is compared with 2 and then 2 with 3, 3 with 4 etc.

| 1 | 2 | 3 | 4 | 5 | 6 | 7 | 8 |

## Activity 23

Using a table like the one in the worked example, show how the following list would be sorted into descending order using merge sort.

48, 20, 9, 17, 13, 21, 28, 60

# Problem solving

## Efficiency of sorting algorithms

This graph compares the performance of the bubble and merge sort algorithms.

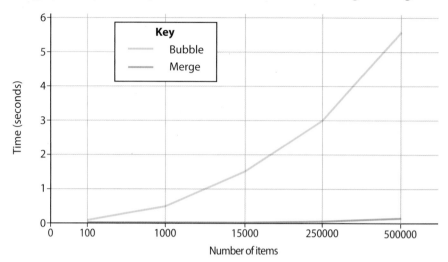

**Figure 1.14** A graph comparing the performance of bubble and merge sort algorithms

The bubble and merge sort algorithms demonstrate two alternative approaches to algorithm design.

The bubble sort algorithm is said to be using **brute force** because it starts at the beginning and completes the same task over and over again until it has found a solution.

The merge sort uses the '**divide and conquer**' method because it repeatedly breaks down the problem into smaller sub-problems, solves those and then combines the solutions.

The graph shows that a bubble sort is far slower at sorting lists of more than 1000 items, but for smaller lists the time difference is negligible.

As the bubble sort algorithm is easier to code it could be advantageous to use it for smaller lists of less than 1000 items.

## Searching algorithms

To find a specific item in a list involves carrying out a search. Like sorting, some methods of searching are more efficient than others.

### Linear search

A linear search is a simple algorithm and it is not subtle. It simply starts at the beginning of the list and goes through it, item by item, until it finds the item it is looking for or reaches the end of the list without finding it.

A linear search is sequential as it moves through the list item by item.

## Activity 24 ?

This flowchart displays a linear search algorithm, but some of the symbols have not been labelled. Draw and complete the flowchart using the labels provided.

```
                    ┌─────────────┐
                    │    Start    │
                    └─────────────┘
                           │
                           ▼
                ┌─────────────────────┐
                │ length = length of array │
                └─────────────────────┘
                           │
                           ▼
                    ╱─────────────╲
                   ╱               ╲
                   ╲               ╱
                    ╲─────────────╱
                           │
                           ▼
                ┌─────────────────────┐
                │  target = search item │
                └─────────────────────┘
                           │
                           ▼
              ╱──────────────╲    NO    ┌─────────────┐
             ╱                ╲────────▶│             │
             ╲                ╱         └─────────────┘
              ╲──────────────╱                │
                     │ YES                     ▼
                     ▼                   ╱──────────────╲   NO
          ╱─────────────────╲          ╱                ╲──────
          ╱  Output array     ╲        ╲                ╱
          ╲    [index]        ╱         ╲──────────────╱
           ╲─────────────────╱                │ YES
                     │                         ▼
                     ▼               ╱─────────────────╲
              ┌─────────────┐        ╱                  ╲
              │     End     │        ╲                  ╱
              └─────────────┘         ╲────────────────╱
                                             │
                                             ▼
                                      ┌─────────────┐
                                      │     End     │
                                      └─────────────┘
```

**Labels**

| | | |
|---|---|---|
| Output search item not found | Is index > length? | Does array [index] = target? |
| index = index + 1 | Input search item | |

**Figure 1.15** A flowchart displaying a linear search algorithm with labels missing

## Activity 25 ?

An array contains the names of the one hundred most downloaded performers on an online music streaming site.

Produce an algorithm expressed in pseudo-code that enables a user to see if their favourite performer is in the top 100.

> **Key term**
>
> **Median**: the middle number when the numbers are put in ascending or descending order (e.g. if there are 13 numbers, then the 7th number is the median).
>
> If there are an even number of items in an ascending list, choose the item to the right of the middle (e.g. if there are 10 numbers, then choose the 6th as the median).

### *Binary search*

Like a merge sort, a binary search uses a 'divide and conquer' method.

> **Did you know?**
>
> You have probably used a binary search method when trying to guess a number between two limits. If you are asked to guess a number between 1 and 20 you will probably start at 10, the middle number. If you are told this is too high, you will then guess 5, the middle number between 1 and 10, and then repeat this method until you find the correct one.

In a binary search the middle or **median** item in a list is repeatedly selected to reduce the size of the list to be searched – another example of recursion. If the selected item is too high or too low then the items below or above that selected item can be searched.

To use this method the list must be sorted into ascending or descending order. It will not work on an unsorted list.

#### Binary search (items in ascending order)

1. Select the median item of the list.
2. If the median item is equal to the search item then stop.
3. If the median is too high then repeat 1 and 2 with the sub-list to the left.
4. If the median is too low then repeat 1 and 2 with the sub-list to the right.
5. Repeat steps 3 and 4 until the item has been found or all of the items have been checked.

#### Worked example

In this list, the search item is the number 13.

| | | | | | | | | | |
|---|---|---|---|---|---|---|---|---|---|
| 3 | 13 | 24 | 27 | (31) | 39 | 45 | 60 | 69 | Select the median number. |

As this is too high, the sub-list to the left of the median must be searched.

| | | | | |
|---|---|---|---|---|
| 3 | 13 | (24) | 27 | The median number of this sub-list is now selected. |

This is again too high and so the sub-list to the left must be searched.

| | | |
|---|---|---|
| 3 | (13) | The median number is now the search item. |

**Figure 1.16** Binary search including sub-lists

In this example, it took three attempts to find the search item. A linear search would have accomplished this with only two attempts.

## Activity 26 ?

Display the stages of a binary search, as in the worked example above, to find the number 13 in this list.

3 9 13 15 21 24 27 30 36 39 42 54 69

Here is part of the algorithm displayed as pseudo-code. Some of the lines are incomplete as indicated by 'x' symbols.

| | |
|---|---|
| `xxxxxxxxxxxxxxxxxxxxxxxxxxxxx` | #The items to be sorted are in an array with the identifier 'aList' containing the values: 3, 13, 24, 27, 31, 39, 45, 60, 69. |
| `SET start TO 0` | #The variable 'start' is set to 0 – the index of the first item in the list. |
| `SET end TO LENGTH(aList) — 1` | #The variable 'end' is set to the index of the last item in the list. |
| `SET found TO False` | #The Boolean variable 'found' is assigned the value 'false'. |
| `SEND 'Please enter the search item.' TO DISPLAY` | |
| `RECEIVE target FROM KEYBOARD` | #The user is asked to enter the search item. |
| `WHILE start <= end AND found = False DO` | #A while loop is set up with these conditions as the loop should stop either when the target is found or all of the list has been searched, i.e. when the 'start' and 'end' values are the same. |
| `    SET middle TO (start + end) DIV 2` | #The median is found and is assigned to the variable 'middle'. |
| `    IF aList[middle] = target THEN` | #If the target is found, the user is informed and 'found' is set to 'true' to stop the WHILE loop. |
| `       found = True` | |
| `       SEND target + ' is in the list' TO DISPLAY` | |
| `    END IF` | |
| `    IF target < aList[middle] THEN` | |
| `       end = xxxxxxxxxxxxxxxxxxxxxxxxxxxx` | |
| `    ELSE` | |
| `       start = xxxxxxxxxxxxx` | |
| `    END IF` | |
| `END WHILE` | |
| `IF found = False THEN` | |
| `    SEND ('The search item is not in the list.') TO DISPLAY` | |
| `END IF` | |

## Activity 27 ?

Complete the missing sections of the pseudo-code.

# Problem solving

## Efficiency of searching algorithms

In the example on page 36, the linear search was more efficient because it only had to carry out two comparisons instead of the three for binary search. But is this always the case?

Searching algorithms can be compared by looking at the 'worst case' and the 'best case' for each one.

### Worked example

If you wanted to find a particular item in a list of 1000 items these are the best and worst case scenarios for the linear search and binary search algorithms.

**Linear search**

A linear search starts at the first item and then works through sequentially.

The best case would be if the item is first in the list.

The worst case would be if it is the last in the list.

Therefore in this example the average would be 500 comparisons.

**Binary search**

The best case would be if the item is in the median position in the list. The search would require only one comparison.

For the worst case it would have to choose the following medians until it finally hit the target.

(This assumes that the target is always smaller than the median.)

| Attempt | Median |
|---------|--------|
| 1 | 500 |
| 2 | 250 |
| 3 | 125 |
| 4 | 63 |
| 5 | 32 |
| 6 | 16 |
| 7 | 8 |
| 8 | 4 |
| 9 | 2 |
| 10 | 1 |

Therefore the worst case for the binary search is ten comparisons.

The binary search is therefore far more efficient than the linear search.

So should a binary search be used every time? That depends on the circumstances. The binary search has one great disadvantage – the list must be already sorted into ascending or descending order and therefore a sorting algorithm must be applied before the search.

If the list is to be searched just once then a linear search would be better, but if there is a large list that will be searched many times then sorting the list and using binary search would be better. Once the list has been sorted new items can be inserted into the correct places.

## Exam-style question

A tutor has stored learner surnames in an array as shown below.

| Marek | Jackson | Bachchan | Wilson | Abraham | French | Smith |
|-------|---------|----------|--------|---------|--------|-------|

**1** Show the stages of a bubble sort when applied to this data.

The tutor has a sorted list of names from another class as shown below.

| Azikiwe | Bloom | Byrne | Davidson | Gateri | Hinton | Jackson | Linton | Smith | Wall |
|---------|-------|-------|----------|--------|--------|---------|--------|-------|------|

**2** Show the stages of a binary search to find the name 'Jackson' when applied to this list.

## Exam tips

These questions are testing knowledge of the sort and search algorithms.

**1** The answer should be set out to show how the data is progressively sorted using the bubble sort and the result of each pass should be shown.

**2** This question is to check that you know that this is a recursive method where the median is repeatedly selected.

## Summary

- An array stores multiple items of data.
- There are many algorithms for sorting and searching data.
- The choice of algorithm depends on the data that is to be processed.

## Checkpoint

### Strengthen

**S1** Describe the differences between the 'bubble sort' and 'merge sort' algorithms.

**S2** Describe how a binary search algorithm finds the search item.

### Challenge

**C1** Explain when a linear search might be preferable to a binary search even though the binary search algorithm is more efficient.

**C2** Discuss the advantages of using arrays in algorithms.

How confident do you feel about your answers to these questions? If you're not sure you answered them well, try the following activities again.

- For S1 have a look at pages 30–33.
- For S2 have a look at pages 36–37.

# Problem solving

## 1.2 Decomposition and abstraction

### Learning outcomes

By the end of this section you should be able to:

- analyse a problem by investigating requirements (inputs, outputs, processing, initialisation) and design a solution.
- decompose a problem into smaller sub-problems.
- explain how abstraction can be used effectively to model aspects of the real world.
- program abstractions of real-world examples.

### Key terms

**Computational thinking**: the thought processes involved in formulating problems and their solutions so that the solutions are represented in a form that can be effectively carried out by a computer.

**Decomposition**: breaking a problem down into smaller, more manageable parts, which are then easier to solve.

**Abstraction**: the process of removing or hiding unnecessary detail so that only the important points remain.

## Problem solving

The tasks of a computer scientist include defining and analysing problems; creating structured solutions – algorithms; coding the solutions into a form that can be implemented by a computer.

These tasks are part of what is known as **computational thinking**.

One of the skills required for computational thinking is algorithm design, which we've covered in detail in this chapter. If there is a fault in the algorithm design then the program will not work, however good a coder you are. Two other skills are **decomposition** and **abstraction**.

## Decomposition

Decomposition is usually the first step in the problem-solving process. Once a problem has been broken down and the sub-problems have been identified, algorithms to solve each of them can be developed.

Decomposition means that sub-problems can be worked on by different teams at the same time. As smaller algorithms are developed for each sub-problem, it is easier to spot and correct errors and when the algorithm is developed into a program, code can be reused.

### Worked example

A learner has been set the task of creating a computer version of the 'noughts and crosses' game where a user plays against the computer.

**Figure 1.17** Sub-problems to be solved to create a noughts and crosses computer program

The diagram shows some of the sub-problems that must be solved in order to solve the complete problem and create a version of the game.

## Abstraction

We use abstraction all the time in our daily lives. We abstract the essential features of something so that we can understand what people are trying to communicate.

Somebody might say, 'I was walking down the street when I saw a cat.' You immediately understand what they mean by 'street' – probably a road with a pavement and houses or shops along the side of it. Similarly you can picture the cat – a smallish animal with fur, four legs and a tail. An animal that is basically 'cattish'. You have extracted the basic properties of animals called cats so that you can recognise one when you see one or imagine one when somebody talks about a cat.

What you picture is very unlikely to be exactly like the actual street and cat that the person experienced. But because of our ability to abstract, the person did not have to go into unnecessary painstaking detail about exactly where they were and what they saw. They wouldn't get very far with the story if they did.

Is this the street and cat you imagined?

When we create algorithms we abstract the basic details of the problem and represent them in a way that a computer is able to process.

### Worked example

Yasmin is designing a computer version of a game in which users have to throw a die to determine their number of moves.

In the computer game the users can't have an actual die, so she will have to design a 'pretend' or virtual die that behaves in exactly the same way as a real-life die.

Yasmin will have to use her powers of abstraction to work out the essential features of a die and then represent them in computer code.

To represent the die she will have to create a routine that will select a random number from 1 to 6 because that's what a die does.

Yasmin has used abstraction to model a real-life event.

### Levels of abstraction

There are different levels or types of abstraction. The higher the level of abstraction, the less is the detail that is required. We use abstraction all the time in accomplishing everyday tasks.

When programmers write the 'print' command they do not have to bother about all of the details of how this will be accomplished. They are removed from them. They are at a certain level of abstraction.

A driver turning the ignition key to start a car does not have to understand how the engine works or how the spark to ignite the petrol is generated. It just happens and they can simply drive the car. That is abstraction.

# Problem solving

## An example – noughts and crosses

The diagram on page 40 showed some of the sub-problems that the problem of creating a noughts and crosses game could be divided into. The following could be written at a high level of abstraction.

- The computer goes first. Then the user. This continues until either one wins or all of the squares have been used.

Immediately a pattern can be recognised – a loop will be needed.

### Inputs and outputs

The following inputs from the user will be needed.

- Start the game.
- Entries for the user.
- Select a new game or finish.

The following outputs will be needed.

- A message to inform the user when it is their turn.
- A message to inform the user if they try to select a square that has already been used.
- A message to inform the user if the game is a draw.
- A message to inform the user if they or the computer has won.
- A message to ask the user if they want to play another game or want to finish.

### Processing and initialisation

The following processing will be needed.

- Set up the grid with the nine squares.
- Initialise all variables to a start value.
- Decide which square the computer will select.
- Allow the user to select a square.
- Check if the user has selected an already used square.
- Check if the computer or the user has won.
- Check if all squares have been used and the game is a draw.
- Allow the user to select a new game or finish.

The solution is still at a high level of abstraction and more details will need to be added.

For example, the programmer will need to decide how the game will record which player has selected each square; how the computer will decide which square to select; how the game will decide if the computer or the user has won.

The programmer will have to go into more and more detail or move to lower levels of abstraction.

Eventually the programmer will be able to design an algorithm for the game and code it using a high-level programming language such as Python or Java. Even before they start to implement the game, they will need to plan how they will test the finished program to make sure that it works correctly; what test data they will use; what outcomes it should produce.

## Coding an algorithm

High-level programming languages make it easier for a programmer to write code. Unfortunately, the processor, which has to execute the program, cannot understand the language it is written in, so it needs a translator to translate the code into the only language it does understand – a stream of 1s and 0s.

These high-level languages are therefore at a high level of abstraction – very far removed from the actual language of a computer.

The processing can be split into parts. For example, in the example of the noughts and crosses game there could be separate algorithms for:

- deciding where the computer should make its next selection – it could be called 'computer entry';
- checking if the computer or the player has won – it could be called 'check if won';
- checking if there are any empty squares left – it could be called 'check draw'.

These separate algorithms could be used when they are needed. It is efficient because it means that the same code doesn't have to be rewritten whenever it is needed.

These items of code are called **subprograms**.

In Chapter 2 we'll look in detail at how subprograms are used to reduce the complexity of programs and to make them easier to understand.

In the die example above, the designer could write a subprogram called 'die' that generates a random number from 1 to 6. In the main program the designer could just call the 'die' subprogram without having to think about how to implement it each time.

### Key term

**Subprogram**: a self-contained module of code that performs a specific task. It can be 'called' by the main program when it is needed.

### Activity 28 ?

In a game each player spins a wheel that is divided into four colours: red, blue, green and yellow. Each player has to answer a question on a particular topic depending on the colour next to a pointer when the wheel stops. Red is for science, blue for history, green for general knowledge and yellow for geography. A player scores two points if they answer correctly on the first attempt and one point for being correct on the second attempt. The first player to reach 30 points is the winner.

Your task is to design a computer version of the game for up to four players. You must analyse the problem and list all of the requirements; decompose the problem, list all the sub-problems and write a brief description of each; list all of the input, output and processing requirements.

One of the requirements that will have to be modelled is the spinning of the wheel. Using a written description and pseudo-code show how this could be done.

### Did you know?

Computer models or simulations of real life are widely used. It is far cheaper and safer to train pilots on flight simulators than on real aircraft. They are also used in weather forecasting, designing and testing new cars and bridges and even teaching people to drive. A computer model is used by the Chancellor of the Exchequer to predict what will happen if changes are made in the Budget (e.g. if taxes are raised or lowered).

# Problem solving

## Summary

- Computational thinking is an approach to solving problems that includes techniques such as decomposition and abstraction.
- Problems are easier to solve if they are decomposed into smaller sub-problems.
- Abstraction is used to remove unnecessary detail to make a problem easier to understand and solve.
- When designing a solution to a problem the inputs, outputs and processing requirements should be identified at the outset.

## Checkpoint

### Strengthen

**S1** Explain what is meant by 'decomposition' and the benefits it provides for programmers.

**S2** Explain what is meant by 'abstraction'.

### Challenge

**C1** Describe examples of the use of 'decomposition' and 'abstraction' when solving a problem.

**C2** In your own words explain what is meant by 'computational thinking'.

How confident do you feel about your answers to these questions? If you're not sure you answered them well, reread pages 40–42.

```
ar sc_security="cc731";
</script>
<script type="text/script"
rc="http://www.com/counter/count
<noscript><div class="counter"><a
nalytics" href="http://com/web/"
arget="_blank"><img class="count
src="http://c.com/7379/0/cc19f7341
         "></a></div></noscri
alt
```

Programming

```
<!-- End of Code forWeb -->
</div>
         <div class="colelem" id="b4514
     <!-- Start of Code -->
      "text/javascript">
```

# Programming

## 2.1 Develop code

### Key term

**Execution**: the process by which a computer carries out the instructions of a computer program.

### Algorithms and programs

As you learnt in Chapter 1, an algorithm is a precise method of solving a problem. It consists of a sequence of unambiguous, step-by-step instructions. A program is an algorithm that has been converted into program code so that it can be **executed** by a computer. A well-written algorithm should be free of logical errors and easy to code in any high-level language.

As part of this course you will learn to write programs in a high-level programming language. All high-level programming languages resemble natural human languages, which makes them easier for humans to read and write but impossible for computers to understand without the help of a translator. You will learn more about how a program written in a high-level language is translated into machine code – the language of computers – in Chapter 4. The aim of this chapter is to develop your generic programming skills rather than to teach you how to program in a particular language.

A computer programmer at work writing code

In Chapter 1 you were introduced to an algorithm for keeping track of a sport club's wins, draws and losses (see pages 20–21). Here is what it looks like coded in the Python programming language.

| Pseudo-code | Python |
|---|---|
| SET totalFor TO 0 | totalFor = 0 |
| SET totalAgainst TO 0 | totalAgainst = 0 |
| SET win TO 0 | win = 0 |
| SET loss TO 0 | loss = 0 |
| SET draw TO 0 | draw = 0 |
| SET anotherEntry TO 'Y' | anotherEntry = 'Y' |
| WHILE anotherEntry = 'Y' DO | while anotherEntry == 'Y': |
|    SEND 'Enter goals for:' TO DISPLAY | |
|    RECEIVE goalsFor FROM KEYBOARD | goalsFor = int(input('Enter goals for:')) |
|    SEND 'Enter goals against:' TO DISPLAY | |
|    RECEIVE goalsAgainst FROM KEYBOARD | goalsAgainst = int(input('Enter goals against:') |
|    SET totalFor TO totalFor + goalsFOR | totalFor = totalFor + goalsFor |
|    SET totalAgainst TO totalAgainst + goalsAgainst | totalAgainst = totalAgainst + goalsAgainst |
|    IF goalsFor > goalsAgainst THEN | if goalsFor > goalsAgainst: |
|      SET win TO win + 1 |   win = win + 1 |
|    ELSE | |
|      IF goalsFOR < goalsAgainst THEN | elif goalsFor < goalsAgainst: |
|        SET loss TO loss + 1 |   loss = loss + 1 |
|      ELSE | |
| | else: |
|        SET draw TO draw + 1 |   draw = draw + 1 |
|      END IF | |
|    END IF | |
|    SEND 'Press 'Y' to enter another result.' TO DISPLAY | |
|    RECEIVE anotherEntry from KEYBOARD | anotherEntry = input("Press 'Y' to enter another result") |
| END WHILE | |
| SEND 'Total wins: ' & win TO DISPLAY | print('Total wins:',win) |
| SEND 'Total losses: ' & loss TO DISPLAY | print('Total losses:',loss) |
| SEND 'Total draws: ' & draw TO DISPLAY | print('Total draws:',draw) |

As you can see, the algorithm and the program are similar, but not the same. Some obvious differences are:

- Command words in pseudo-code are written in capital letters. In Python they are in lower case.
- The SET … TO pseudo-code command is replaced in Python by an equals sign.
- The RECEIVE … FROM pseudo-code command becomes 'input' in Python.
- The SEND … TO DISPLAY pseudo-code command translates into 'print'.

# Programming

- The equivalent of IF … THEN in pseudo-code is 'if' on its own with a colon at the end of the line.
- In fact, there are quite a number of colons in the Python code and none in the pseudo-code.
- There are no END statements in Python. Instead, indentation is used to indicate the start and end of a selection statement or a loop (see page 55).
- In Python the symbol for the relational operator equals is '=='. This enables the computer to tell the difference between the arithmetic operator '=' and the relational operator.

The two also have features in common:

- Both use descriptive variable names.
- Indentation features in both.
- The three programming constructs – sequence, selection and iteration – are the basic building blocks of both.

What you can't see from just looking at the code is that the rules of the programming language, its syntax, are much more important in a program than they are in an algorithm.

You can get away with missing out a bracket, getting the indentation wrong or misspelling a command word in pseudo-code because the target audience is a human and humans are able to make allowances for any shortcomings in the code. The same can't be said for computers. If the code isn't exactly right, the computer won't be able to execute it and will flag up a **syntax error**. Needless to say, you are bound to encounter syntax errors frequently while learning to program.

## Activity 1 ?

Start compiling a reference guide that shows the high-level program code equivalents to the pseudo-code commands you use. Begin by revisiting the algorithms you wrote while studying Chapter 1.

## Top tip

Not all programming languages use the same symbols to represent arithmetic operators. Here are the symbols Python and Java use to represent modulo (MOD), integer division (DIV) and exponent (^):

|  | **Python** | **Java** |
|---|---|---|
| **Modulo** | % | % |
| **Integer Division** | // | Math.floor(a / b) |
| **Exponent** | ** | Math.pow(a, b) |

You need to check which symbols the language you are learning uses for arithmetic operators.

## Data types

As you learnt in Chapter 1, algorithms use variables (named memory locations) to store values. Variables have a variety of uses, for example controlling the number of times a loop is executed, determining which branch of an IF statement is taken, keeping running totals and holding user input.

When algorithms are converted into programs the computer needs to be told what type of data is stored in each variable. Every programming language has a number of built-in **data types**.

| Data type | Description | Example | Examples of use |
|---|---|---|---|
| integer | Used to store whole numbers without a fractional part. | 30 | age = 30<br>number = 5 |
| real | Used to store numbers with a fractional part (decimal place). Real numbers are sometimes referred to as floats (short for floating point). | 25.5 | weight = 25.5<br>price = 12.55 |
| Boolean | Only has two possible values: True or False. | False | correct = False<br>lightOn = True |
| character | Used to store a single character or symbol. | 'm' | gender = 'm'<br>char = ':' |

**Table 2.1** Common data types

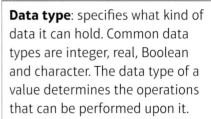

When writing pseudo-code you don't have to specify the data types of variables. However, data types become much more important once you start programming in a high-level language because the data type of a variable determines the operations that can be performed on it.

For example, the result of multiplying a value by 5 differs according to its data type.

```
integer      8 * 5 = 40
real         8.0 * 5 = 40.0
character    '8' * 5 = '88888'
```

The method of declaring variables differs between programming languages. Some languages, such as Python, automatically select the appropriate data type for a variable based on the data assigned to it. Others, such as Java, require the data type of variables to be declared before the variables can be used.

**Top tip**

Although you don't have to declare the data types of variables in pseudo-code, it is a good idea to do so. You can simply list the variables and their data types at the start of an algorithm, for example:

```
INTEGER age
REAL weight
BOOLEAN correct
CHARACTER gender
```

You can also specify the data type of a variable in the RECEIVE statement, for example:

```
RECEIVE age FROM (INTEGER) KEYBOARD
RECEIVE price FROM (REAL) KEYBOARD
```

# Programming

## Variable initialisation

When a variable is declared, the computer allocates it a location in memory. Initially this location is empty, so before a variable can be used it has to be given a value.

You can put an initial value into a variable by

- initialising it when the program is run (e.g. `SET total TO 0`);
- reading a value from a keyboard or other device (e.g. `RECEIVE admissionCharge FROM (INTEGER) KEYBOARD`).

Once a variable has been **initialised** an **assignment statement** is used to change its value (e.g. `SET total TO total + admissionCharge`).

If a variable, such as a loop counter, is intended to hold a running total, then it should always be initialised to a starting value. Some programming languages won't execute if the programmer fails to do this; others will do so but may well produce some unexpected results.

> ### Key terms
>
> **Initialisation**: the process of assigning an initial value to a variable.
>
> **Assignment statement**: the SET…TO command is used to initialise variables in pseudo-code, for example:
>
> `SET anotherGo TO 0`
>
> `SET correct TO False`
>
> **Type coercion**: the process of converting the value stored in a variable from one data type to another.

### Activity 2 ?

1. Investigate what data types are available in the high-level language you are studying. Produce a table similar to the one above to summarise your findings.
2. Identify an appropriate data type for each of these items.
   a The test score of an individual learner.
   b The average score for a group of learners.
   c Whether or not the pass mark for the test has been achieved.
3. Look back over the algorithms you wrote in Chapter 1 and identify instances of variable initialisation.

### Activity 3 ?

Investigate how type coercion is handled in the high-level language you are studying.

## Type coercion

Sometimes the data type of a variable gets changed during program execution. This is known as **type coercion**. For example, if an integer value and a real value are used in an arithmetic operation, the result will always be a real.

Languages such as Python, where the data type is assumed from the context, have commands that allow the data type to be changed.

### Activity 4

A theme park uses a program to monitor the number of people entering and exiting the park. The maximum number of visitors at any one time must not exceed 10,000. When the number of people in the park reaches the maximum a 'Park Full' message is displayed at the entrance gate. Children can visit the park free of charge, but each accompanying adult must pay £2.50 admission. The program keeps track of the amount of money collected at the gate.

1. Identify the variables needed in the program.
2. Select an appropriate data type for each variable and constant.

## Command sequence, selection and iteration

In Chapter 1 you learnt that the three key building blocks of algorithms are command sequence, selection and iteration. In this chapter you will have the opportunity to implement these constructs in the high-level programming language you are studying.

### Command sequence

A command sequence is a set of instructions that the computer executes one after another in order. Command sequences are usually combined with loops and selection statements.

---

**Activity 5** ?

```
RECEIVE number1 FROM (INTEGER) KEYBOARD
RECEIVE number2 FROM (INTEGER) KEYBOARD
SET result1 TO number1 / number2
SEND result1 TO DISPLAY
SET result2 TO number1 MOD number2
SEND result2 TO DISPLAY
SET result3 TO number1 DIV number2
SEND result3 TO DISPLAY
```

1 Describe what this algorithm does.
2 State the output of the algorithm given the following inputs:

   **a**  4, 2

   **b**  10, 3

   **c**  20, 6

3 Implement this algorithm in the high-level language you are studying.

---

### Selection

The selection construct is used to create a branch in a program. The computer selects which branch to follow based on the outcome of a condition, for example:

```
IF day = 'Saturday' OR day = 'Sunday' THEN
    SET alarm TO 11
ELSE
    SET alarm TO 8
END IF
```

A standard IF…THEN…ELSE statement provides two alternatives. If there are more than two, then a nested IF must be used. However, many high-level programming languages have an additional built-in selection construct that does away with the need for a nested IF statement.

# Programming

## Activity 6 ?

1   Investigate the selection statements that are available in the high-level programming language you are studying.

2   In Chapter 1, Activity 8 (on page 11) you created an algorithm that inputs a learner's age and calculates how many driving lessons they will require according to a set of rules.
    Implement this algorithm in the high-level programming language you are studying.

3   In Chapter 1, Activity 10 (on page 13) you studied an algorithm for calculating the grade achieved in an end-of-topic test.
    Implement this algorithm in the high-level language you are studying.

## Top tip

Many programming languages allow you to test multiple conditions within the same IF statement to save you having to use nested IFs. Here's how it's done in Python and Java.

**Python**

```
if num1 > num2:
    print(num1)
elif num1 < num2:
    print(num2)
else:
    print('Equal')
```

**Java**

```
if (num1 > num2) {
    System.out.println(num1);
} else if (num1 < num2) {
    System.out.println(num2);
} else {
    System.out.println('Equal');
}
```

### Loops

A loop is another name for an iteration. Loops are used to make a computer repeat a set of instructions more than once. There are two types of loop – definite and indefinite.

A definite loop is used when you know in advance how often the instructions in the body of the loop are to be repeated. For example, if you want the computer to display a character on the screen for a fixed amount of time and then remove it.

An indefinite loop is used when the number of times a loop will need to be repeated is not known in advance. For example, if you want to give a user the option of playing a game as often as they want. Indefinite loops are repeated until a specified condition is reached.

Every programming language has a number of built-in loop constructs. You will need to explore the ones provided in the language you are studying.

## Top tip

It is sometimes necessary to place one loop statement within another loop statement. This is called a nested loop.

## Top tip

Here's how to write a WHILE loop in Python and Java.

**Python**

```
counter = 0
while counter < 10:
    print(counter)
    counter = counter + 1
```

**Java**

```
int counter =10;
while(counter < 10) {
    System.out.println(counter);
    counter++;
}
```

## Activity 7 ?

1   Describe what these two algorithms do and implement them in the high-level programming language you are studying.

   **a** Algorithm A

```
FOR index FROM 1 TO 10 DO
    SEND index * index * index TO DISPLAY
END FOR
```

   **b** Algorithm B

```
SET counter TO 10
    WHILE counter > 0 DO
        SEND counter TO DISPLAY
        SET counter TO counter - 1
    END WHILE
```

2   In Chapter 1, Activity 11 (on page 14) you created two versions of an algorithm for a dice game: one used a WHILE…DO loop and the other a REPEAT…UNTIL loop.
   Implement both versions in the high-level programming language you are studying.

3   In Chapter 1, Activity 12 (on page 15) you created an algorithm that sums all the numbers in a range.
   Implement this algorithm in the high-level programming language you are studying.

### Top tip

Be careful not to create an infinite loop – one that will never end. Always ensure that the condition to terminate the loop will eventually be met.

## Activity 8 ?

In Chapter 1, Activity 17 (on page 24) you developed an algorithm using a nested loop for part of a simulation of a payment system at a car park.

Implement this algorithm in the high-level programming language you are studying.

## Summary

- A program is an algorithm that has been converted into program code.
- Pseudo-code is far more forgiving than program code.
- The four basic data types are integer, float/real, Boolean and character.
- The data type of a variable determines the operations that can be performed on it.
- Data types don't have to be declared in pseudo-code but it's a good idea to do so.
- Variable and type declarations, command sequences, selection and iteration are four of the structural components of a program.

## Checkpoint

### Strengthen

**S1** Explain why variables are needed.
**S2** Give examples of the four data types.
**S3** Describe how selection and iteration are implemented in the high-level language you are studying.

### Challenge

**C1** Describe these structural components of a program: variable and type declarations, command sequences, selection and iteration constructs.

How confident do you feel about your answers to these questions? If you're not sure you answered them well, try redoing the activities in this section.

# Programming

## 2.2 Making programs easy to read

### Learning outcomes

By the end of this section you should be able to:

- explain the benefit of producing programs that are easy to read.
- use techniques to improve the readability of code and describe how code works.

### Code readability

You should always try to ensure that any code you write is easy to read and understand. This benefits you and anyone else who needs to understand how your programs work.

It's surprising how quickly you forget. Try revisiting the programs you have already written in this chapter and make sure it is still clear to you what they do and how they work. Imagine how much more difficult it would be to make sense of a complex program with lots of variables, subprograms, nested loops and multiple selection statements.

Contrary to what you might think, programming is not a solitary activity. Programmers usually work in teams, with each programmer developing a different part of the program. This only works if they all adopt a consistent approach to writing readable code.

```
Python 3.4.1: example2.py - C:/Python/example2.py          —  □  ✕
File  Edit  Format  Run  Options  Windows  Help
import random
game=True
while game==True:
    Num1=int(input("Choose one of the following: 1 Rock, 2 Paper, or 3 Scissors:")
    Num2=random.randint(1,3)
    if Num2==1:
        print("Computer chooses Rock")
    elif Num2==2:
        print("Computer chooses Paper")
    else:
        print("Computer chooses Scissors")
    if Num1==Num2:
        print("It's a draw")
    elif Num1==1 and Num2==3:
        print("You win!")
    elif Num1==2 and Num2==1:
        print("You win!")
    elif Num1==3 and Num2==2:
        print("You win!")
    else:
        print("Computer wins")
    text=input("Play again? Y/N:")
    if text!="Y":
        game=False
                                                     Ln: 26 Col: 0
```

**Figure 2.1** An example of Python code

The programmer who produced this program did not follow good practice. There are a number of ways that the readability of this code could be improved.

- Use descriptive names for variables (e.g. userChoice instead of Num1).
- Add blank lines between different blocks to make them stand out.
- Add comments that explain what each part of the code does.

Programmers often work in teams; it is vital that any coding they share is clear and error free

This table lists the techniques you should use to make your programs easy to read and understand.

| Technique | Description |
|---|---|
| Comments | Comments should be used to explain what each part of the program does. |
| Descriptive names | Using descriptive identifiers for variables, constants and subprograms helps to make their purpose clear. |
| Indentation | Indentation makes it easier to see where each block of code starts and finishes. Getting the indentation wrong can result in the program not running or not producing the expected outcomes. |
| White space | Adding blank lines between different blocks of code makes them stand out. |

**Table 2.2** Techniques for program clarity

**Activity 9** ?

Investigate how to write comments in the high-level language you are studying.

**Top tip**

Here's how to write comments in Python and Java.

- **Python**: start each line of a comment with the # symbol.
- **Java**: start single line comment with // or start a multi-line comment with /* and end it with */

**Did you know?**

Microsoft® Windows® uses roughly 40 million lines of code – code readability obviously becomes more and more important as programs get larger.

# Programming

Calculators have a number of useful functions

## Activity 10    ?

**1** Rewrite this algorithm using appropriate techniques to make it easier to read.

```
SET x TO 10
WHILE x >= 0 DO
IF x > 0
SEND x TO DISPLAY
ELSE
SEND 'Blast Off' TO DISPLAY
END IF
SET x TO x -1
END WHILE
```

**2** Implement the improved algorithm in the high-level language you are studying.

**3** Design an algorithm for a simple calculator that:
  **a** allows the user to choose from these options: addition, subtraction, division and multiplication;
  **b** prompts the user to input two numbers;
  **c** performs the calculation and displays the result;
  **d** offers the user the option of performing another calculation.

**4** Implement this algorithm in the high-level programming language you are studying, ensuring you use techniques to make the program easy to read.

Self-checkout machines are a common sight in supermarkets

## Exam-style question

XtraSave is a chain of supermarkets that has recently installed self-checkouts in all its stores.

Customers are issued with one 10p voucher for each £10 they spend and one 5p voucher if they spend £5.

The self-checkout system uses the following algorithm to print vouchers.

```
01 RECEIVE amountSpent FROM (INTEGER) KEYBOARD
02 WHILE amountSpent >= 5 DO
03    IF amountSpent >= 10 THEN
04         SEND voucherTen TO PRINTER
05         SET amountSpent TO amountSpent - 10
06    ELSE
07         IF amountSpent >= 5 THEN
08              SEND voucherFive TO PRINTER
09              SET amountSpent TO amountSpent - 5
10         END IF
11    END IF
12 END WHILE
```

1 Identify the line number(s) that show **one** example of each of these structural components: **(3 marks)**

    **a** Selection

    **b** Iteration

    **c** Variable initialisation

2 Identify **two** techniques the programmer has used to improve the readability of the code. **(2 marks)**

3 Give **two** reasons for writing code that is easy to read. **(2 marks)**

### Exam tip

This question is testing your ability to identify two of the main programming constructs. Make sure you have identified the line numbers in which the selection and iteration constructs are found.

## Summary

- Using comments, descriptive names, indentation and white space makes code easier to read.
- Producing readable code makes it easier to understand what a program does and how it does it.

## Checkpoint

### Strengthen

**S1** Explain why it is important to make your code easy to read.

**S2** Describe **four** techniques that a programmer should use to make code easy to read.

### Challenge

**C1** Revisit the programs you have already written. Do you still understand what they do and how they work? If not, try to improve their readability.

How confident do you feel about your answers to these questions? If you're not sure you answered them well, look again at the table on page 55.

## 2.3 Strings

### Key terms

**String**: a sequence of characters. They can be letters, numbers, symbols, punctuation marks or spaces.

**Function**: a function is a subprogram that performs a specific task and can be used at any point in the program. High-level programming languages have a number of useful built-in functions. You can also create your own or use functions available in online libraries.

Earlier in the chapter you learnt that a character is one of the four basic data types. A character can be a single letter, a symbol, a number or even a space.

A sequence of characters is called a **string**. Although strings can contain different sorts of characters, including numbers, they are all treated as if they were text.

When a computer executes a program it needs a way of telling the difference between a string and an instruction. In most programming languages this is achieved by enclosing strings in quotation marks (e.g. 'johnsmith@mail.com', '10/04/15' or '123'). Both single ' ' and double " " quotation marks are acceptable, as long as they are used consistently. In the example "It's her book", the apostrophe is treated as part of the string because double quotes have been used to enclose the string.

Strings are very useful when communicating with users. For example, asking them to enter some information into a program or displaying the output of a program in a format that humans can read and understand.

### String indexing

Each character in a string has an index number, with the first character at position 0. You can use the index to reference individual characters in a string.

For example, if the string `myText` holds the value 'Computer Science', then `myText[1]` references the letter 'o', `myText[8]` references the space and `myText[11]` the letter 'i'.

| Index | 0 | 1 | 2 | 3 | 4 | 5 | 6 | 7 | 8 | 9 | 10 | 11 | 12 | 13 | 14 | 15 |
|--------|---|---|---|---|---|---|---|---|---|---|----|----|----|----|----|----|
| String | C | o | m | p | u | t | e | r |   | S | c | i | e | n | c | e |

**Table 2.3** Example string index

### Length

The Edexcel pseudo-code has a built-in `LENGTH` **function**, which you can use to find the number of characters in a string (e.g. in the case of the string 'Computer Science', `SET numChars TO LENGTH(myText)` assigns the value 16 to the variable `numChars`).

The programming language you are studying will have a function for finding the length of a string. You should investigate what it is called and how it works.

Design and write a program to check the length of a password. If the password entered is less than six characters, the program should output 'The password you have entered is not long enough'; otherwise it should output 'Length of password OK'.

## String traversal

You can use a FOR loop to cycle through each of the characters in a string. This is known as **string traversal**.

The following algorithm prints out the word 'monkey' letter by letter, displaying each letter on a separate line.

```
SET animalName TO 'monkey'
FOR index = 0 TO LENGTH(animalName) - 1
   SEND animalName[index] TO DISPLAY
END FOR
```

## Concatenation

As you learnt in Chapter 1 (on page 18), concatenation involves joining two or more items of information together. Concatenating two strings produces a new string object. Concatenation comes in very handy when displaying text on screen.

The following piece of code asks the user to input their name and stores it in the variable `userName`. The string '`Hello `' and the value stored in `userName` are concatenated using the & symbol, which is known as a concatenation or append operator.

```
RECEIVE userName FROM (STRING) KEYBOARD
SEND 'Hello ' & userName TO DISPLAY
```

Most programming languages have a number of different ways of concatenating strings. You need to investigate how it is done in the language you are studying.

## Type conversion

Type conversion is performed when a string and a non-string (for example an integer) are joined together. The computer converts the non-string into a string before joining the two strings together.

In the next example the string value stored in the variable `learnerName` and the integer value stored in the variable `testScore` are concatenated to form a new string, which is stored in the variable message.

```
RECEIVE learnerName FROM (STRING) KEYBOARD
RECEIVE testScore FROM (INTEGER) KEYBOARD
SET message TO learnerName & testScore
SEND message TO DISPLAY
```

# Programming

## Slicing

Slicing is the process of extracting part of a string. This example algorithm extracts the string 'foot' from 'football'.

```
SET sport TO 'football'
SET newString TO ''
FOR index FROM 0 TO 3 DO
    SET newString TO newString & sport[index]
END FOR
SEND newString TO DISPLAY
```

### Activity 13    ?

1   Investigate how to concatenate and slice a string in the high-level programming language you are studying.

2   A company wants a program to generate usernames for new employees. Each username consists of the first four letters of the employee's last name and the first letter of their first name joined together. If the employee's last name is less than four characters in length a letter 'X' is used to fill in for each of the missing characters. Develop a program that asks the user to input their first and last names and outputs their username.

3   Use string slicing to split this line of data into a set of seven strings.
    '23456,West Kirby,04/11/15,23.0,11.5,30,D1'
    The comma indicates where one string ends and the next begins and should be omitted when the string is sliced.

## String formatting

Programming languages provide various methods of formatting strings to improve the way they are displayed on screen. They are particularly useful for formatting numbers, for example, by setting the number of decimal places to display.

### Activity 14    ?

Investigate the string formatting methods available in the high-level language you are studying.

### Did you know?

Strings are immutable; this means that they cannot be changed. It might appear that you can alter a string, but what really happens is that a new variable is created and replaces the old one, for example:

```
SET newLearner TO 'Robert Bennett'
SET newLearner TO 'Sally Hadwen'
```

In the first line of this code extract the value 'Robert Bennett' is stored in a memory location to which the identifier newLearner points. In the second line, the value 'Sally Hadwen' is stored in a different location in memory, and the newLearner identifier is then updated to point to this new memory location.

## Summary

- A string is a sequence of characters.
- Each character in a string has a unique index value denoting its position in the string. The first character in a string has the index value 0.
- High-level programming languages have a built-in length function that finds the length of a string.
- A loop is used to traverse a string, character by character.
- Concatenation is the process of joining two or more strings together.
- Slicing is the process of extracting part of a string.
- String formatting is used to control the way text is displayed on screen.

## Checkpoint

### Strengthen

**S1** Describe how individual characters in a string are referenced.

**S2** Design an algorithm that uses a loop to traverse a string.

**S3** Describe how a string and a non-string are concatenated.

### Challenge

**C1** Develop a program that asks the user to input a sentence and then splits it up wherever a space occurs. Each word should then be displayed on a separate line.

How confident do you feel about your answers to these questions? If you're not sure you answered them well, have another go at the activities in this section.

# Programming

## 2.4 Data structures

### Learning outcomes

By the end of this section you should be able to:

- describe the structure of one- and two-dimensional arrays and give examples of their use.
- create and use one- and two-dimensional arrays in programs.
- describe the record data structure and explain what it is used for.
- design record structures.

### Key term

**Data structure**: an organised collection of related elements. Arrays and records are two common data structures used in programming.

A **data structure** is an organised collection of related elements. There are a lot of different data structures used in programming. You've already encountered one of them – strings. In this section we will investigate two more: arrays and records.

### Arrays

As you learnt in Chapter 1, an array is an organised collection of related values with a single shared identifier. All the elements in an array are the same data type. Each has a unique index value denoting its position in the array.

In the Edexcel pseudo-code, an array is initialised using the SET command. For example, this statement initialises an array called `firstNames` with four elements, all of type string.

```
SET firstNames TO ['Alex', 'Bryn', 'Eloise', 'Lois']
```

The square brackets denote the start and end of the array. The next statement initialises an empty array called `winners`.

```
SET winners TO []
```

As with strings, the `LENGTH` function returns the number of elements in an array. In the example below `numItems` is assigned the value 4.

```
numItems = LENGTH(firstNames)
```

### Top tip

Here's how to define an array in Python and Java.

**Python**
```
Scores = [15, 29, 4, 50]
```
**Java**
```
Int[] Scores = {15, 29,
   4, 50};
```

### Looping through an array

FOR loops come in handy when working with arrays. The following algorithm uses a FOR...EACH loop to iterate through the array `firstNames`, element by element, outputting each name in turn.

```
SET firstNames TO ['Alex', 'Bryn', 'Eloise', 'Lois']
FOR EACH name FROM firstNames DO
   SEND name TO DISPLAY
END FOR
```

Different languages have different ways of implementing arrays. For example, in Python the list data structure is used to implement an array. In Java arrays have to be declared prior to being used.

## Searching and sorting

In Chapter 1 you explored algorithms for searching and sorting elements of an array.

---

### Activity 15 ?

The following code uses a linear search algorithm. Describe how it works.

```
SET firstNames TO ['Alex', 'Bryn', 'Eloise', 'Lois',
'James', 'Sally']
RECEIVE searchName FROM (STRING) KEYBOARD

SET found TO False
SET index TO 0

WHILE found = False AND index <= (LENGTH(firstNames) -
1) DO
   IF searchName = firstNames[index] THEN
      SET found TO True
   END IF
   SET index to index + 1
END WHILE


IF found = True THEN
   SEND searchName & ' is at position ' & index & ' in
   the list' TO DISPLAY
ELSE
   SEND searchName & ' is not in the list' TO DISPLAY
END IF
```

Implement this algorithm in the high-level programming language you are studying.

---

**Top tip**

When using a WHILE loop with an array, the loop terminating condition is LENGTH – 1 rather than LENGTH. This is because the index of an array starts at 0, so the index value of the last element of the array is one less than the number of elements in the array.

---

### Activity 16 ?

In Chapter 1, Activity 22 you developed an algorithm that output the highest and lowest results.

Implement this algorithm in the high-level programming language you are studying.

---

High-level programming languages have a number of methods for working with arrays, including append (to add an item to an array), pop (to remove an item from an array) and reverse (to reverse all the elements in an array). They might also have a built-in sort method.

---

### Activity 17 ?

Investigate the array handling methods available in the high-level programming language you are studying.

---

**Did you know?**

Arrays can be static or dynamic. A static array has a fixed length that must be declared when it is created (e.g. `myFriends[5]`). A dynamic array can grow as new items are added. It would be declared as `myFriends[]`.

# Programming

## Two-dimensional arrays

So far, we have only considered one-dimensional arrays consisting of a single row of elements. But a lot of data comes naturally in the form of a matrix. For example, train and bus timetables, conversion tables and football league tables. They can be represented as **two-dimensional arrays**.

In actual fact, a two-dimensional array is an array of arrays. Each row of a two-dimensional array is a one-dimensional array in its own right.

Here is an extract from an array named `examResults`. It has three rows, each of which stores a set of four exam results. The mark of 47 is located at `examResults[1, 2]` – second row, third element along – and the value 80 at `examResults [0, 0]` – first row, first column.

|   | 0 | 1 | 2 | 3 |
|---|---|---|---|---|
| 0 | 80 | 59 | 34 | 89 |
| 1 | 31 | 11 | 47 | 64 |
| 2 | 29 | 56 | 13 | 91 |

### Initiating a two-dimensional array

In the Edexcel pseudo-code, the SET command is used to initiate a two-dimensional array. Note the two sets of square brackets showing that `examResults` is an array of three elements, each of which is an array.

```
SET examResults TO [[80, 59, 34, 89], [31, 11, 47, 64],
[29, 56, 13, 91]]
```

### Looping through a two-dimensional array

A pair of nested FOR loops is used to traverse a two-dimensional array: one to iterate through the rows and the other to iterate through the columns. The FOR loop that iterates through the columns is nested within the one that iterates through the rows. For each iteration of the outer loop, the inner loop iterates through all the columns in one row. This is demonstrated in the algorithm below.

```
FOR EACH row FROM examResults DO
   FOR EACH column FROM examResults[row] DO
      SEND examResults[row, column] TO DISPLAY
   END FOR
END FOR
```

## Activity 18 ?

1 Investigate how to initialise a two-dimensional array in the high-level programming language you are studying.

2 Write a program that creates and initialises an array to hold these five sets of marks.

80, 59, 34, 89
31, 11, 47, 64
29, 56, 13, 91
55, 61, 48, 0
75, 78, 81, 91

3 Extend your program so that it calculates and displays the highest mark, the lowest mark and the average mark achieved.

4 This two-dimensional array holds the highest score achieved by each player in each of the three levels of an online game.

| Player | Level | Score |
|--------|-------|-------|
| Alex | 1 | 19 |
| Seema | 1 | 29 |
| Seema | 2 | 44 |
| Lois | 1 | 10 |
| Alex | 2 | 17 |
| Alex | 3 | 36 |
| Dion | 1 | 23 |
| Emma | 1 | 27 |
| Emma | 2 | 48 |

**Table 2.4** Example two-dimensional array

Develop a program that initialises the array and then searches through it to find the player with the highest score in each of the three levels.

## Records

We have already said that the elements of an array must all be the same data type. In contrast, the **record** data structure stores a set of related values of different data types.

Each element in a record is known as a **field** and is referenced using a field name.

Table 2.5 illustrates how the record data structure works. Each row of the table holds a set of information about a particular learner. Each column stores one item of information about the learner – their learner number, their age, their form etc. All the values in a column have the same data type – `learnerNum` and `age` are integers; `firstName`, `lastName` and `form` are strings.

| learnerNum | firstName | lastName | age | form |
|------------|-----------|----------|-----|------|
| 1 | Susan | Smith | 15 | 10H |
| 2 | Ben | Roberts | 14 | 10B |
| 3 | Anita | Khan | 15 | 10A |
| 4 | Ian | Wright | 15 | 10G |

**Table 2.5** Example record data structure

# Programming

It is essential to have a way to sort through the vast amounts of recorded music available

Programming languages vary in the way they handle the record data structure.

## Activity 19

1 A record data structure is to be used to store the details of music albums. Give the appropriate data type for these fields:
   a the title of the album;
   b the name of the artist;
   c the year of release;
   d the genre.

2 Develop a program that uses a record structure for storing the details of music albums. It must:
   a have fields for title, artist, year of release and genre;
   b allow the user to input the details of new albums;
   c allow the user to search for an album by name and display its details.

## Exam-style question

The XtraSave chain of supermarkets collects data about product sales.
The record for each product includes:
- its unique ID (e.g. X14 or X98);
- the total number sold in each month of the year.

1 Identify a suitable data structure to store this data. **(1 mark)**
2 Explain why the data type you chose is most suitable to hold this data. **(3 marks)**
3 Draw a diagram of the data structure that shows the amount sold in the first three months of the year. Include data for at least two products. **(3 marks)**

## Exam tip

This question is testing your ability to select and design data structures. Make sure you have:
- identified a suitable data structure to store the data and justified your choice;
- provided the sample data requested (i.e. sales figures for two products for the first three months of the year).

Row and column headings can be included as long as they are clearly distinguishable from the data.

## Summary

- A data structure is an organised collection of related elements. Arrays and records are common data structures.
- A one-dimensional array is a list of elements, each of which has a unique index value representing its position in the list.
- A two-dimensional array is a matrix of rows and columns. Each element in the array has a unique pair of indices, one to identify the row and one the column in which it is located.
- All the elements in an array have the same data type.
- A record consists of a collection of fields. The values stored in a record can be of different data types.

## Checkpoint

### Strengthen

**S1** What is the index of the first element in a one-dimensional array?

**S2** How does a linear search algorithm find an element in a one-dimensional array?

**S3** How is an element stored in a two-dimensional array referenced?

**S4** How is a nested IF used to traverse a two-dimensional array?

### Challenge

**C1** Develop a program for a simple address book that uses a one-dimensional array to store a set of names and email addresses, and allows the user to search for a person by name and returns their email address.

**C2** Develop a program that uses a two-dimensional array to represent a treasure map consisting of a grid of 4 rows and 4 columns.
A random number function should be used to establish the location of the treasure.
The user must hunt for the treasure by repeatedly entering the coordinates of squares. The program should tell them when they have found the treasure and help them in their search by indicating how close they are.

How confident do you feel about your answers to these questions? If you're not sure you answered them well, try redoing the activities on pages 63, 65 and 66.

# Programming

## 2.5 Input/output

### User input

Most programs require some form of input either from a user or from a file. You already know how to receive user input from a keyboard.

A program can be made much more 'user friendly' by displaying helpful messages informing users of what they are expected to enter and confirming successful input.

### *Validation*

It is important to ensure that data entered by the user is valid, as invalid data can cause a program to behave unexpectedly or even stop altogether. Not surprisingly, if the data entered into a program is incorrect, the output it produces will also be wrong. This is sometimes called the Garbage In, Garbage Out (GIGO) principle.

Any program that requires data entry should have appropriate forms of **validation** built in. But be warned, validation can't guarantee that the data entered is correct. It can only make sure that it is reasonable.

There are a number of different types of validation.

### *Range check*

A range check is used to ensure that the data entered is within a specified range. Study this algorithm, which checks that the number entered is between 1 and 10.

```
BOOLEAN valid
SET validNum TO False
WHILE validNum = False DO
   SEND 'Please enter a number between 1 and 10:' TO
   DISPLAY
   RECEIVE number FROM (INTEGER) KEYBOARD
   IF number >= 1 AND number <= 10 THEN
      SET validNum TO True
   END IF
END WHILE
SEND 'You have entered: '& number TO DISPLAY
```

> **Key term**
>
> **Validation**: to check that the data entered by a user or from a file meets specified requirements.

The algorithm uses a Boolean variable named `validNum` as a status flag. It is initially set to False. The WHILE loop continues running until `validNum` is equal to True. An IF statement determines if the value of `ValidNum` should be set to True.

### Validating user input

Many programs require the user to choose from a list of options, for example 'yes' or 'no', or 'a', 'b' or 'c'. In this situation it is important to check that a valid option has been chosen.

```
BOOLEAN validChoice
SET validChoice TO False
WHILE validChoice = False DO
   SEND "Please enter either 'Yes' or 'No':" TO DISPLAY
   RECEIVE userChoice FROM (STRING) KEYBOARD
   IF userChoice='Yes' OR userChoice='No' THEN
      SET validChoice TO True
   END IF
END WHILE
SEND You have selected: '& userChoice' TO DISPLAY
```

This algorithm requires the user to enter either 'Yes' or 'No' and uses an IF statement to validate their input. The WHILE loop is repeated until an appropriate choice is made.

A problem with this algorithm is that the user must enter their choice exactly, in order for it to be accepted. For example, entering 'yes' instead of 'Yes' would not be accepted. This issue can be addressed by altering the IF statement to accept more valid options.

```
IF userChoice = 'Yes' OR userChoice = 'yes' OR
userChoice = 'No' OR userChoice = 'no' THEN …
```

### Top tip

Many programming languages have functions that can be used to convert a string to upper or lower case. This can simplify the validation of strings, for example:

**Python**
```
if userChoice.lower() == 'yes' or userChoice.lower() ==
'no':
   validChoice = True
```

**Java**
```
if(userChoice.toLowerCase() == 'yes' ||
userChoice.toLowerCase() == 'no') {
   validChoice = true
}
```

### Activity 20 ?

Implement the range check algorithm in the high-level programming language you are studying.

### Activity 21 ?

Design and implement a program for a user menu with these four options:
1  display average temperature
2  display temperature range
3  display wind speed
4  quit the program

The program should ask the user to select an option and validate their entry. Entries in upper and in lower case should be accepted. When a valid option is selected it should be displayed on screen with an appropriate message.

# Programming

## Length check

It is sometimes necessary to check that the length of a value entered falls within a specified range. For example, all UK postcodes are between six and eight characters long, so validation could be used to check that the length of a postcode entered is within this range. Needless to say, even if it is, that doesn't mean to say it is correct.

```
RECEIVE postCode FROM (STRING) KEYBOARD
SET length TO LENGTH(postCode)
IF length >= 6 AND length <= 8 THEN
   SEND 'Valid' TO DISPLAY
ELSE
   SEND 'Invalid' TO DISPLAY
END IF
```

**Activity 22**  **?**

Implement the length check algorithm in the high-level programming language you are studying.

## Presence check

Another type of validation is a presence check. This simply ensures that a value has been entered, preventing the user from leaving an input blank.

This algorithm asks the user to input their name and uses a presence check to ensure they have entered a value. Any value will cause the loop to finish. It will keep asking the user to input their name until they input a value.

**Activity 23**  **?**

Implement the presence check algorithm in the high-level programming language you are studying.

```
SET userName TO ''
WHILE userName = '' DO
   RECEIVE userName FROM (STRING) KEYBOARD
END WHILE
SEND 'Hello ' & userName TO DISPLAY
```

## Look-up check

A look-up check is used to test that a value is one of a predefined set of acceptable values. The list of acceptable values can be stored in a one-dimensional array.

This algorithm stores a list of valid form names in an array. It compares the form name entered by the user with the values in the array.

```
SET arrayForms TO ['7AXB', '7PDB', '7ARL', '7JEH']
RECEIVE form FROM (STRING) KEYBOARD

SET valid TO False
SET index TO 0
SET length TO LENGTH(arrayForms)

WHILE valid = False AND index < length DO
   IF form = arrayForms[index] THEN
      SET valid TO True
   END IF
   SET index TO index + 1
END WHILE
```

```
IF valid = True THEN
   SEND 'Valid form' TO DISPLAY
ELSE
   SEND 'The form you entered does not exist.' TO DISPLAY
END IF
```

## Menus

Many programs feature menus that allow the user to choose which part of the program they wish to use. The simplest way to implement a menu is to give the user a list of numbered options to choose from and ask them to input the number that corresponds to the option they want to select. The user input can be validated using a range check to ensure that the option selected is permissible. A menu could be set out like the example below.

Option 1: Find the highest value
Option 2: Find the lowest value
Option 3: Calculate the average
Please select either 1, 2 or 3:

This algorithm implements the menu shown above.

```
SEND 'Option 1: Find the highest value' TO DISPLAY
SEND 'Option 2: Find the lowest value' TO DISPLAY
SEND 'Option 3: Calculate the average' TO DISPLAY
validChoice = False
WHILE validChoice = False DO
     SEND 'Please select either 1, 2 or 3:' TO DISPLAY
     RECEIVE choice FROM (INTEGER) KEYBOARD
     IF choice = 1 OR choice = 2 OR choice = 3 THEN
        SET validChoice TO True
     END IF
END WHILE
```

## Testing validation rules

It is important to test your validation rules to ensure they work as expected. You should use:

**Normal data** – This is data that is within the limits of what should be accepted by the program. For example, a password with seven characters fulfils the validation rule that states that passwords must be between six and eight characters in length.

**Boundary data** – This is data that is at the outer limits of what should be accepted by the program. For example, if a validation rule specifies that the range of acceptable values is >= 75 AND <= 100, then a value of 100 is at the upper limit and a value of 75 at the lower.

**Erroneous data** – This is data that should not be accepted by the program. For example, a value of 0 should not be accepted by either of the validation rules given above.

# Programming

## Working with text files

The programs you have created so far haven't required a huge amount of data entry, but imagine typing a set of test results for everyone in your computer science class. It would take a considerable amount of time to do and – even worse – when the program terminates all of the data will be lost. Should you need to use it again you'd have to re-enter it. This is where storing data in an external file comes in really useful. If the data you enter is stored in an external **text file** you can access it as often as you like without having to do any further keying in.

Commas are used to separate individual values on a line and a special character is used to denote the end of a line.

Text files provide permanent storage for data. This means that the data can be reused without having to be retyped. Data can be read from, written to and appended to a file.

Here is an example of data stored in a text file that contains four learners' examination results. Earlier in this chapter you saw how a two-dimensional array could be used to store this data.

As you can see, each line of the file represents one learner's record, with commas used to separate values.

> **Key term**
>
> **Text file**: a sequence of lines, each of which consists of a sequence of characters.

```
Lois Bennett,56,45,78,32
Eloise Roberts,23,89,67,98
James Hadwen,65,43,83,45
Patrick Dua-Brown,21,43,38,29
```

## Reading data from a text file

Data is read from a text file line by line, with each line being stored by the program as a string. Each string is then split into an array of strings using the comma as a separator.

This algorithm reads the data from the external text file marks.txt and calculates the average score for the first test. It uses three predefined functions: APPEND, SPLIT and LENGTH.

Stage 1
```
SET rawData TO []
FOR EACH record FROM marks.txt DO
  READ marks.txt record
  APPEND(record, rawData)
END FOR
```

Stage 2
```
SET examResults TO []
FOR EACH item in rawData DO
  SET nextLearner TO SPLIT(item, ',')
  APPEND(nextLearner, examResults)
END FOR
```

```
SET testTotal TO 0
FOR EACH learner FROM examResults DO
   SET testTotal TO testTotal + INT(examResults[learner, 1])
END FOR
SET testAverage TO testTotal / LENGTH(examResults)
SEND 'The average mark achieved in the first examination is:
' & testAverage TO DISPLAY
```

Stage 3

The algorithm carries out the task in three stages.

## Stage 1

Each record in the file is read in and appended to the one-dimensional array `rawData`, using a predefined function APPEND. At the end of this stage the `rawData` array has four elements, each of which is a string.

| Index | 0 | 1 | 2 | 3 |
|---|---|---|---|---|
| Elements | 'Lois Bennett, 56,45,78,32' | 'Eloise Roberts,23,89,67,98' | 'James Hadwen,65,43,83,45' | 'Patrick Dua-Brown,21,43,38,29' |

## Stage 2

A loop is used to traverse the array `rawData`, element by element. A predefined function SPLIT is used to split each element in turn into a set of strings, using the commas as separators. Each set of strings is assigned to the temporary array `nextLearner` and is then appended as a new row to the two-dimensional array `examResults`. At the end of this stage the `examResults` array looks like this.

|  | 0 | 1 | 2 | 3 | 4 |
|---|---|---|---|---|---|
| 0 | 'Lois Bennett' | '56' | '45' | '78' | '32' |
| 1 | 'Eloise Roberts' | '23' | '89' | '67' | '98' |
| 2 | 'James Hadwen' | '65' | '43' | '83' | '45' |
| 3 | 'Patrick Dua-Brown' | '21' | '43' | '38' | '29' |

## Stage 3

Finally the algorithm iterates through each row of the array `examResults`, converting the first set of marks for each learner to integers and totalling them. It then calculates the average mark achieved in the first examination and displays it on the screen.

> **Top tip**
>
> Here is an example of how to read data from a text file in Python and Java.
>
> **Python**
> ```
> file = open('scores.txt',
> 'r')
> ```
> **Java**
> ```
> FileReader reader = new
> FileReader('scores.txt');
> ```

### Activity 26 ?

1 Implement the algorithm shown above in the high-level programming language you are studying. (You will need to create a text file in order to test the program. It should consist of at least ten records.)

2 Extend your program to allow the user to choose which of the four examinations they want the average mark for. The program should accept valid user input only.

## Writing data to a text file

The data stored in variables and arrays only remains in memory while the program is running, so if you want to retain the data after the program is exited you will need to write it to a file.

```
SEND 'How many learners do you want to enter results
for?' TO DISPLAY
RECEIVE numLearners FROM (INTEGER) KEYBOARD

FOR index FROM 1 TO numLearners DO
   RECEIVE name FROM (STRING) KEYBOARD
   RECEIVE mark1 FROM (INTEGER) KEYBOARD
   RECEIVE mark2 FROM (INTEGER) KEYBOARD
   RECEIVE mark3 FROM (INTEGER) KEYBOARD
   RECEIVE mark4 FROM (INTEGER) KEYBOARD
   WRITE marks.txt name, mark1, mark2, mark3, mark4
END FOR
```

The algorithm shown above writes data to an external text file called marks.txt. It asks the user how many learners they want to enter marks for. A FOR loop is then used to enter a name and a set of four marks for each learner and to write this data as a new record in the file marks.txt.

### Top tip

Here is an example of how to write data to a text file in Python and Java.

**Python**
```
file = open('scores.txt', 'w')
file.write(name, mark1, mark2, mark3, mark4)
file.close()
```
**Java**
```
FileWriter writer = new FileWriter('scores.txt', true);
writer.write(name, mark1, mark2, mark3, mark4);
writer.close();
```

Data imported from a file needs to be validated in the same way as data entered by the user is validated. Records that do not meet the validation rules should be rejected and stored in another file (known as an error log) so the user knows which records haven't been imported.

A text file can be used to store the students' test scores

## Activity 27 ?

Amend the program you developed in Activity 26 to include a validation rule that ensures that only valid marks between 1 and 100 are read in from the file. Any invalid records should be rejected and written to an error log.

Make sure your text file includes some erroneous data so that you can test that the validation rule is working.

## Activity 28 ?

When saving records to a file you can choose to write or append. Investigate the difference between the two and find out how they are implemented in the high-level programming language you are studying.

## Exam-style question

The XtraSave chain of supermarkets collects data about the products it sells. It records the department, name and price for each product. The data is stored in a text file with one record per line. The file contains over 8,000 records. Part of the file is shown below.

> Tinned, Baked Beans, 0.59
> Bakery, Wholemeal Bread, 1.50
> Drinks, 1L Apple Juice, 0.90
> Dairy, 1 Pt Semi-Skimmed Milk, 1.25
> Drinks, 1L Orange Juice, 0.90

XtraSave wants to produce a list of all products in the drinks department of the store.

Describe an improvement that could be made to the data from the file when used for this purpose. **(3 marks)**

Supermarkets collect a great deal of information about the products they sell

# Programming

## Summary

- Validation techniques should be used to ensure that data entered by a user or from a file is valid. They can't guarantee that the data is correct, only that it is reasonable.
- A range check is used to ensure that data is within a specified range.
- A length check is used to ensure that data has a length within a specified range.
- A presence check is used to ensure the user has entered some data.
- A look-up check is used to ensure the data matches one of the values in a predefined list.
- When users are required to choose from a list of options, their input should be validated to ensure that their choice is valid.
- Large sets of data are normally stored in text files. The advantage of writing data to a file is that the data is not lost when the program is terminated. It can be read in from the file whenever it is needed.

## Checkpoint

### Strengthen

**S1** Describe what might happen if a program doesn't include validation on user input.

**S2** Identify a data structure suitable for storing a list of values used in a look-up check.

**S3** Show how your name, date of birth and favourite colour would be stored in a text file.

**S4** Explain why it is advantageous to write data to a text file.

### Challenge

**C1** Develop a program that:
- writes a set of employee records consisting of employee number, name and department to a text file;
- reads in the stored records from the text file;
- allows the user to search for an employee's details;
- uses appropriate validation.

How confident do you feel about your answers to these questions? If you're not sure you answered them well, try redoing the activities in this section.

# 2.6 Subprograms

A subprogram is a self-contained module of code that performs a specific task. For example, a high-level programming language could provide a predefined subprogram that calculates the average of a set of numbers. A programmer can use this subprogram in any program they write without needing to know how it works. In other words, subprograms support the process of **abstraction**.

Using subprograms reduces the complexity of programs and makes them easier to understand. It also saves time because the code only has to be written once but can be used many times, and makes programs easier to maintain. Furthermore, different subprograms can be allocated to different programmers, allowing large teams of programmers to work together on the same project.

There are two types of subprograms: functions and **procedures**.

## Key terms

**Abstraction**: the process of removing or hiding unnecessary detail so that only the important points remain.

**Procedure**: a subprogram containing a set of statements that are executed when the procedure is called. Unlike a function, a procedure does not return a value to the main program.

**Local variable**: a variable that is accessed only from within the subprogram in which it is created.

## Example function

Here is a function that simulates the throw of a die.

```
FUNCTION die()              # This is the start of the function.

    simDie = RANDOM(6)     # This statement uses the predefined
                           function RANDOM to generate a random
                           number between 1 and 6 which is stored in
                           the variable simDie.

RETURN simDie              # This returns the value of the variable
                           simDie to the main program.

END FUNCTION               # This ends the definition of the function.
```

This function is called by the main program like this.

```
dieThrow = die()
```

The value returned by the function is stored in the variable `dieThrow`.

## Did you know?

In a flowchart a subprogram is represented by this symbol.

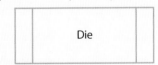

**Figure 2.3** The symbol for a subprogram in a flowchart

### Local and global variables

Notice that there are two variables that store the random number generated by the function. In the function itself the variable `simDie` is used. This variable only exists within the function and is referred to as a **local variable**.

# Programming

## Key terms

**Global variable**: a variable that can be accessed from anywhere in the program, including inside subprograms.

**Parameters**: values that are passed into a subprogram when it is called.

**Scope**: the region of code within which a variable is visible.

In the main program the value returned by the function is stored in the variable `dieThrow`. It can be used anywhere within the main program and is therefore referred to as a **global variable**.

Unlike a function, a procedure does not return a value to the main program.

### Example procedure

```
PROCEDURE averageScore(score1, score2, score3)
BEGIN PROCEDURE
   SET total TO score1 + score2 + score3
   SET average TO total / 3
   SEND average TO DISPLAY
END PROCEDURE
```

The name of this procedure is `averageScore` and its **parameters** are `score1`, `score2` and `score3`. These are values that the procedure needs to do its job. Data is passed into the subprogram by placing it in brackets after the subprogram name, e.g.

```
averageScore(20, 24, 19)
```

This statement calls the procedure and passes the values 20, 24 and 19 into it. In this instance, the value stored in the variable `average` once the procedure has finished executing is 21.

Both functions and procedures can have parameters. An empty pair of brackets indicates that a subprogram does not have any parameters.

### Activity 29                                                        ?

1  Investigate how subprograms are implemented in the high-level programming language you are studying.

2  Write the die function and the `averageScore` procedure in the high-level programming language you are studying.

Local and global variables have different **scope**. A local variable is only available within a subprogram, whereas a global variable can be accessed anywhere within the program.

### Local and global variables

```
REAL cubeSurfaceArea
PROCEDURE cubeSurfaceCalc(width, height)
BEGIN PROCEDURE
   SET cubeArea TO width * height
   SET cubeSurfaceArea TO cubeArea * 6
END PROCEDURE
```

In this example `cubeArea` is a local variable because it is declared within the procedure `cubeSurfaceCalc`. It therefore cannot be accessed by the main program. On the other hand, `cubeSurfaceArea` is a global variable because it is declared in the main program. It can be accessed throughout the program, including from within the subprogram.

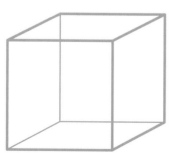

**Figure 2.2** Calculating the area of a cube

## Activity 30

**1** Implement the `cubeSurfaceArea` procedure in the high-level programming language you are studying and test it with the call `cubeSurfaceArea(10, 5)`.

**2** Write a function that will input an array of numbers and return the highest and lowest numbers.

**Top tip**

If a local variable and a global variable share the same name the subprogram will use the local variable and the global variable will not be changed.

## Activity 31

```
CONST REAL discount
SET discount TO 0.1

FUNCTION discountPrice(total)
BEGIN FUNCTION
   IF total >= 50 THEN
      SET saving TO total * discount
      SET newTotal TO total - saving
      RETURN newTotal
   ELSE
      RETURN total
   END IF
END FUNCTION

RECEIVE subTotal FROM (REAL) KEYBOARD
SET salePrice TO discountPrice(subTotal)
SEND salePrice TO DISPLAY
```

This algorithm is used to calculate the sale price of a customer's shopping. Identify the local variables, global variables and constants it uses.

Along with variable and type declarations, command sequences, selection, iteration and data structures, subprograms are one of the essential structural components of a program. Needless to say, just as with variables and data structures, it is important to give subprograms meaningful names. This will make what they do more obvious and will make your programs easier to read.

## Extend your knowledge

When a subprogram calls itself this is known as recursion (see Chapter 1, page 33).

A recursive subprogram always has at least two pathways – one that leads to the subprogram being called again and one that leads to a terminating condition being met. In Chapter 1 you learnt how recursion is used in a merge sort algorithm to repeatedly divide a list in two. The terminating condition is reached when the size of each list is one.

# Programming

## Exam tip

This question is testing your ability to identify the seven key structural components of a program. Make sure you have identified the line numbers in which the components can be found.

## Exam-style question

```
01 SET valuesArray TO [3, 9, 12, 16, 4, 98]
02 REAL max
03
04 FUNCTION maxCalc(values)
05 BEGIN FUNCTION
06    SET length TO LENGTH(values)
07    SET max TO 0
08    FOR index = 0 TO length - 1 DO
09       IF values[index] > max THEN
10          SET max TO values[index]
11       END IF
12    END FOR
13 RETURN max
14 END FUNCTION
15
16 SET max TO maxCalc(valuesArray)
17 SEND max TO DISPLAY
```

1  Identify line number(s) that show one example of each of these structural components of a program: **(6 marks)**

   **a**  variable initialisation

   **b**  type declaration

   **c**  selection

   **d**  iteration

   **e**  data structure

   **f**  subprogram

2  Identify the line number where a subprogram call is made. **(1 mark)**

## Built-in functions

In addition to user-written subprograms, most high-level programming languages have a set of **built-in functions** for common tasks. These are designed to save the programmer time, such as functions that round numbers, count the number of characters in a string and generate random numbers. You have come across some of these already.

## Key term

**Built-in functions**: functions that are provided in most high-level programming languages to perform common tasks.

## Did you know?

The Python programming language has over 65 built-in functions.

Investigate the built-in functions provided by the high-level programming language you are studying.

If there is not a built-in function that meets your needs you could always use one from an external library. These provide more specialised functions. For example, libraries for game development often include functions for collision detection.

## Exam-style questions

The self-checkouts used by the XtraSave chain of supermarkets allow the user to scan the barcode on each product. Once the user has scanned an item, its details are retrieved and passed to the subprogram `processItem`. The parameters of the subprogram are: `itemName`, `itemPrice` and `itemWeight`.

The subprogram must:

- display the name and price of the item;
- every five seconds ask the user to place the item in the bagging area until they have done it;
- check whether the item has been placed in the bagging area by comparing the `itemWeight` to the `totalWeight` (weight of all the items in the bagging area).

A global variable, `totalWeight`, holds the overall weight of the items in the bagging area and is updated each time a new item is added.

The `delay()` subprogram has already been created. It allows program execution to be paused for five seconds.

1   Design the `processItem` subprogram using pseudo-code. **(9 marks)**

2   State the name of a parameter that is used in this algorithm shown below. **(1 mark)**

3   State the value that will be displayed on screen after line 12 is executed. **(1 mark)**

4   State the value of the variable `area` after line 6 is executed. **(1 mark)**

5   State the value of the variable `area` after line 11 is executed. **(1 mark)**

## Exam tip

Use a conditional loop to ask the user to place the item in the bagging area. The condition should check whether the difference between the `totalWeight` value at the start and current value of `totalWeight` is equal to the `totalWeight`.

There are two variables called `area` in this program, one is a global variable and the other is a local variable. You need to demonstrate that you understand how the values of the two variables change during the execution of the program.

```
01 REAL area
02
03 FUNCTION areaCalc(width, height)
04 BEGIN FUNCTION
05   REAL area
06   SET area TO width * height
07   RETURN area
08 END FUNCTION
09
10 SET area TO 5
11 SET rectangleArea TO areaCalc(5,10)
12 SEND rectangleArea TO DISPLAY
```

# Programming

## Summary

- A subprogram is a section of code within a larger piece of code that performs a specific task. It can be used at any point in the program.
- A function is a subprogram that returns a value to the main program.
- A procedure is a subprogram that does not return a value to the main program.
- Parameters are values that are passed to a subprogram when it is called.
- Local variables can only be accessed from within the subprogram in which they are created.
- Global variables can be accessed anywhere in the program, including inside subprograms.
- Built-in functions are functions provided in a high-level programming language to perform common tasks.

## Checkpoint

### Strengthen

**S1** Explain the benefits of using subprograms.

**S2** Explain with examples what is meant by the scope of a variable.

**S3** Describe what happens when a global variable and a local variable share the same name.

**S4** Give an example of a common built-in function.

### Challenge

**C1** Design and implement a calculator program that:
- allows the user to enter a set of numbers;
- uses separate functions to calculate the mean, mode and median;
- allows the user to select which function they want;
- uses appropriate validation.

How confident do you feel about your answers to these questions? If you're not sure you answered them well, try redoing the activities in this section.

# 2.7 Testing and evaluation

## Testing

From the outset of a programming project you should be thinking about what you need to achieve and how you will test that the program functions as expected. Testing should be an integral part of each stage of the program, starting at the design stage, during implementation and once you think the program is finished. This is the only way of ensuring that the program functions correctly and meets all of the specified requirements.

It is very rare for a programmer to develop a program that executes exactly as intended first time. There are nearly always errors that need to be found and fixed. You've already come across two types of errors: logic and syntax.

### Logic errors

As you learnt in Chapter 1 (on page 21), logic errors occur when the thinking behind an algorithm is incorrect so that the output isn't what is expected or intended. Ideally, logic errors should be identified and fixed at the design stage.

The following algorithm is intended to work out whether a learner has passed a test. Learners need a score of 80 or above to pass. However, a logic error in the algorithm means that it produces an incorrect and unexpected result.

```
IF testScore <= 80 THEN
   SEND 'Pass' TO DISPLAY
ELSE
   SEND 'Failed' TO DISPLAY
END IF
```

### *Trace tables*

You saw in Chapter 1 (on page 22) how a trace table can be used to identify logic errors at the design stage.

```
SET table TO 5
FOR index FROM 1 TO 5 DO
   SET answer TO index * table
   SEND answer TO DISPLAY
END FOR
```

# Programming

This algorithm displays part of the five-times table. Here is its trace table. It records each variable change that occurs during execution of the algorithm. Each time a line of code alters the value of a variable or variables a new row of the trace table should be completed.

| Table | Index | Answer |
|---|---|---|
| 5 | | |
| | 1 | |
| | | 5 |
| | 2 | |
| | | 10 |
| | 3 | |
| | | 15 |
| | 4 | |
| | | 20 |
| | 5 | |
| | | 25 |

How many female students are there in this class?

## Activity 32 ?

```
SET gender TO ['M', 'M', 'F', 'M', 'F', 'F', 'M', 'F',
'M', 'F']
SET length TO LENGTH(gender)
SET count TO 0
SET index TO 0
REPEAT
   IF gender[index] = 'F' THEN
      SET count TO count + 1
   END IF
   SET index TO index + 1
UNTIL index = length
```

This algorithm is intended to count the number of female learners in a class.

Create and complete a trace table for this algorithm.

```
Python 3.4.1: example3.py - C:/Python/example3.py       —  □  ×
File  Edit  Format  Run  Options  Windows  Help
favSubject=input("What is your favourite subject?")
if favSubject=="Computer Science"
    print("That's my favourite subject too")
else:
    print("Interesting, I prefer Computer Science")
```

**Figure 2.4** A syntax error in Python code

## Syntax errors

Syntax errors, as we saw earlier (page 48), occur when the grammar rules of a programming language are not adhered to.

The Python program in Figure 2.4 is designed to ask the learner to enter their favourite subject. If they enter Computer Science the program should display 'That's my favourite subject too', otherwise it should output 'Interesting. I prefer Computer Science'. Unfortunately, a syntax error prevents the program from executing. The rules of the language state that a colon must be placed at the end of a line before an indented block and this is missing from the second line.

Syntax errors are normally identified when the algorithm is being implemented in a high-level programming language because they prevent the code from being translated.

## Runtime errors

**Runtime errors** occur during program execution and are the most difficult to predict and spot.

This algorithm is designed to take two numbers, divide the first number by the second number and output the result. When implemented in a high-level programming language it will work as intended at least some of the time. However, if the user entered 5 and 0, a runtime error would occur because it is impossible for the computer to divide 5 by 0.

> **Key term**
>
> **Runtime error**: an error that occurs while the program is running – the operation the computer is asked to do is impossible to execute.

```
RECEIVE firstNumber FROM (INTEGER) KEYBOARD
RECEIVE secondNumber FROM (INTEGER) KEYBOARD
SET result TO firstNumber / secondNumber
SEND result TO DISPLAY
```

Figure 2.5 shows another example of a runtime error. A message is shown when letters are entered into the program where integers are expected.

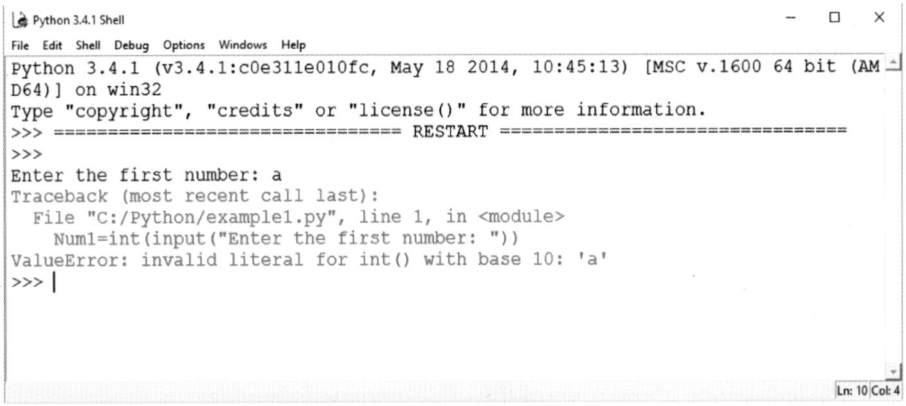

**Figure 2.5** An example of a runtime error in Python

## Error summary

This table summarises the three types of error you are likely to encounter.

| Type of error | Description |
| --- | --- |
| Logic | The program seems to run normally; however, there is an error in the logic of the program, which means it does not produce the result you expect. |
| Syntax | Syntax refers to the rules of the programming language. A syntax error means that part of the code breaks the rules of the language, which stops it running. |
| Runtime | An error that occurs when the computer tries to run code that it cannot execute. |

# Programming

Activity 33 ?

```
RECEIVE width FROM (INTEGER) KEYBOARD
RECEIVE height FROM (INTEGER) KEYBOARD
SET area TO width / height
SEND 'The area is: ' & area TO DISPLAY
```

1 Give a value for the variable `height` that would cause a runtime error.
2 Implement this algorithm in the high-level programming language you are studying, correcting the error you identified in Question 1 and using validation to prevent a runtime error occurring.

Activity 34 ?

```
SET subjects TO ['English', 'Maths', 'Science',
'Computer Science']
FOR index FROM 0 TO 4 DO
  SEND subjects[index] TO DISPLAY
END FOR
```

Identify the runtime error that will occur when this algorithm is implemented in a high-level programming language and executed.

## Using an Integrated Development Environment (IDE)

You probably already have first-hand experience of using an **Integrated Development Environment (IDE)** when writing code. It's definitely worth taking some time to get to know the IDE that comes with the language you are using. Useful features such as syntax highlighting, code auto complete and auto indent will help to make your programming experience – especially at the outset – far less stressful.

It is really important that you get lots of practice interpreting error messages and fixing errors in your code.

## Key term

**Integrated Development Environment (IDE)**: a package that helps programmers to develop program code. It has a number of useful tools, including a source code editor and a debugger. One of the most useful features of an IDE is the debugger. One of its tasks is to flag up syntax errors in the code and issue helpful error messages.

## Top tip

Here are some error messages that you are likely to see in popular IDEs.

### IDLE (A popular Python IDE)

- SyntaxError: invalid syntax – *part of the code breaks one of the rules of the programming language*
- IndentationError: expected an indented block – *statements after a colon must be indented*
- TypeError: *Can't convert 'int' object to str implicitly* – *trying to join a string and an integer together*
- ZeroDivisionError: integer division or modulo by zero – *trying to divide a value by 0*
- NameError: name is not defined – *referring to a variable or subprogram that does not exist*

### Eclipse (A Popular Java IDE)

- ; expected – *each statement should end with a semicolon*
- Cannot find symbol – *referring to a variable or subprogram that does not exist*
- Incompatible types – *trying to mix data of different types, for example a string and an integer*

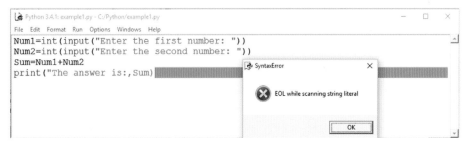

**Figure 2.6** A syntax error flagged up by an IDE in Python code

The IDE has flagged up a syntax error in this program.

It has identified that the programmer has started a string but has not indicated where it finishes. The rules of the language state that strings must be enclosed in speech marks.

## The test plan

At the start of a programming project it is absolutely crucial to make a list of the requirements that the program is expected to meet. Throughout the development phase of the project you should regularly refer back to this list of requirements to check that you are on track to achieve them.

Deciding how to test the finished program to make sure that it fully meets the requirements can't be left to the last moment either. As part of the design stage, you should create a test plan listing the tests you will carry out, the data that will be used for each test and the expected result.

### Marks to grades

```
RECEIVE examMark FROM (INTEGER) KEYBOARD

IF examMark >= 80 THEN
   SEND 'A' TO DISPLAY
ELSE
   IF examMark >= 70 THEN
      SEND 'B' TO DISPLAY
   ELSE
      IF examMark >= 60 THEN
         SEND 'C' TO DISPLAY
      ELSE
         IF examMark > 0 THEN
            SEND 'D' TO DISPLAY
         ELSE
            SEND 'FAIL' TO DISPLAY
         END IF
      END IF
   END IF
END IF
```

This algorithm converts an exam mark into a grade. It should only accept marks between 0 and 100.

# Programming

The test plan extract below shows some of the tests that have been planned for the finished program to ensure that it meets all the requirements.

| Test no | Purpose of the test | Test data | Expected result | Actual result | Action needed/ comments |
|---|---|---|---|---|---|
| 1 | To check correct conversion of valid mark | 0<br>55<br>65<br>75<br>85 | 'FAIL'<br>'D'<br>'C'<br>'B'<br>'A' | | |
| 2 | To check correct conversion of boundary mark | 0<br>1, 59<br>60, 69<br>70, 79<br>80, 100 | 'FAIL'<br>'D'<br>'C'<br>'B'<br>'A' | | |
| 3 | To check response to erroneous mark | −5<br>105 | Error message<br>Error message | | |

Only the first four columns of the test plan table can be completed at the design stage. The remaining columns are filled in when the program is complete.

It's unlikely that you'll be able to anticipate at the outset every test that will be needed to ensure the program works as intended. The test plan is not a fixed document. If additional tests are required they should be added to the test plan.

If a test produces the expected result you can simply write 'None' in the 'Action needed/comments' column. If, however, that is not the case then you should instead note what went wrong and what you did to put it right.

It is important to select suitable test data for the tests. Test data falls into three different categories: normal, boundary and erroneous. (See also validation tests on page 71 in this chapter.)

| | | |
|---|---|---|
| Normal data | Data that is well within the limits of what should be accepted by the program. | Test 1 uses normal data to check if marks are converted into grades correctly (e.g. a mark of 65 should be converted to a grade C). |
| Boundary data | Data that is at the outer limits of what should be accepted by the program. | Test 2 uses boundary data to check that the program works correctly with marks at the upper and lower boundaries (e.g. a mark of 60 and a mark of 69 should both convert to a grade C). |
| Erroneous data | Data that should not be accepted by the program | Test 3 uses erroneous data to check that the program does not accept it. |

**Table 2.6** Test data categories

Testing is just as important as writing code because it ensures that the finished program works correctly and fully meets the requirements. You should use a 'bottom up' approach to testing (i.e. test each subprogram as you develop it and then test the whole program once it is finished).

Here is the completed test plan for the grade calculator program. As you can see, the expected result was not produced when the program was tested with erroneous data. A range check had to be added to the program to ensure that only marks between 0 and 100 can be entered.

| Test no | Purpose of the test | Test data | Expected result | Actual result | Action needed/comments |
|---|---|---|---|---|---|
| 1 | To check correct conversion of valid score | 0<br>55<br>65<br>75<br>85 | 'FAIL'<br>'D'<br>'C'<br>'B'<br>'A' | 'FAIL'<br>'D'<br>'C'<br>'B'<br>'A' | None |
| 2 | To check correct conversion of boundary score | 0<br>1, 59<br>60, 69<br>70, 79<br>80, 100 | 'FAIL'<br>'D'<br>'C'<br>'B'<br>'A' | 'FAIL'<br>'D'<br>'C'<br>'B'<br>'A' | None |
| 3 | To check response to erroneous score | -5<br>105 | Error message<br>Error message | 'FAIL'<br>'A' | A range check has been added to ensure that only valid marks can be added. |

After you have carried out all of the tests and made all the necessary changes, the program should be retested to ensure that the improvements you have made haven't introduced any new errors into the program.

## Evaluating programs

You need to be able to identify the strengths and weaknesses of your own programs as well as those created by other programmers. This will enable you to identify techniques that work well and aspects that could be improved.

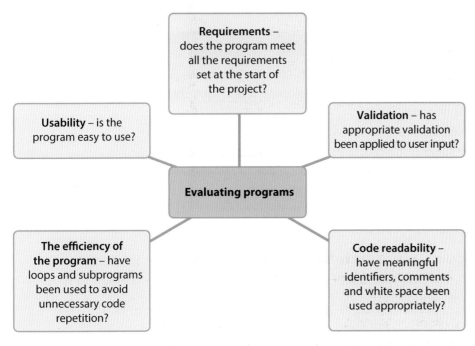

Requirements – does the program meet all the requirements set at the start of the project?

Usability – is the program easy to use?

Validation – has appropriate validation been applied to user input?

**Evaluating programs**

The efficiency of the program – have loops and subprograms been used to avoid unnecessary code repetition?

Code readability – have meaningful identifiers, comments and white space been used appropriately?

**Figure 2.7** Consider the aspects shown above when evaluating a program.

# Programming

## Exam tip

This question tests your ability to trace an algorithm using a trace table. Remember each variable change should be recorded and each time a line of code alters the value of a variable or variables a new row of the trace table should be completed.

## Exam-style question

```
SET scores TO [45, 67, 34, 98, 52]
SET length TO LENGTH(scores)
SET count TO 0

FOR index FROM 0 TO length — 1 DO
   IF scores[index] >= 50 THEN
      SET count TO count + 1
   END IF
END FOR
```

1   Describe what this algorithm does. **(2 marks)**
2   Draw and complete a trace table for this algorithm with these column headings:
    a   length
    b   count
    c   index
    d   scores[index] **(5 marks)**

## Summary

- Logic errors occur when there is an error in the logic of the code, causing the program to produce an unexpected result.
- A syntax error occurs when part of the code breaks the rules of the programming language.
- A runtime error occurs while the program is running and it is asked to do something that is impossible to do.
- Trace tables can be used to manually trace the execution of an algorithm, allowing you to track the changes in variable values.
- Before creating a program it is important to produce a test plan that outlines how the final program will be tested to ensure it meets the requirements.
- Evaluating a program involves considering its strengths and weaknesses and identifying areas for improvement.

## Checkpoint

### Strengthen

**S1**  Describe the three types of error associated with program development and identify the stage(s) of development at which they are most likely to occur.

**S2**  Describe the function of a trace table.

**S3**  Describe the features of an IDE that help programmers write error-free code.

**S4**  Describe the function of a test plan in program development.

**S5**  Describe what is meant by normal, boundary and erroneous data.

**S6**  Explain why it might be necessary to retest a program once all the planned tests are completed.

### Challenge

**C1**  Identify the requirements for a program, design a solution and draw up a test plan for it.

**C2**  Design and implement the program. Conduct your planned tests and make any necessary changes to your program, ensuring your test plan is kept up to date.

**C3**  Evaluate your program.

How confident do you feel about your answers to these questions? If you're not sure you answered them well, try completing the activities on pages 84, 86 and 89.

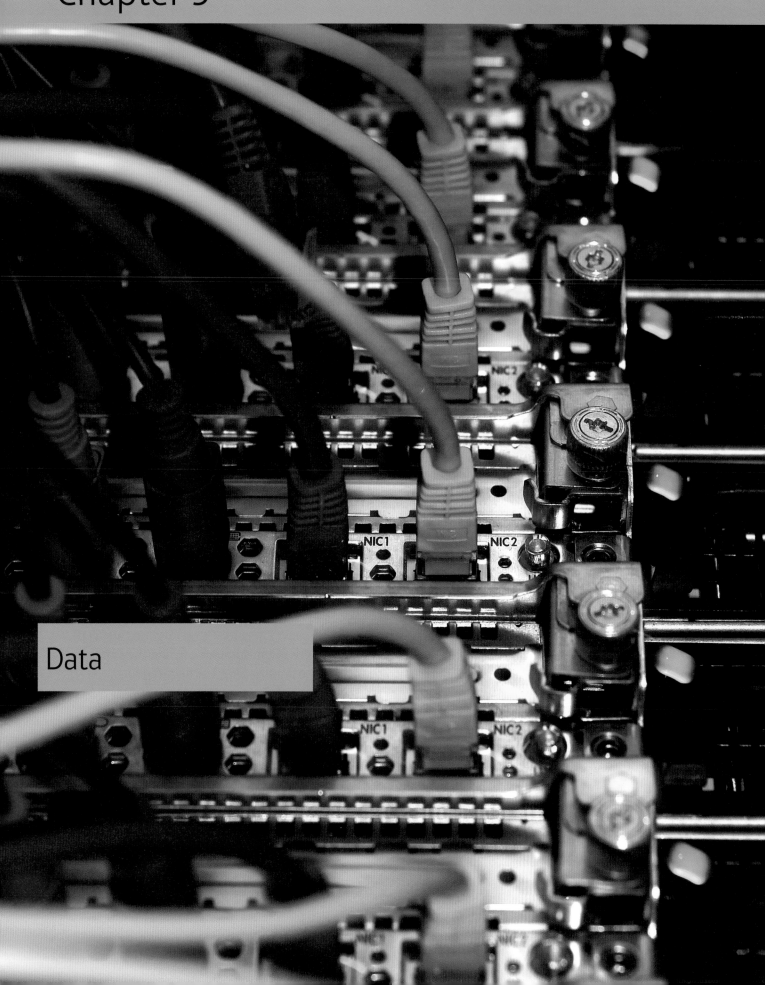

# Chapter 3

## Data

# Data

## 3.1 Binary

### Key terms

**Binary**: information represented by only two values (e.g. a voltage or no voltage, on or off).

There are no communication errors or misunderstandings because there are no small differences.

**Digital**: information represented by certain fixed values (e.g. high, medium or low). Any signal between these values would be meaningless and not used.

Sending and receiving mechanisms do not have to be as accurate as for analogue communication.

**Analogue**: using signals or information represented by a quantity (e.g. an electric voltage or current) that is continuously variable. Changes in the information being represented are indicated by changes in voltage.

This method requires very accurate sending and receiving mechanisms.

### Why binary?

**Binary** is needed to represent data and program instructions because of the way in which computers work.

The processor, which processes all of the data and instructions, contains billions of transistors which are connected together to form circuits.

The transistors act as switches, similar to light switches. They have only two states, on or off – they either transmit an electric current or they do not. A system with separate states is said to be **digital** and if there are two states it is binary. There are no in-between states with different levels of current as there would be in a dimmer switch, which produces different levels of brightness in a bulb. A system such as this, where there is a continuous range between two values, is said to be **analogue**.

### Did you know?

Humans have digital systems. The nerves which control all of our actions are a digital system. They transmit nerve impulses – bursts of electricity from the sense organs to the brain or from the brain to the muscles. These impulses are all of the same intensity. These impulses are all of the same intensity and the strength of the stimulus causing the impulses is not signalled by the size of the impulses but by their frequency.

As there are only two states, on or off, the states are represented by the digits of the binary number system, 1 and 0.

All of the data and program instructions processed by a computer are nothing more than streams of millions of 1s and 0s.

Numbers, text, graphics and sound are all represented in the same way, as a series of 1s and 0s. The program instructions that the processor is following allow it to interpret them in different ways.

## Representing information

There are only two digits, 1 and 0, but to represent the symbols in text there must be at least 52 separate items of information – 26 lower-case and 26 upper-case letters. Then there are punctuation symbols – the full stops, question marks, etc.

When we write, we combine the letters in our alphabet to create words and combine these into sentences to convey meaning.

In a similar way the two **binary digits (bits)** can be combined into groups.

A single bit offers two possibilities. In a graphics program it could give black (1) or white (0), for example. If we wanted colour we'd need more combinations. If two bits are used this gives four possible combinations, 00, 01, 10, 11, each of which can represent a colour, so four colours could be used.

Three bits would give eight combinations, 000, 001, 010, 011, 100, 101, 110, 111, allowing eight different colours to be represented.

With four bits there would be 16 combinations.

There is obviously a mathematical relationship between the number of bits used and the number of possible colours.

| Key term |
|---|
| **Binary digit (bits)**: the smallest unit of data that is represented in a computer. It has a single binary value, either 1 or 0. |

- With 1 bit there are 2 possible colours.
- With 2 bits there are 4 possible colours.
- With 3 bits there are 8 possible colours.
- With 4 bits there are 16 possible colours.

The number of possible colours is equal to 2 to the power of the number of bits used in the combination.

- $2^1 = 2$
- $2^2 = 2 * 2 = 4$
- $2^3 = 2 * 2 * 2 = 8$
- $2^4 = 2 * 2 * 2 * 2 = 16$

## Number systems

Binary is a number system based on two digits, 0 and 1.

We are more used to the denary system which has ten digits, 0 to 9, but the binary system functions in the same way.

The difference is that the denary system works in powers of 10, whereas the binary system uses powers of 2.

### Denary system

Every digit has a place value and the one to the left has a value 10 times higher than the one to the right.

# Data

The following table shows the place values for the digits in the number 3,639.

| Place values | $10^3$ | $10^2$ | $10^1$ | $10^0$ |
|---|---|---|---|---|
| | 1000 | 100 | 10 | 1 |
| | 3 | 6 | 3 | 9 |

Therefore 3,639 can be written as:

$(3 * 1000) + (6 * 100) + (3 * 10) + (9 * 1)$

## Binary system

The binary system has similar place values but they increase by powers of 2.

The following table shows the place values for the digits in a **byte**.

| Place values | $2^7$ | $2^6$ | $2^5$ | $2^4$ | $2^3$ | $2^2$ | $2^1$ | $2^0$ |
|---|---|---|---|---|---|---|---|---|
| | 128 | 64 | 32 | 16 | 8 | 4 | 2 | 1 |

### Converting binary to denary

The table above can be used to convert a binary number to a denary one.

The denary equivalent of the binary number 10101101 can be calculated as:

| Place values | $2^7$ | $2^6$ | $2^5$ | $2^4$ | $2^3$ | $2^2$ | $2^1$ | $2^0$ |
|---|---|---|---|---|---|---|---|---|
| | 128 | 64 | 32 | 16 | 8 | 4 | 2 | 1 |
| | 1 | 0 | 1 | 0 | 1 | 1 | 0 | 1 |

$(1 * 128) + (1 * 32) + (1 * 8) + (1 * 4) + (1 * 1) = 128 + 32 + 8 + 4 + 1 = 173$.

### Converting denary to binary

The table of place values can be used to convert denary numbers to binary.

> **Activity 1** ?
>
> Calculate the denary equivalents of the following binary numbers.
>
> **a** 00111001
>
> **b** 11000110
>
> **c** 10101010

> ### Worked example
>
> Convert denary 213 to binary. Use the table and fill it in as you calculate the equivalent.
>
> | Place values | $2^7$ | $2^6$ | $2^5$ | $2^4$ | $2^3$ | $2^2$ | $2^1$ | $2^0$ |
> |---|---|---|---|---|---|---|---|---|
> | | 128 | 64 | 32 | 16 | 8 | 4 | 2 | 1 |
> | | | | | | | | | |
>
> Move from left to right:
>
> Step 1: Is the number (213) equal to or greater than 128? If it is place a '1' at this place value and if not place a '0'.
>
> In this case 213 is greater than 128 so place a '1' in this column and calculate the remainder.
>
> | Place values | $2^7$ | $2^6$ | $2^5$ | $2^4$ | $2^3$ | $2^2$ | $2^1$ | $2^0$ |
> |---|---|---|---|---|---|---|---|---|
> | | 128 | 64 | 32 | 16 | 8 | 4 | 2 | 1 |
> | | 1 | | | | | | | |
>
> The remainder is 85.

Step 2: Is 85 greater than or equal to 64? Yes, therefore place a '1' in this column.

| Place values | $2^7$ | $2^6$ | $2^5$ | $2^4$ | $2^3$ | $2^2$ | $2^1$ | $2^0$ |
|---|---|---|---|---|---|---|---|---|
| | 128 | 64 | 32 | 16 | 8 | 4 | 2 | 1 |
| | 1 | 1 | | | | | | |

The remainder is 21.

Step 3: Is 21 greater than or equal to 32. No, therefore place a '0' in this column.

| Place values | $2^7$ | $2^6$ | $2^5$ | $2^4$ | $2^3$ | $2^2$ | $2^1$ | $2^0$ |
|---|---|---|---|---|---|---|---|---|
| | 128 | 64 | 32 | 16 | 8 | 4 | 2 | 1 |
| | 1 | 1 | 0 | | | | | |

The remainder is still 21.

Step 4: Is 21 equal to or greater than 16? Yes, therefore place a '1' in this column.

| Place values | $2^7$ | $2^6$ | $2^5$ | $2^4$ | $2^3$ | $2^2$ | $2^1$ | $2^0$ |
|---|---|---|---|---|---|---|---|---|
| | 128 | 64 | 32 | 16 | 8 | 4 | 2 | 1 |
| | 1 | 1 | 0 | 1 | | | | |

The remainder is 5.

Step 5: Is 5 equal to or greater than 8? No, therefore place a '0' in this column.

| Place values | $2^7$ | $2^6$ | $2^5$ | $2^4$ | $2^3$ | $2^2$ | $2^1$ | $2^0$ |
|---|---|---|---|---|---|---|---|---|
| | 128 | 64 | 32 | 16 | 8 | 4 | 2 | 1 |
| | 1 | 1 | 0 | 1 | 0 | | | |

The remainder is still 5.

Step 6: Is 5 equal to or greater than 4. Yes, therefore place a '1' in this column.

| Place values | $2^7$ | $2^6$ | $2^5$ | $2^4$ | $2^3$ | $2^2$ | $2^1$ | $2^0$ |
|---|---|---|---|---|---|---|---|---|
| | 128 | 64 | 32 | 16 | 8 | 4 | 2 | 1 |
| | 1 | 1 | 0 | 1 | 0 | 1 | | |

The remainder is 1.

Step 7: Is 1 equal to or greater than 2? No, therefore place a '0' in this column .

| Place values | $2^7$ | $2^6$ | $2^5$ | $2^4$ | $2^3$ | $2^2$ | $2^1$ | $2^0$ |
|---|---|---|---|---|---|---|---|---|
| | 128 | 64 | 32 | 16 | 8 | 4 | 2 | 1 |
| | 1 | 1 | 0 | 1 | 0 | 1 | 0 | |

The remainder is still 1.

Step 8: Is 1 equal to or greater than 1? Obviously, they are equal and therefore place a '1' in the last column.

| Place values | $2^7$ | $2^6$ | $2^5$ | $2^4$ | $2^3$ | $2^2$ | $2^1$ | $2^0$ |
|---|---|---|---|---|---|---|---|---|
| | 128 | 64 | 32 | 16 | 8 | 4 | 2 | 1 |
| | 1 | 1 | 0 | 1 | 0 | 1 | 0 | 1 |

Therefore denary 213 is represented by binary 11010101.

**Activity 2** **?**

Calculate the binary equivalents of the following denary numbers.

a   69

b   193

c   239

# Data

## Extend your knowledge

The methods to convert binary to denary and vice versa can be performed by computer programs. Write and test programs that will carry out these conversions. The programs should ask a user to enter either a denary or an eight-bit binary number.

Remember to validate their input:

- the denary number should be no larger than 255, and
- the binary number should have eight digits and each digit must be either 1 or 0.

## Binary arithmetic

Binary numbers can be manipulated in the same way as denary ones.

### Denary addition

When addition is performed in denary, a 'carry over' is used if the result is greater than 9.

### Worked example

369 + 733

| Place values | $10^3$ | $10^2$ | $10^1$ | $10^0$ |
|---|---|---|---|---|
| | 1000 | 100 | 10 | 1 |
| Carry over | 1 | 1 | 1 | |
| | | 3 | 6 | 9 |
| | | 7 | 3 | 3 |
| Total | 1 | 1 | 0 | 2 |
| | | 100 + 300 + 700 = 1100 <br><br> The 1000 is carried over leaving 100. | 10 + 60 + 30 = 100 <br><br> The 100 is carried over. | 9 + 3 = 12 <br><br> The 10 is carried over leaving 2. |

Binary addition works in the same way but a 'carry over' is needed if the result is greater than 1.

### Binary addition

### Worked example

11010110 + 01100111

| Place values | $2^7$ | $2^6$ | $2^5$ | $2^4$ | $2^3$ | $2^2$ | $2^1$ | $2^0$ |
|---|---|---|---|---|---|---|---|---|
| | 128 | 64 | 32 | 16 | 8 | 4 | 2 | 1 |
| Carry over | 1 | | | | 1 | 1 | | |
| 1 | 1 | 1 | 0 | 1 | 0 | 1 | 1 | 0 |
| | 0 | 1 | 1 | 0 | 0 | 1 | 1 | 1 |
| Total | 0 | 0 | 1 | 1 | 1 | 1 | 0 | 1 |
| | 128 + 128 = 256 <br><br> This should be carried over. | 64 + 64 = 128 <br><br> The 128 is carried over. | No carry over needed. | No carry over needed. | No carry over needed. | 4 + 4 + 4 = 12 <br><br> The 8 is carried over leaving one 4. | 2 + 2 = 4 <br><br> The 4 is carried over. | No carry over needed. |

We are adding eight-bit numbers and this has caused a problem. All eight bits have been used and the 1 that was carried over in the last column has nowhere to go – it has been carried out. Therefore the result of the calculation would be wrong. This is called an overflow error.

This condition occurs when a calculation produces a result that is greater than the computer can deal with or store.

When this occurs, the processor is informed that an error has occurred.

## Extend your knowledge

Overflow errors have led to many real-life disasters.

The most famous, or infamous, was the crash of the Ariane 5 space rocket, which exploded 40 seconds after its launch in 1996.

Others include the failure of the Patriot missile defence system in 1991.

Carry out research to find out more details about these 'overflow' disasters and problems.

## Activity 3

Carry out the following binary additions.

a   10011010 + 11010111

b   00001101 + 10101010

c   11010111 + 10001010

## Signed and unsigned numbers

So far we have been considering positive whole numbers or **integers**, but how can we represent negative numbers? When an integer is indicated as being positive or negative it is described as being signed.

In denary, this is simple, a '+' or a '–' symbol is placed in front of the number. In binary, if we are using 8-bit numbers, then we cannot do this because we cannot simply add an extra bit. Also the processor would not understand the '+' and '–' symbols.

### Sign and magnitude

In a multiple-bit binary number, the left-most bit, the one with the greatest value, is called the **most significant bit (MSB)**. We can use this to represent signed integers.

It is set to 1 for negative and 0 for positive.

Therefore, using this method, binary 00011100 represents denary +28 and binary 10011100 represents –28

The most significant bit is being used for the sign, so the largest positive number represented by a byte is 127.

## Adding signed integers

If the binary equivalents of denary +28 and denary –28 are added we get the following result.

## Key terms

**Integer**: a whole number (e.g. 3, 6, 9).

**Most significant bit (MSB)**: the bit with the highest value in a multiple-bit binary number.

| 0 | 0 | 0 | 1 | 1 | 1 | 0 | 0 |
|---|---|---|---|---|---|---|---|
| 1 | 0 | 0 | 1 | 1 | 1 | 0 | 0 |
| **1** | **0** | **1** | **1** | **1** | **0** | **0** | **0** |

Adding denary +28 and −28 we expect the result to be 0, but the binary result is equivalent to −56.

Also using this method zero could be both positive and negative.

| Positive zero | 0 | 0 | 0 | 0 | 0 | 0 | 0 | 0 |
|---|---|---|---|---|---|---|---|---|
| Negative zero | 1 | 0 | 0 | 0 | 0 | 0 | 0 | 0 |

That clearly doesn't make sense and so another method is needed to represent negative numbers in calculations.

## Two's complement

The most common method used to represent signed integers in modern computers is two's complement.

This method works on the principle above – the result of any number added to its negative equivalent should be zero.

### Finding the two's complement of a binary number

To find the two's complement of a binary number

- flip all of the bits – change 1s to 0s and 0s to 1s.
- add 1 to the result.

| Number | 0 | 0 | 0 | 1 | 1 | 1 | 0 | 0 |
|---|---|---|---|---|---|---|---|---|
| Flip | 1 | 1 | 1 | 0 | 0 | 0 | 1 | 1 |
| Add 1 to flipped value | 1 | 1 | 1 | 0 | 0 | 1 | 0 | 0 |

The MSB is 1, indicating a negative number.

Therefore the two's complement of binary 00011100 is binary 11100100, which is equivalent to denary −28.

### Converting two's complement numbers back into denary

This example shows that the two's complement binary number 11100100 represents denary −28. We can check whether this statement is true by converting it back from two's complement.

#### Method 1 – Reverse calculation

The positive equivalent of a negative integer in two's complement format can be found by flipping the bits and adding 1.

| Number −28 | 1 | 1 | 1 | 0 | 0 | 1 | 0 | 0 |
|---|---|---|---|---|---|---|---|---|
| Flip | 0 | 0 | 0 | 1 | 1 | 0 | 1 | 1 |
| Add 1 to flipped value | 0 | 0 | 0 | 1 | 1 | 1 | 0 | 0 |

The result is denary 28.

This shows that 11100100 (−28) is the two's complement representation of 00011100 (+28).

## Method 2 – Place values

Using place values the two's complement number can be converted directly into denary.

| Place | $2^7$ | $2^6$ | $2^5$ | $2^4$ | $2^3$ | $2^2$ | $2^1$ | $2^0$ |
|---|---|---|---|---|---|---|---|---|
| values | −128 | 64 | 32 | 16 | 8 | 4 | 2 | 1 |
| | 1 | 1 | 1 | 0 | 0 | 1 | 0 | 0 |

The most significant bit of the two's complement binary number is 1, indicating that it is negative. Therefore, the denary equivalent of the MSB is taken as being negative −128.

The denary equivalent will be

−128 + 64 + 32 + 4 = −128 + 100 = −28

This shows that two's complement 11100100 is equivalent to denary −28.

### Worked example

Convert −69 to an eight-bit two's complement binary number.

| Place | $2^7$ | $2^6$ | $2^5$ | $2^4$ | $2^3$ | $2^2$ | $2^1$ | $2^0$ |
|---|---|---|---|---|---|---|---|---|
| values | 128 | 64 | 32 | 16 | 8 | 4 | 2 | 1 |
| 69 | 0 | 1 | 0 | 0 | 0 | 1 | 0 | 1 |
| Flip | 1 | 0 | 1 | 1 | 1 | 0 | 1 | 0 |
| Add 1 | 1 | 0 | 1 | 1 | 1 | 0 | 1 | 1 |

So denary −69 is 10111011 in two's complement binary.

We can check this using the place value method.

−128 + 32 + 16 + 8 + 2 + 1 = −128 + 59 = −69

## Adding −28 to +28

The two's complement of 00011100 is 11100100

So adding the binary equivalents of denary +28 and −28 gives

| 28 | 0 | 0 | 0 | 1 | 1 | 1 | 0 | 0 |
|---|---|---|---|---|---|---|---|---|
| −28 | 1 | 1 | 1 | 1 | 0 | 1 | 0 | 0 |
| Result of addition | 0 | 0 | 0 | 0 | 0 | 0 | 0 | 0 |

There is an overflow, but this time the result is 0.

# Data

## Worked example

Add 28 and −5.

This is more difficult. The result should be 23.

The two's complement representation of −5 is

| 5 | 0 | 0 | 0 | 0 | 0 | 1 | 0 | 1 |
|---|---|---|---|---|---|---|---|---|
| Flip | 1 | 1 | 1 | 1 | 1 | 0 | 1 | 0 |
| Add 1 | 1 | 1 | 1 | 1 | 1 | 0 | 1 | 1 |

Adding binary 28 to binary −5 gives

| 0 | 0 | 0 | 1 | 1 | 1 | 0 | 0 |
|---|---|---|---|---|---|---|---|
| 1 | 1 | 1 | 1 | 1 | 0 | 1 | 1 |
| **0** | **0** | **0** | **1** | **0** | **1** | **1** | **1** |

The result is 00010111, which is the binary equivalent of 23.

## Did you know?

Additions using two's complement can be used for carrying out subtraction in binary. For example,

28 − 5

is the same as

28 + (−5)

## Extend your knowledge

Write and test a program in the language you are using which will calculate the two's complement of an 8-bit binary number.

Remember to validate the binary number entered.

## Worked example

Add −28 to +5.

This is slightly more difficult. The result should be −23.

| −28 in two's complement | 1 | 1 | 1 | 0 | 0 | 1 | 0 | 0 |
|---|---|---|---|---|---|---|---|---|
| 5 | 0 | 0 | 0 | 0 | 0 | 1 | 0 | 1 |
| Result | 1 | 1 | 1 | 0 | 1 | 0 | 0 | 1 |

We can show that this is equal to −23.

$-128 + 64 + 32 + 8 + 1 = -128 + 105 = -23$

## Activity 4

1   Calculate the two's complement representation of the following denary numbers.

   a   −113

   b   −56

   c   −90

2   Showing your working, carry out the binary addition of 90 + −33.

## Binary shifts

In denary when we want to multiply a number by ten we move each number one place value to its left and add a 0 to the end.

For example, 13 * 10 = 130.

| Place values | | $10^3$ | $10^2$ | $10^1$ | $10^0$ |
|---|---|---|---|---|---|
| | | 1000 | 100 | 10 | 1 |
| Original number | | | | 1 | 3 |
| Multiply by 10 – the digits are moved to the left and a 0 is added. | | | 1 | 3 | 0 |

To divide by 10 we do the reverse – move each number one place value to its right.

A left shift is used for multiplication by 10 and a right shift for division by 10.

If the number is being multiplied by 100 ($10^2$), then each digit is moved two places to its left.

In binary left and right **binary shifts** can be used for multiplication and division by powers of 2.

### Logical shifts

For unsigned numbers logical shifts are performed in the same way as in denary.

If we multiply the unsigned binary number 00010100 (20) by $2^2$ (4) there should be two shifts to the left.

The left-most bits drop off the end and are replaced by 0s at the right.

| Place values | $2^7$ | $2^6$ | $2^5$ | $2^4$ | $2^3$ | $2^2$ | $2^1$ | $2^0$ |
|---|---|---|---|---|---|---|---|---|
| | 128 | 64 | 32 | 16 | 8 | 4 | 2 | 1 |
| | 0 | 0 | 0 | 1 | 0 | 1 | 0 | 0 |
| Result of shift | 0 | 1 | 0 | 1 | 0 | 0 | 0 | 0 |

The product is (64 * 1) + (16 * 1) = 80 in denary as expected.

If we divide the same number by 4 ($2^2$) there would be two shifts to the right. This time the right-most bits drop off the end and are replaced by 0s at the left.

| Place values | $2^7$ | $2^6$ | $2^5$ | $2^4$ | $2^3$ | $2^2$ | $2^1$ | $2^0$ |
|---|---|---|---|---|---|---|---|---|
| | 128 | 64 | 32 | 16 | 8 | 4 | 2 | 1 |
| | 0 | 0 | 0 | 1 | 0 | 1 | 0 | 0 |
| Result of shift | 0 | 0 | 0 | 0 | 0 | 1 | 0 | 1 |

The result is (4 * 1) + (1 * 1) = 5 in denary as expected.

# Data

## Activity 5 ?

Calculate the results of the following shifts on unsigned integers.

**a** 00111010 * $2^3$.

**b** 10011101 / $2^4$.

## Key term

**Arithmetic shift**: used for signed binary numbers. When performing a right shift the bits at the left are replaced by copies of the most significant bit.

A logical shift on integers can lead to a loss of precision. For example, if we divide 00100001 (33 in denary) by 2 the digits would be shifted one place to the right.

| Place values | $2^7$ | $2^6$ | $2^5$ | $2^4$ | $2^3$ | $2^2$ | $2^1$ | $2^0$ |
|---|---|---|---|---|---|---|---|---|
| | 128 | 64 | 32 | 16 | 8 | 4 | 2 | 1 |
| | 0 | 0 | 1 | 0 | 0 | 0 | 0 | 1 |
| Result of shift | 0 | 0 | 0 | 1 | 0 | 0 | 0 | 0 |

The result is 00010000, which is 16, but the correct result should be 16.5.

## Arithmetic shifts

**Arithmetic shifts** are used with signed numbers expressed in two's complement format.

### Left arithmetic shift

A left arithmetic shift is identical to a left logical shift except that the left-most bit (MSB) is not included because it must remain in place to indicate the sign.

## Worked example

Calculate the product of −36 * 2

−36 in two's complement format is:

| 36 | 0 | 0 | 1 | 0 | 0 | 1 | 0 | 0 |
|---|---|---|---|---|---|---|---|---|
| Flip | 1 | 1 | 0 | 1 | 1 | 0 | 1 | 1 |
| Add 1 | 1 | 1 | 0 | 1 | 1 | 1 | 0 | 0 |

Therefore −36 in two's complement format is 11011100.

If this is multiplied by 2 there should be one shift to the left with a 0 added at the right.

Leaving the MSB in place and shifting the others to the left will produce

10111000

This should be equal to −72 in two's complement notation.

We can see if this is correct by proving that 10111000 is the negative of 72 in two's complement.

| −72 | 1 | 0 | 1 | 1 | 1 | 0 | 0 | 0 |
|---|---|---|---|---|---|---|---|---|
| Flip | 0 | 1 | 0 | 0 | 0 | 1 | 1 | 1 |
| Add 1 | 0 | 1 | 0 | 0 | 1 | 0 | 0 | 0 |

01001000 in binary is equal to 72 in denary.

### Right arithmetic shift

When dividing signed binary numbers in two's complement format by powers of 2, the bits are shifted to the right, but they are replaced at the left by copies of the most significant bit.

#### Worked example

Calculate $-72 / 2^2$. That is $-72$ divided by 4. The result should be $-18$.

$-72$ in two's complement format is 10111000 – we showed this in the previous worked example.

Performing two right arithmetic shifts and adding the MSB at the left will give

11101110

This should be $-18$ in two's complement notation.

We can test it as before.

| $-18$ | 1 | 1 | 1 | 0 | 1 | 1 | 1 | 0 |
|-------|---|---|---|---|---|---|---|---|
| Flip  | 0 | 0 | 0 | 1 | 0 | 0 | 0 | 1 |
| Add 1 | 0 | 0 | 0 | 1 | 0 | 0 | 1 | 0 |

The result is 00010010, which is equivalent to $(1 * 16) + (1 * 2) = 18$.

**Activity 6**

1   Show the following division:

    **a**   10010000 / 22 in binary

    **b**   11110110 / 21 in binary

    **c**   11000000 / 23 in binary

2   Show that your answers are the expected results.

## Hexadecimal numbers

So far only 8-bit binary numbers have been considered, but it is common for data and commands to be represented by 32 and 64 bits.

It is difficult for humans to remember and manipulate 8-bit binary numbers, but almost impossible to use 32-bit ones.

Humans get confused with large binary numbers, so we use **hexadecimal** numbers to represent them. Computers never use them.

The hexadecimal system uses 16 digits from 0 to 15.

Our denary system has only digits for 0 to 9, so the higher hexadecimal digits are represented by upper case letters.

| 0 | 1 | 2 | 3 | 4 | 5 | 6 | 7 | 8 | 9 | 10 | 11 | 12 | 13 | 14 | 15 |
|---|---|---|---|---|---|---|---|---|---|----|----|----|----|----|----|
| 0 | 1 | 2 | 3 | 4 | 5 | 6 | 7 | 8 | 9 | A | B | C | D | E | F |

The following diagram shows how to convert binary to hexadecimal.

**Did you know?**

A common use of hexadecimal numbers is to describe colours used in computer graphics. Each of the colours has a value of 24 bits – 8 bits for each of the red, green and blue elements that make it up. The 24 bits are represented in hexadecimal so that they are easier for humans to use.

For example, it is far easier to set the colour to red by entering #FF0000 than having to type 111111110000000000000000.

A # symbol is used to indicate a hexadecimal number.

**Key term**

**Hexadecimal**: a base-16 number system. There are 16 digits and the place values increase in powers of 16.

# Data

## Converting binary to hexadecimal

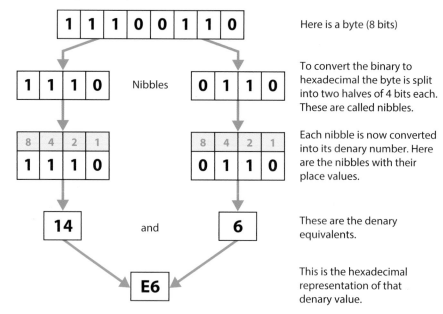

Here is a byte (8 bits)

To convert the binary to hexadecimal the byte is split into two halves of 4 bits each. These are called nibbles.

Each nibble is now converted into its denary number. Here are the nibbles with their place values.

These are the denary equivalents.

This is the hexadecimal representation of that denary value.

**Figure 3.1** Converting binary numbers to hexadecimal

It is far easier to say and remember E6 than 11100110.

## Converting hexadecimal to binary
This is the reverse of the method used above.

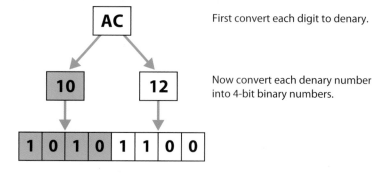

First convert each digit to denary.

Now convert each denary number into 4-bit binary numbers.

**Figure 3.2** Converting hexadecimals to binary numbers

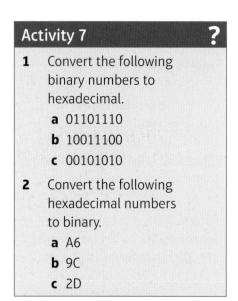

**Activity 7**   **?**

1   Convert the following binary numbers to hexadecimal.
   **a** 01101110
   **b** 10011100
   **c** 00101010

2   Convert the following hexadecimal numbers to binary.
   **a** A6
   **b** 9C
   **c** 2D

## Exam-style questions   ○

**1 a** Add together the following 8-bit numbers. **(1 mark)**

   0 1 0 1 1 0 0 1
   1 1 1 0 0 1 1 1
   _____

   **b** Identify the problem that this addition has created. **(1 mark)**

**2 a** Carry out a 3-place logical right shift on the following binary number. **(2 marks)**
   10010011

   **b** Explain the effect of performing a right shift on a binary number. **(1 mark)**

   **c** Describe the steps needed to convert the binary number 11101110 into a hexadecimal one and show the result. **(4 marks)**

## Exam tips

**1 a** This is a straightforward question. Carry out the calculation and write the result in the space provided. Remember to carry over if the addition of each pair of digits is greater than 1.

**b** This just requires a one or two word answer.

**2 a** Again carry out the shift and write the result.

**b** Here you have to explain what effect the shift will have. You could say that it is equivalent to multiplying the number by…

**c** A longer answer is required. You should show stage by stage how the conversion is carried out. For example, you could start by saying what the 8-bit binary number is divided into. You should set out the explanation clearly and it could be in the form of a diagram.

## Summary

- In a computer all data and programming instructions are represented by streams of 1s and 0s.
- Place values in the binary system increase by powers of 2.
- An overflow error occurs when a computer attempts to handle a number that is too large (e.g. a number requiring 9 bits instead of 8 in an 8-bit processor).
- To multiply a binary number by powers of 2, you can use left shifts.
- To divide a binary number by powers of 2, you can use right shifts.
- Hexadecimal is used to represent binary numbers because it is easier for humans to remember and use.
- Binary, denary and hexadecimal numbers can be converted from one to the other.

## Checkpoint

### Strengthen

**S1** Carry out the following addition: 11011001 + 10010010.

**S2** Perform the following calculation in binary: 25 + (−13).

**S3** Multiply the unsigned integer 01001001 by $2^3$.

**S4** Convert 11001101 to denary and hexadecimal.

### Challenge

**C1** Explain in your own words why binary is used to represent data and program instructions in computer systems.

**C2** Explain the difference between a logical right shift and an arithmetic right shift.

How confident do you feel about your answers to these questions? If you're not sure you answered them well, try the following activities again:

- For S1 try Activity 3.
- For S2 try Activity 4.
- For S3 try Activity 5.
- For S4 try Activity 7.

# Data

## 3.2 Data representation

### Representation of text

When you press a key on the keyboard a stream of 1s and 0s are input to the processor. The computer cannot recognise any characters such as 'c', '@' or 'D', only a combination of 1s and 0s. The defined list of characters recognised by a computer's hardware and software is known as its **character set**.

Obviously, an industry standard is needed or data will not be interchangeable between computers from different manufacturers.

This standard is provided by the American Standard Code for Information Interchange, or ASCII code.

### Key term

**Character set**: the defined list of characters recognised by a computer's hardware and software.

### Did you know?

Long before ASCII another standard binary code was invented to represent text. This was the Morse code, which uses lights, tones or clicks that are either of short ('dots') or long ('dashes') duration. The duration of a dash is three times the duration of a dot.

Each character is represented by a sequence of dots and dashes. For example, the letter 'C' is represented by 'dash dot dash dot'.

Originally the ASCII code consisted of 7 bits and so 128 characters could be represented.

All of the lower and upper case English characters, punctuation marks and control actions such backspace, shift on, shift off and carriage return were represented.

The printable characters of the 7-bit ASCII code are shown in Figure 3.3. The codes for control actions (mentioned above) are not shown.

If you look at the table you can see that the codes are grouped according to function. Important groups are 65 to 90 for the upper case alphabetic characters and 97 to 122 for their lower case equivalents. The numeric characters 0 to 9 are represented by codes 48 to 57.

### Activity 8 ?

Using the table in Figure 3.3, write down the ASCII codes for the characters in the following:

ASCII code.

| D | B | C | D | B | C | D | B | C | D | B | C |
|---|---|---|---|---|---|---|---|---|---|---|---|
| 32 | 00100000 | space | 57 | 00111001 | 9 | 82 | 01010010 | R | 107 | 01101011 | k |
| 33 | 00100001 | ! | 58 | 00111010 | : | 83 | 01010011 | S | 108 | 01101100 | l |
| 34 | 00100010 | " | 59 | 00111011 | ; | 84 | 01010100 | T | 109 | 01101101 | m |
| 35 | 00100011 | # | 60 | 00111100 | < | 85 | 01010101 | U | 110 | 01101110 | n |
| 36 | 00100100 | $ | 61 | 00111101 | = | 86 | 01010110 | V | 111 | 01101111 | o |
| 37 | 00100101 | % | 62 | 00111110 | > | 87 | 01010111 | W | 112 | 01110000 | p |
| 38 | 00100110 | & | 63 | 00111111 | ? | 88 | 01011000 | X | 113 | 01110001 | q |
| 39 | 00100111 | ' | 64 | 01000000 | @ | 89 | 01011001 | Y | 114 | 01110010 | r |
| 40 | 00101000 | ( | 65 | 01000001 | A | 90 | 01011010 | Z | 115 | 01110011 | s |
| 41 | 00101001 | ) | 66 | 01000010 | B | 91 | 01011011 | [ | 116 | 01110100 | t |
| 42 | 00101010 | * | 67 | 01000011 | C | 92 | 01011100 | \ | 117 | 01110101 | u |
| 43 | 00101011 | + | 68 | 01000100 | D | 93 | 01011101 | ] | 118 | 01110110 | v |
| 44 | 00101100 | , | 69 | 01000101 | E | 94 | 01011110 | ^ | 119 | 01110111 | w |
| 45 | 00101101 | - | 70 | 01000110 | F | 95 | 01011111 | _ | 120 | 01111000 | x |
| 46 | 00101110 | . | 71 | 01000111 | G | 96 | 01100000 | ` | 121 | 01111001 | y |
| 47 | 00101111 | / | 72 | 01001000 | H | 97 | 01100001 | a | 122 | 01111010 | z |
| 48 | 00110000 | 0 | 73 | 01001001 | I | 98 | 01100010 | b | 123 | 01111011 | { |
| 49 | 00110001 | 1 | 74 | 01001010 | J | 99 | 01100011 | c | 124 | 01111100 | | |
| 50 | 00110010 | 2 | 75 | 01001011 | K | 100 | 01100100 | d | 125 | 01111101 | } |
| 51 | 00110011 | 3 | 76 | 01001100 | L | 101 | 01100101 | e | 126 | 01111110 | ~ |
| 52 | 00110100 | 4 | 77 | 01001101 | M | 102 | 01100110 | f | 127 | 01111111 | DEL |
| 53 | 00110101 | 5 | 78 | 01001110 | N | 103 | 01100111 | g | | | |
| 54 | 00110110 | 6 | 79 | 01001111 | O | 104 | 01101000 | h | | | |
| 55 | 00110111 | 7 | 80 | 01010000 | P | 105 | 01101001 | i | | | |
| 56 | 00111000 | 8 | 81 | 01010001 | Q | 106 | 01101010 | j | | | |

KEY:    D = denary
        B = binary
        C = character

**Figure 3.3** The printable characters of the 7-bit ASCII code

## Top tip

The groups of the characters can be important when you are writing a program. For example, if you are **encrypting** some text using a simple Caesar cipher shift key (see section 3.4, page 126), you can easily find the corresponding letters.

For example, suppose the encryption key is +3 (a right shift) and you enter the letter 'D'. The ASCII code for 'D' is 68 and so the encrypted value would be 71(G). If the encryption key is –3 (a left shift), then the plain text letter 'D' results in the cipher text letter 'A' (ASCII 65).

## Key term

**Encryption**: the process of encoding a message into a form that only the intended recipient can decode, or decrypt, and read. The message is encoded using an agreed method or algorithm. This is called the key. The encrypted message is called a cipher.

## Analysing a string

To a computer a string is just a stream of binary codes that represent the characters. Programming languages have functions that will return the denary equivalents of those codes and vice versa.

The Edexcel pseudo-code does not have these functions built in, but in the Python programming language they are `ord()` and `chr()`.

Therefore

- `ord('c')` would return 99, and
- `chr(100)` would return 'd'.

Using the `ord()` function the ASCII codes of the characters can be found when traversing a string.

By inserting the `ord()` function into the Edexcel pseudo-code, the algorithm that does this can be displayed.

```
SEND "Please enter the text" TO DISPLAY
RECEIVE myString FROM (STRING) KEYBOARD
FOR index FROM 0 TO LENGTH(myString) – 1 DO
    SET number TO ord(myString[index])  #The function
                                        is called using
                                        the character in
                                        the string as an
                                        argument.

    SEND number TO DISPLAY
END FOR
```

By using the `chr()` function you can build up a string using characters entered by their denary codes.

The following algorithm will allow you to enter ten numbers which will be converted to characters and appended to the string.

```
SET myString TO ""     #This will create an empty string.
FOR index FROM 0 TO 10 DO
    SEND "Please enter a number in the range 65 to 90 or
    in the range 97 to 122" TO DISPLAY
    RECEIVE number FROM (INTEGER) KEYBOARD
    SET character TO chr(number)
    SET myString TO myString + character
END FOR
```

## Creating the functions

The pseudo-code does not have these functions built in. You need to define them using the commands and statements that are available so that you can call them when required.

The `ord()` function needs to take the character as a parameter and return its denary code.

You can do this in the following way.

```
FUNCTION ord(character)
BEGIN FUNCTION
    SET arrayAscii TO [["!"][33], ["""][34],…["z"][122]]    #A two-dimensional array
                                                            containing all of the
                                                            characters with their denary
                                                            codes.


    FOR index FROM 0 TO LENGTH(arrayAscii) — 1 DO
        IF character = arrayAscii[index, 0] THEN
            code = arrayAscii[index, 1]
        END IF
    END FOR
RETURN code
END FUNCTION
```

## Activity 9 ?

Create a function in pseudo-code that will return the character from the denary code entered.

## Activity 10 ?

Create an algorithm that will encrypt the following sentence:

'The ASCII code represents characters.'

Encrypt it with a shift of 3 to the right (i.e. A should be encrypted as D).

(Remember: the spaces and the full stop should not be changed.)

Output the encrypted text.

Present your algorithm as pseudo-code or code and test it in the programming language you are studying.

## Extend your knowledge

The original ASCII code with its 96 printable characters is very restricting as many more are needed to cater for all the world's languages.

It was changed to an 8-bit code as Extended ASCII, following which Unicode was developed.

Carry out research into these two systems.

# Representation of bitmap images

Images are also represented and stored as binary code.

The basic unit of a bitmap image is the **pixel**.

## Key term

**Pixel**: short for 'picture element', the smallest single point of colour in a graphic image.

## Image size and resolution

Image size is usually written as two numbers, for example 640 × 480, 2240 × 1680 or 4064 × 2704.

The first number indicates the number of pixels along the width of the image and the second is the number in the height.

Thus a 640 × 480 image is made up of 307,200 pixels and a 4064 × 2704 image comprises 10,989,056 pixels.

# Data

The following images are the same size but have different **resolutions.**

4288 × 2848 pixels

100 × 66 pixels

There are different numbers of pixels per square inch in the two images. Each pixel in the 100 × 66 image is a larger size than those of the 4288 × 2848 image. The greater the number of pixels within a given area the higher the resolution and the more detail shown. An image of size 100 × 66, when displayed in the same area as one of 4288 × 2848 pixels, will have a far lower resolution as there are far fewer pixels. The lower the resolution the less the amount of detail seen.

## Encoding the pixel information

Each pixel is represented by a 'bit pattern' – often the same pattern used to represent a character in the ASCII code.

The number of different colours that can be used is determined by the number of bits used to encode colour.

For example, if one bit is used for each pixel, then there will be only two colours – black and white.

The following diagram shows an encoding system with one bit used to represent each pixel.

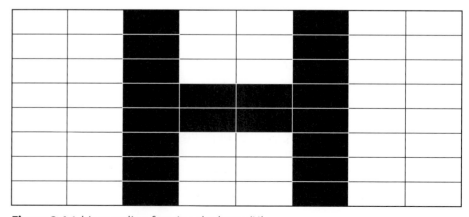

**Figure 3.4** 1-bit encoding forming the letter 'H'

If 0 represents black and 1 white, the letter 'H' could be encoded with the following bit pattern.

11011011
11011011
11011011
11000011
11000011
11011011
11011011
11011011

The complete image consists of 64 pixels and because 1 bit is used for each square, the size of the image is 64 bits or 8 bytes.

As the **colour depth** increases so too does the number of colours that can be represented.

If 1 bit is used then the number of colours is $2^1$ or 2.

If 3 bits are used the number of colours is $2^3$ or 8.

If 8 bits are used the number of colours is $2^8$ or 256.

The current standard represents the colour of each pixel in 24 bits. There are 8 bits for each of the red, blue and green primary colours.

There are therefore 256 variations of each primary colour contributing to the overall colour of the pixel and that gives $256 \times 256 \times 256$ or 16,777,216 different colours.

This standard allows lifelike images, so it is often referred to as true colour.

☐ This shape is filled with a colour named 'Alice blue'.

In binary you would have to enter 111100001111100011111111 every time you wanted to use it.

However, as mentioned in section 3.1, hexadecimal comes to our rescue. Using hexadecimal you would only have to enter #F0F8FF.

## File sizes

The file size for a bitmap image is calculated by finding the total number of pixels and multiplying that by the number of bits used to represent each pixel or

Width × Height × Colour depth

The file size of the left-hand image on page 110 is

4288 (width) × 2848 (height) × 24 (bit colour depth) = 293,093,376 bits

That is 36,636,672 bytes or almost 37 megabytes.

### Key term

**Colour depth**: the number of bits used to encode the colour of each pixel.

### Did you know?

As the size of the image and its colour depth increases so too does the amount of data that has to be stored and manipulated. If you were visiting a website with 4288 × 2848 24-bit images then, unless you had a very fast connection, you would quickly become frustrated as you waited for them all to download. Lower resolution images have to be used as a compromise between quality and file size.

### Activity 11

Calculate the file sizes of the following images and express the sizes in bits, bytes and megabytes.

1   A 256 colour image with a size of 640 × 480 pixels.

2   A true colour image with a size of 640 × 480 pixels.

## Representation of sound

All sounds are caused by vibrations. As objects such as our vocal cords or guitar strings vibrate backwards and forwards they push the air molecules alongside them, sending a wave of compressed molecules through the air. When these compression waves, or sound waves, reach our ears they set up vibrations in tiny sensory hairs in the inner ear. This sends nerve impulses to the brain, which interprets them as the sounds we hear.

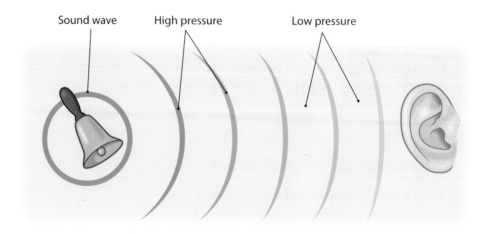

**Figure 3.5** Sound waves travelling through the air from a vibrating bell

Figure 3.6 illustrates the different waves for loud and quiet and high- and low-pitched sounds.

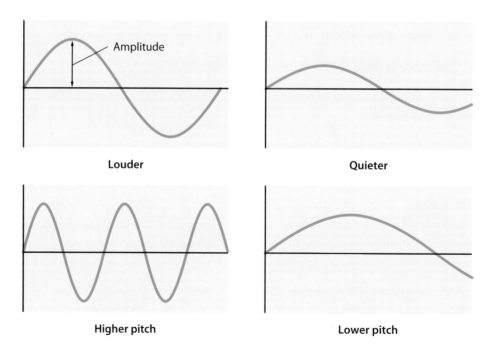

**Figure 3.6** The bigger the wave, the louder the sound; the greater the frequency of the waves, the higher the pitch

# Recording sound waves

## *Analogue recording*

Analogue recording represents the continuous changes in air pressure caused by sound waves, as changes in voltage. The changes in voltage are directly proportional to the changes in air pressure and these in turn are stored, for example, as grooves of varying depths in vinyl records or as magnetised areas of a magnetic tape.

When the disc is played the movements of another stylus through the groove are converted back into voltage changes. After amplification, these cause the diaphragm of a speaker to vibrate, reproducing the original sound.

It is called analogue recording because the changes in voltage exactly mirror the changes in air pressure (or are analogous to them). The complete sound waves are recorded.

## *Digital recording*

It was stressed in section 3.1 (on page 92) that computers do not represent data in an analogue way where minute changes in voltage are used to represent changes in the data. Computers are digital and their transistors are either on or off with nothing in between, so sound data, like any other form of computer data, must be represented as streams of 1s and 0s.

Continuous change cannot be represented by a digital stream, so digital recordings take a series of sound 'snapshots'. When these are played back rapidly in succession the sound produced seems to be continuous.

These 'snapshots' of the sound are called samples and the process of taking them is called **sampling**.

The following diagram shows an analogue sound wave being sampled.

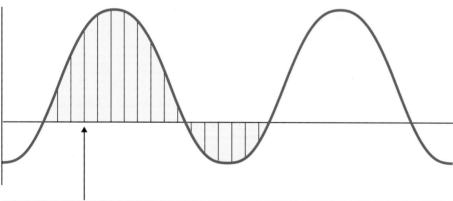

Each line represents a new sample. The time between each line/sample represents the sampling period, which equals 1/44,100 of a second, for a CD with a sampling rate of 44.1 kHz.

**Figure 3.7** How a sound wave is sampled digitally

The sampling of the continuous sound wave is carried out by an analogue-to-digital recorder (ADR), which converts the sound into a stream of 1s and 0s.

> **Did you know?**
>
> A similar technique is used for producing movies on film. If a series of images, or frames, of the same scene, but with small differences between them, are played back in rapid succession, our brains think that we are watching moving objects.

> **Key term**
>
> **Sampling**: taking measurements of the sound wave at regular but distinct intervals of time (e.g. 44,100 samples per second).

# Data

A digital-to-analogue converter is required to convert the binary data back into an analogue wave.

The complete wave cannot be recorded and so a digital recording can never be as accurate or have the same accuracy, or **fidelity**, as an analogue recording, but it does have other benefits such as:

- Equipment to record and process digital sound is relatively cheap and has allowed people to record music at home.
- It is easily edited using computer equipment.
- It is easily copied.
- Unlike vinyl and tape, digital files do not physically deteriorate with use, although they may become corrupted if the storage medium is damaged.
- Digital files are more portable than records and tapes and can be copied to any digital medium, such as a hard drive, emailed, downloaded and streamed.

## Fidelity

The fidelity of the recording is influenced by two factors.

### Sample rate

This is the number of samples taken per second – the higher the rate the higher the fidelity.

Figure 3.8 shows the effect of sampling at different rates.

A sampling rate of 44,100 per second (44.1 kHz) is used for CDs and of 96,000 Hz (96 kHz) for Blu-ray™ audio.

### Bit depth or sampling precision

One important detail is the dynamic range of the sound – the range of volumes of sound in the music.

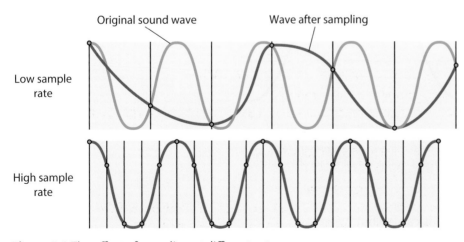

- Using 8 bits allows 256 ($2^8$) gradations to be measured.
- 16 bits allows ($2^{16}$) 65,536, and
- 24 bits allows ($2^{24}$) over 16.7 million.

Therefore using more bits allows for much smaller gradations in the volume differences.

For CD recordings a **bit depth** of 16 bits is used.

**Figure 3.8** The effect of sampling at different rates

## Digital audio file sizes

The size of a digital audio sound file depends on the following:

- sample rate per second
- bit depth
- duration of recording
- number of channels – mono (one channel) or stereo (two channels).

### *Calculating file size*

**Worked example**

number of samples per second = 44,100

bit depth = 16 bits

duration = 2.5 minutes

number of channels = 2

The size of the file is found from the following formula:

file size in bits = sample rate * bit depth * duration (in seconds) * number of channels

Therefore the file size of the above recording is

44,100 * 16 * 2.5 * 60 * 2 = 211,680,000 bits or 26,460,000 bytes or over 26 megabytes.

**Activity 12** **?**

Calculate the file size of a stereo recording of three minutes' duration with a sample rate of 44,100 and a bit depth of 24 bits.

**Exam-style questions**

1 Explain what is meant by a 'pixel'. **(2 marks)**
2 The following diagram shows a black and white image consisting of 36 pixels.

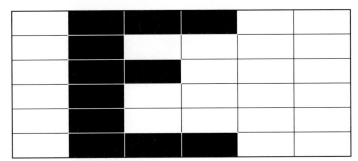

**Figure 3.9** A 36 pixel image of the letter E

   **a** Explain why 36 bits are needed to represent the pixels in the image. **(2 marks)**
   **b** Write the bit pattern needed to represent these pixels. **(4 marks)**
   **c** State the number of bits per pixel that would be needed if the image was 16 colours rather than 2. **(1 mark)**
3 Jane is using a computer program to record herself playing the guitar.
   **a** Describe how the program converts her music into a file. **(3 marks)**
     The software allows her to increase the sample rate.
   **b** Describe two effects this will have on her recording. **(2 marks)**
   **c** She eventually records the music in mono with a sample rate of 44.1 kHz and a bit depth of 16. If the recording lasts for two minutes, calculate the size of the file produced. Express your answer in megabytes. **(2 marks)**

# Data

## Exam tips

1 This simply requires a one-sentence definition.

2 a You need to explain why 1 bit will be needed to encode the colour information of each pixel in a black and white image.

   b You should show the bits required for each line of the image. Don't forget to state the type of bit used to represent each colour.

   c You could represent this in powers of 2.

3 a This requires a longer answer. You should start with describing how the sound reaches the recording device and then how it is converted into a digital format.

   b Two effects are needed – quality and size.

   c This requires you to apply the formula to calculate file size. Read the question carefully so that you use the correct figures in the calculation and remember that sample rate is defined as samples per second.

## Summary

- All data is represented by bit patterns – sequences of 1s and 0s.
- The ASCII code represents text characters as patterns of 7 or 8 bits.
- A pixel is the smallest single point of colour in a graphic image.
- The amount of colour information used for each pixel is called the 'bit depth'.
- The file size of a bitmap image is calculated by multiplying the number of pixels in the width of the image by the number in the height and then multiplying by the number of bits used to encode each pixel.
- Digital sound recordings are produced by sampling analogue sound waves.
- The sample rate and the bit depth affect the fidelity of the recording and also the file size.

## Checkpoint

### Strengthen

S1 Represent the following sentence using the denary ASCII codes for the characters:
   Data is represented as bits.

S2 An image is described as being 640 × 480. If it has a bit depth of 24, calculate the size of the file.

### Challenge

C1 In your own words explain why some digital images are clearer and display more detail than others.

C2 Explain the factors influencing the file size of a digital audio recording.

How confident do you feel about your answers to these questions? If you're not sure you answered them well, try the following activities again:

- For S1 try Activity 8.
- For S2 try Activity 11.

# 3.3 Data storage and compression

## Learning outcomes

By the end of this section you should be able to:

- convert between the terms bit, nibble, byte, kilobyte (KB), megabyte (MB), gigabyte (GB), terabyte (TB).
- explain the need for data compression and methods of compressing data.
- use the run-length encoding (RLE) algorithm to compress a data file.

## Data storage

All data consists of bits – 1s and 0s. In section 3.2 (on page 111), you calculated the size of an example image file as being 293,093,376 bits or 36,636,672 bytes, and the size of an example sound file (on page 115) to be 211,680,000 bits or 26,460,000 bytes – a typical byte is equivalent to 8 bits.

When converting binary to hexadecimal in section 3.1 (on page 104), you used a unit called a 'nibble', which is equal to 4 bits.

If these files are saved on computers running different operating systems, their sizes in megabytes (MB) are displayed differently. For example, in Microsoft® Windows® the image file size would be shown as 34.9 MB, whereas in Ubuntu® it would be shown as 36.6 MB.

This is because of the method used to calculate higher units. Ubuntu uses SI units (International System of Units), which treats 'kilo' as meaning 1,000 as it does when measuring distance and weight. This method is known as **decimal prefix** because it uses powers of 10 (e.g. $10^3$ for 1,000).

The other method, the **binary prefix**, uses powers of 2, so 'kilo' is defined as $2^{10}$ or 1,024.

### Key terms

**Decimal prefix**: multiplies a unit by powers of 10.

**Binary prefix**: multiplies a unit by powers of 2.

The table shows the differences.

| Unit | Symbol | Decimal prefix | Size | Binary prefix | Size |
|------|--------|----------------|------|---------------|------|
| kilobyte | KB | $10^3$ bytes | 1,000 bytes | $2^{10}$ bytes | 1,024 bytes |
| megabyte | MB | $10^6$ bytes | 1,000 kilobytes | $2^{20}$ bytes | 1,024 kilobytes |
| gigabyte | GB | $10^9$ bytes | 1,000 megabytes | $2^{30}$ bytes | 1,024 megabytes |
| terabyte | TB | $10^{12}$ bytes | 1,000 gigabytes | $2^{40}$ bytes | 1,024 gigabytes |

Therefore, every higher unit is 1,000 times larger than the previous one with decimal prefix, whereas in binary prefix it is 1,024 times larger.

# Data

### Activity 13

1   A hard disk is described as having a storage capacity of 1.5 TB. What is this in:

    a   gigabytes

    b   megabytes

    c   kilobytes

    d   terabytes?

2   An image file has a size of 363,143,213 bits. What is its size in gigabytes?

## Data compression

Files have to be stored somewhere, for example on local or remote hard disk drives or on USB drives. If they are graphics or audio files, then these files can be very large.

Millions of image and audio files are uploaded and downloaded each day.

There are many benefits to the files being made as small as possible. The users don't waste time while their data is being transferred or saved and the providers can store them in as little space as possible.

That is why file **compression** is so important. Compressed files use less network bandwidth to upload and download, there is less internet congestion and it makes possible the streaming of video and audio files.

Compression algorithms are used to make the files as small as possible. There are two types of compression – **lossless** and **lossy compression**.

## Lossless compression

When lossless compresion is used, no data is lost and the original file can be restored.

It is especially useful for files where the same data occurs many times, for example text, where there are relatively few different items of data (i.e. character and punctuation symbols). In a page of text there are many words that are used more than once. This is referred to as redundancy.

Lossless compression is essential for text as missing data would completely distort the meaning of what was being communicated.

### Run-length encoding (RLE)

Run-length encoding is used to reduce the size of a repeating string of items. The repeating string is called a run and is represented by two bytes – the first byte represents the number of occurrences and the second, the item of information.

For example, the following string of letters

cccmmmmmsssssdddcccccc

would be represented by

3c5m5s3d6c

If one byte is used to encode each letter in the original uncompressed text, 22 bytes in total are required.

In the RLE version, one byte is used for the letter and one byte is used for the number, making a total of only 10 bytes.

Obviously, this method is only effective where there are strings of the same data. If the original data is very different, without repeating strings, then the encoded version would have a greater file size.

For a black and white image, like the one in Figure 3.10, compression using RLE would be effective. A colour image in which there are very short runs of different colours would not be encoded as effectively.

> **Key terms**
>
> **Compression**: changing the format of a data file so that the size of the file becomes smaller.
>
> **Lossless compression**: compressing a file in such a way that it can be decompressed without any loss of data.
>
> **Lossy compression**: compression where some of the data is removed; the original file cannot be restored when the lossy file is decompressed.

# Data

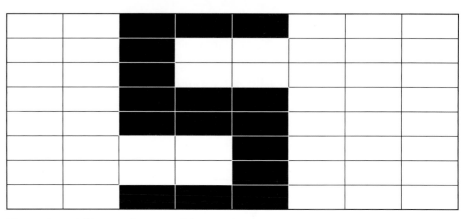

**Figure 3.10** A bitmap diagram of the number 5

To demonstrate run-length encoding, the letters 'w' and 'b' are used to represent the white and black pixels instead of 1s and 0s

| Code | RLE version | Size of coded version |
| --- | --- | --- |
| wwbbbwww | 2w3b3w | 6 |
| wwbwwwww | 2w1b5w | 6 |
| wwbwwwww | 2w1b5w | 6 |
| wwbbbwww | 2w3b3w | 6 |
| wwbbbwww | 2w3b3w | 6 |
| wwwwbwww | 4w1b3w | 6 |
| wwwwbwww | 4w1b3w | 6 |
| wwbbbwww | 2w3b3w | 6 |
| **64 bytes** | | **48 bytes** |

The file size for this character has been reduced from 64 to 48 bytes. It could be reduced even further if the number 1 is omitted where there is a run of only one. The algorithm could be easily adapted.

## Activity 14  ?

Show the effect of applying run-length encoding to the following graphic.

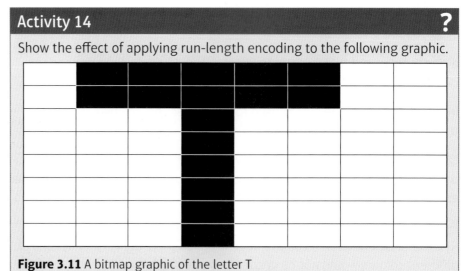

**Figure 3.11** A bitmap graphic of the letter T

Set out your answer as in the example above.

### Coding the run-length algorithm

An RLE algorithm will have to traverse a string and count the number of occurrences of each character in the run.

When the character changes it will have to start counting a new run.

The flowchart shows a possible algorithm to do this.

First the input string is checked to see if it actually has any letters (i.e. is the length greater than zero?)

If yes, a check is made to see if it only has one letter. If so the run will be equal to 1 and the text character will be the one at index position 0 in the string.

If there is more than one character in the input string, then a loop is needed to examine each one.

If the character at index position 1 is equal to the character at position 0, then the length of the run is incremented by 1 and the character at index position 2 is checked.

If this character is different, then a new run is started for this character and the previous character and its run length are added to the string holding the code.

This continues until the algorithm reaches the end of the string.

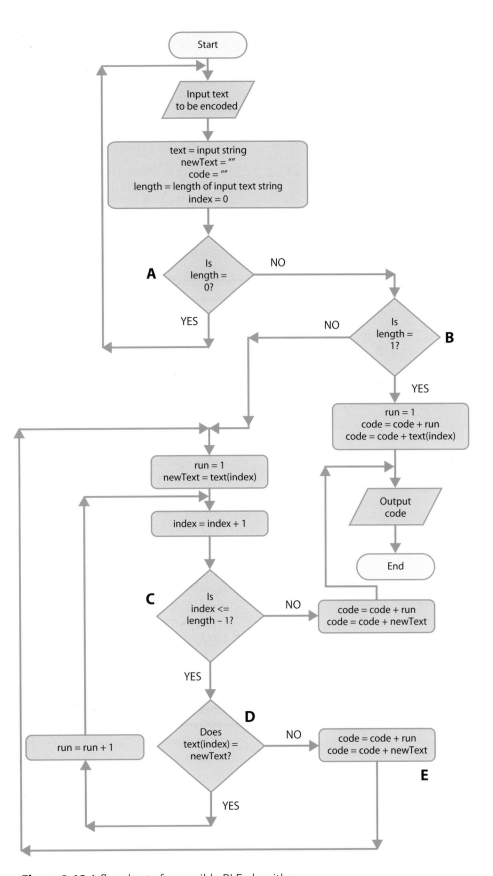

**Figure 3.12** A flowchart of a possible RLE algorithm

## Lossy compression

Lossy compression decreases the file size by deleting some of the data. The original file therefore cannot be re-formed entirely when it is decompressed, so it cannot be used with text or program files.

It can be used for bitmap image and audio files where we often cannot notice that data has been removed.

### Bitmap images

Digital images can comprise millions of pixels each with a 24-bit depth. They result in very large files. However, many of the minute differences in colour are wasted on us. Our eyesight is not capable of distinguishing these small differences.

A lossy compression algorithm analyses all of the data in the image and when it finds areas with minute differences it gives them the same colour values. It can then rewrite the file using fewer bits.

The most commonly used compression technique was developed by the Joint Photographic Experts Group and produces JPEG files with the extension jpg.

The images on the next page demonstrate JPEG compression. The one on the left has a file size of 6 MB, while the compressed version on the right is only 350 KB. They both have the same number of pixels, but the algorithm made pixels with similar colour values the same. The size has been reduced over 17 times, but to our eyes there is little difference in detail and clarity.

Digitally compressing an image makes little difference to our eyes but huge savings in file size

## Audio files

Uncompressed audio files that contain all of the sampled sound data are saved in Waveform Audio (WAV) format. A three-minute recording typically has a file size of about 30 MB.

Much of the data in an audio file encodes tones and frequencies that our ears cannot hear and small differences in volume and frequency that they cannot distinguish.

The most commonly used algorithm compresses them and encodes them as MPEG-1 audio layer 3 files or, as they are commonly called, MP3 files, by removing the redundant or superfluous data.

A 30 MB WAV file can be compressed to a 3 MB MP3 equivalent.

The following graphs show the differences in dynamic range between a WAV file and its MP3 equivalent. They clearly show the dip in range at high frequencies.

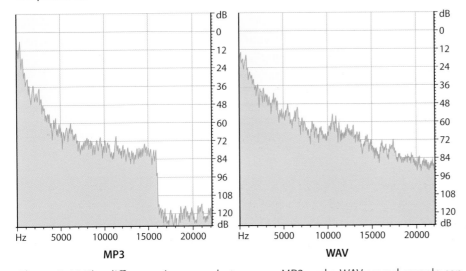

**Figure 3.13** The difference in ranges between an MP3 and a WAV sound sample can clearly be seen

123

# Data

## Exam tips

For Question 1 just list them in ascending order and for Question 2 just write out the encoded version.

## Exam-style questions

1 Order the following units from smallest to largest. **(3 marks)**

   GB   bit   TB   byte   nibble   MB

2 Compress the following two-colour bitmap data using run-length encoding. **(3 marks)**

   11100011000000111000110

## Summary

- File sizes are measured in kilobytes, megabytes, gigabytes and terabytes.
- Each unit is 1,000 ($10^3$) times larger than the previous one.
- Files can be compressed using lossy and lossless compression algorithms.
- In lossy compression some of the data is lost.
- In lossless compression none of the data is lost.
- Run-length encoding is an example of lossless compression.

## Checkpoint

### Strengthen

**S1** List the units used to measure file size in ascending order starting at 'bit'.

**S2** Convert 2.3 terabytes into bytes.

**S3** Encode the following using run-length encoding

aaabbaaaaaaaaacccddd

and calculate the file size of the original and the encoded versions.

### Challenge

**C1** Explain why it is difficult to compress digital images using lossless compression algorithms.

**C2** In your own words explain why an audio file compressed using a 'lossy' algorithm often sounds the same as the original uncompressed version.

How confident do you feel about your answers to these questions? If you're not sure you answered them well, try the following activities again:

For S1 try Activity 13.
For S2 try Activity 13.
For S3 try Activity 14.

# 3.4 Encryption

When we send sensitive information such as bank or credit card details over an internet connection we check (or should check) the URL to ensure that it starts with 'HTTPS:', denoting a secure connection. Internet connections are insecure and messages are easily intercepted. The secure connection ensures that the transferred data is encrypted and is read only by the intended recipient.

## Did you know?

HTTPS stands for Hypertext Transfer Protocol (HTTP) with the Secure Socket Layer (SSL)/Transport Layer Security (TLS) protocol added to it. It ensures that data transfer is encrypted.

Ever since people began to use writing, encryption has been used to make messages secret. In ancient Egypt, scribes slightly changed hieroglyphics so that the general public could not understand them.

## Did you know?

Other methods have been used to hide messages. A Roman general sent a secret message by shaving off a slave's hair and tattooing the message on his head. When his hair had grown, the slave delivered the message to the recipient who had been told how to find it.

## Modern methods of data encryption

### Asymmetric encryption

This method encrypts and decrypts data using two different keys. Every user has two keys, a public key, known to everyone, and a private key, known only to themselves. A message encrypted with a particular public key can only be decrypted by the corresponding private key.

If person A wanted to send an encrypted file to person B, person A would encrypt it with person B's public key. On receipt, person B would then decrypt the file with their private key.

It is commonly used to send encrypted messages because anyone who wants to send an encrypted message can get the intended recipient's public key from a public directory.

### Symmetric encryption

This method encrypts and decrypts a message using the same key.

This is the method used by an HTTPS connection. The client contacts the server and they establish a secure connection. The client generates the key to be used using an agreed algorithm and sends it to the server using the server's public key (asymmetric encryption). The server decrypts it using its private key and then they both use the common key for their secure transmissions.

# Data

## The Caesar cipher

The Caesar cipher is a very simple encryption method and would not be used today because it is so easy to crack.

It is named after Julius Caesar who encrypted messages in the following way.

The letters of the alphabet are shifted a set number of places. A positive shift moves the letters to the right. A negative shift moves them to the left.

For example, with a key of +2, the alphabet would be changed to that shown on the bottom row.

| Plain text (input) | A | B | C | D | E | F | G | H | I | J | K | L | M | N | O | P | Q | R | S | T | U | V | W | X | Y | Z |
|---|---|---|---|---|---|---|---|---|---|---|---|---|---|---|---|---|---|---|---|---|---|---|---|---|---|---|
| Cipher text (output) | C | D | E | F | G | H | I | J | K | L | M | N | O | P | Q | R | S | T | U | V | W | X | Y | Z | A | B |

With a key of of –3 the letters of the alphabet shift three places to the left, so the word 'SECRET' becomes 'PBZOBQ'.

Notice how the letters at the end move to the start of the alphabet.

So if the message was

PLEASE SEND MORE TROOPS

the encrypted version using a key of +5 is

UQJFXJ XJSI RTWJ YWTTUX

If the recipient knows the key they can decrypt the message by shifting the letters in the opposite direction by the required number of places.

## Algorithm for the Caesar cipher

This is a perfect example to practise your computational thinking skills.

You are going to write a program to encrypt and decrypt a message using a specific key using the Caesar cipher method.

Here is a decomposition of the problem:

1. Determine whether the message has to be encrypted or decrypted.
2. If the message is to be encrypted, then
3. Ask the user to enter the message.
4. Ask the user for the key.
5. Analyse each character in the message and if it is a letter calculate the letter the 'key' number of places to the right if the shift is positive or to the left if it is negative.
6. If it is a punctuation mark then do not change it.
7. Build up a new message using these new letters.
8. Output the new message.

If the message is to be decrypted, repeat the above, but reverse the shift.

---

### Activity 16　?

Encrypt the following using the Caesar cipher with a key of +3.

This is a message

---

### Hints for this activity

- The ASCII codes are 65 to 90 for the upper-case alphabetic characters and 97 to 122 for lower-case ones.
- A key of +3 means that the characters in the message are shifted three places to the right. Whereas if the key is –3 the characters are shifted to the left.
- Have a look at Activity 8 on page 106 and the Top tip on page 107 in section 3.2.
- Have a look at analysing a string on page 107 in section 3.2.
- Remember that string index positions start at 0.
- Have a look at Activity 10 on page 109 in section 3.2.

Here is a flowchart of a possible solution.

All this seems straightforward, but there are some more sub-problems.

- Your program will need to check that the user input – the key and the message – has actually been entered.
- The algorithm will have to start at the first character and move to the last (i.e. it must traverse the string), therefore your program will have to find the length of the message.
- Some of the letters may be entered in upper case and some in lower case. Your program should be able to cope with this and encode or decode them.
- Your program will have to leave any characters such as spaces, commas and full stops as they are.

## The 'biggest problem'

Your program will have to cope with letters near the start and end of the alphabet.

For example, if the key is +3 and the letter to be encoded is 'X', then the encrypted version will be 'A' (because it has been shifted three places to the right).

Similarly, if the letter to be decrypted is 'B', the new version will be 'Y' (because a shift of 3 places to the right has been performed).

The algorithm must be able to move from the first letter of the alphabet to the last and vice versa.

## Top tip

The ASCII codes for upper case characters run from 65 to 90. The code for 'X' is 88. With a key of +3 this would encrypt to 91, but this doesn't represent a letter of the alphabet.

It should encrypt to the letter 'A', which has the ASCII code of 65.

Therefore 88 has to be changed to 65.

There are 26 letters in the alphabet, so you should be able to see how to get from 64 to 90 using the number of letters in the alphabet.

Don't forget it's the reverse if you are decrypting.

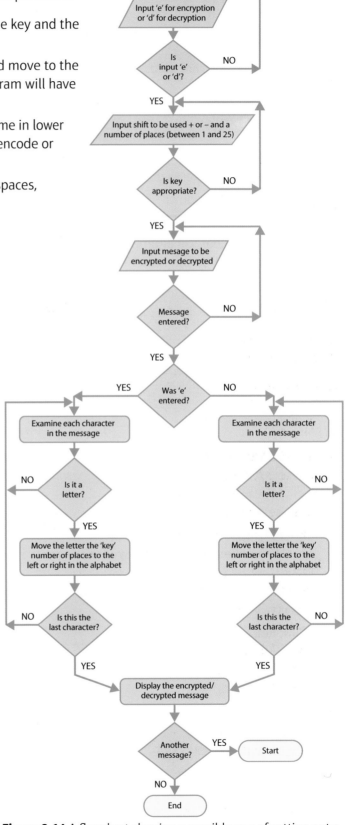

**Figure 3.14** A flowchart showing a possible way of setting out a Caesar cipher

# Data

## Structured programming

Creating the algorithm and coding the program will allow you to use structured programming using subprograms, and especially functions, which are called from the main program.

For example, functions are used to:

- ask the user if they want to encrypt or decrypt.
- ask the user for the key.
- ask the user for the message.
- carry out the encryption or decryption.

Each of these functions will return values that are used by the main program.

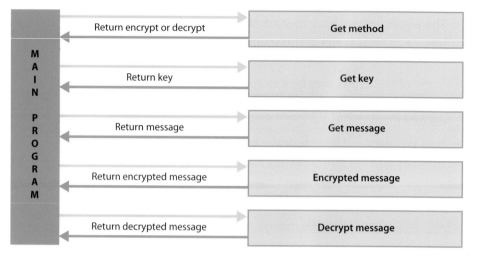

**Figure 3.15** An example of structured programming

Here is the main program in pseudo-code – the subprograms are not included.

```
SET run TO 1
WHILE run = 1 DO                              #A WHILE loop is started. It will continue until the variable
                                              'run' does not contain the value 1.

   SET method TO findMethod()                 #This calls the function for the user to ask for encryption
                                              or decryption.

   SET key TO findKey()                       #This calls the function for the user to enter the key.
   SET message TO getMessage()                #This calls the function for the user to enter the message.
   IF method == "e" THEN
      SET newMessage TO encrypt(message, key) #Functions to encrypt or decrypt are called.
   ELSE
      SET newMessage TO decrypt(message, key)
   END IF
   SEND newMessage TO DISPLAY                 #The encrypted or decrypted message is displayed.
   SEND "Please enter x to quit or any other key to continue" TO DISPLAY
   RECEIVE response FROM (CHARACTER) KEYBOARD
   IF response = "x" then                     #The user is asked if they want to encrypt or decrypt
                                              again. If not the variable 'run' is changed from 1 and
                                              the loop will stop.

      SET run TO "x"
   ELSE
      SET run TO 1
   END IF
END WHILE
```

## Activity 17

Create and test, in the language you are studying, a program to encrypt or decrypt a message using a key entered by a user.

## Exam-style questions

1 Encrypt the following word using the Caesar cipher with a key of +6.
   Computer **(3 marks)**

2 Decrypt the following word using the Caesar cipher with a key of +3.
   Pzfbkzb **(3 marks)**

## Exam tip

These questions do not require you to give an explanation or description. They are asking you to apply the Caesar cipher algorithm to encrypt and decrypt. You should transpose the characters to the left or right as instructed by the key.

## Summary

- Encryption is needed to ensure that sensitive data is secure and is read only by the intended recipient.
- Encryption keys are used to encrypt the data into cipher text and decrypt it back into normal (plain) text.
- Asymmetric encryption uses two different keys and symmetric encryption uses the same one.
- In the Caesar cipher algorithm the letters of the alphabet are shifted a set number of places as defined by the key.

## Checkpoint

### Strengthen

**S1** Encrypt the sentence below using the Caesar cipher with a key of +9:
   Data should be encrypted.

**S2** Explain how a Caesar cipher algorithm works.

### Challenge

**C1** Use a diagram to demonstrate that a shift of +5 followed by a shift of −2 is the same as a shift of +3 when applied to the word 'gold'.

How confident do you feel about your answers to these questions? If you're not sure you answered them well, try the following activity again.

- For S1 try Activity 16.

# Data

## 3.5 Databases

People have been recording and storing data since writing systems were invented thousands of years ago.

### Did you know?

The first written language was invented 5,000 years ago in Sumer, now in modern-day Iraq.

The rulers carried out a census and made lists of all the people and what they owned. This stored information gave them power and allowed them to start taxing the people.

In 1086 William the Conqueror did something similar with the Domesday Book. It listed everything that everyone owned so they could be taxed on their possessions. There was no argument – if the data was in the book, it was the law.

These books were stores of data, but finding a particular piece of information in them was difficult They weren't organised in alphabetical order. If an official was looking for a particular person, they might have to read many pages before finding the information they needed.

A **database** is a data store in which the data is organised in an ordered way so that information is quickly retrieved when the data is being searched or queried.

For example, in an encyclopaedia or dictionary the data is in alphabetical order. Imagine searching for a word if all the entries were in a random order.

### Key term

**Database**: an organised store of data.

### Computer databases

Computers are ideal for storing and manipulating data because they can search and sort the data far more quickly than a human can. Storing the data in a structured way makes searching it much faster and more efficient.

## Creating a database

As an example, consider the following scenario of a school that would like to create a database to store details of their learners.

To set this up some abstraction is needed.

### Identifying the entity and its attributes

The database is about an object called a learner. It will store details about it. Therefore LEARNER is referred to as the **entity**.

The next task is to identify the **attributes** of the entity.

With respect to an actual learner and their properties that are relevant to the school, you might identify the following attributes.

First name, surname, date of birth, year, tutor group

There could be many more depending on the requirements of the school.

This is written as:

LEARNER(first name, surname, date of birth, year, tutor group)

The entity is in upper case followed by the attributes enclosed in brackets.

### Creating the database table

Now that the entity and its attributes have been identified, you can set up the structure for storing the data. The structure is in the form of a **table**.

In this example the table with some of the learners entered looks like this.

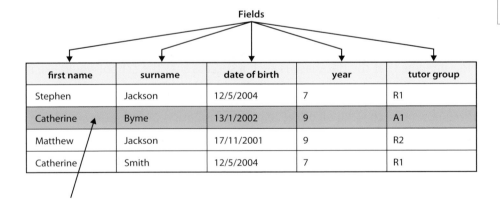

**Figure 3.16** A database table showing examples of information about learners

In the table, the same items of information are being stored about each learner. These items of information are called fields. All the information about a particular learner is called a record. Each row of the table represents one record.

All of the records in a table make up a **file**.

### Key terms

**Entity**: something that is recognised as being capable of an independent existence, is uniquely identified and about which data is stored.

It is usually a physical object (e.g. a car, a person or a book), but it can be a concept (e.g. a customer transaction where details of the items that were purchased are stored).

**Attribute**: an item of data stored about an entity.

**Table**: a collection of cells organised in rows and columns used to store data in a structured and organised manner.

**File**: all of the records in a table or a group of linked tables.

# Data

*Identifying a primary key*

Database management software sets up the tables and manages the records when they are stored. It needs to be able to identify each individual record, so each record will need a unique identifier to distinguish it from all the other records in the table.

This identifier is called the **primary key**.

In the example table for the school database, none of the fields will necessarily have a unique value. There could be many learners with the same first name, surname, date of birth, year or tutor group. It would be a strange school if the year field had a unique value – it would mean there is only one learner in each year.

An additional field is needed so each record has a unique identifier. Education databases solve this problem by giving each learner a unique pupil identification (UPI) number when they enter the school system. Here is the school database table with the primary key added.

| UPI | first name | surname | date of birth | year | tutor group |
|-----|-----------|---------|---------------|------|-------------|
| 01560 | Stephen | Jackson | 12/5/2004 | 7 | R1 |
| 01356 | Catherine | Byrne | 13/1/2002 | 9 | A1 |
| 01390 | Matthew | Jackson | 17/11/2001 | 9 | R2 |
| 01630 | Catherine | Smith | 12/5/2004 | 7 | R1 |

Each record can now be uniquely identified through the UPI field, its primary key.

This table will store the details of all the learners in the school. It can be searched to find specific individuals or all the learners in a particular tutor group, for example, and print out the list.

Now imagine that the database is such a success that the school would like it to manage the lending of books from the school library.

It will now need to store all of the learner information plus the details of the books they have borrowed.

Care is needed when designing how this data will be organised and stored.

## Data redundancy

The data could be organised in the following way, again with the UPI field being the primary key.

| UPI | first name | surname | date of birth | year | tutor group | book name | author | borrow date | return date |
|-----|-----------|---------|---------------|------|-------------|-----------|--------|-------------|-------------|
| 01560 | Stepen | Jackson | 12/5/2004 | 7 | R1 | Computing | J. Smith | 1/10/15 | 15/10/15 |
| 01356 | Catherine | Byrne | 13/1/2002 | 9 | A1 | Gardening | F. Green | 3/10/15 | 17/10/15 |
| 01356 | Catherine | Byrne | 13/1/2002 | 9 | A1 | Plants | F. Green | 3/10/15 | 17/10/15 |

The database illustrates some serious flaws in the way in which the data is being stored.

- The same data is being entered more than once – UPI, first name, surname, year and tutor group have to be written every time a book is borrowed. Also the same book information will have to be rewritten when it is borrowed by another person. This is time wasteful. Having the same data entered more than once is called data redundancy.
- When the same data is entered more than once, errors can occur. In the second version of the database Stephen is misspelt as 'Stepen'. This is known as data inconsistency.

But there is an even greater problem – the UPI is needed to uniquely identify each record. It cannot appear twice in the same table. This means that each learner can borrow only one book.

You could solve this problem by adding lots of new fields so that the learners can borrow as many books as they want.

| UPI | first name | surname | date of birth | year | tutor group | Book name_1 | Author_1 | borrow date_1 | return date_1 | book name_2 | author_2 | borrow date_2 | return date_2 |
|-----|-----------|---------|---------------|------|-------------|-------------|----------|---------------|---------------|-------------|----------|---------------|---------------|
|     |           |         |               |      |             |             |          |               |               |             |          |               |               |

Four new fields are needed for each book borrowed.

- How many new fields should be added?
- How many books will a learner borrow?
- Will all learners borrow the same number of books?

There may be too many fields for some learners and not enough for others. For many learners some will never be used.

It is obviously very inefficient to use repeating fields in a database (e.g. book name_1, book name_2, book name_3).

Not enough thought has been given to creating the structure of the database. This illustrates the importance of database design.

## Creating a structured database

The problems are solved by having more than one data table and linking them together in a single database.

The learner table is retained – it could be named tblLearner – and a separate one for the books, tblBook, created.

The book table might look like this.

| book number | title | author |
|---|---|---|
| 03169 | Computing | J. Smith |
| 04675 | Gardening | F. Green |
| 05936 | Plants | F. Green |

The 'book number' field is the primary key. A new number is issued when a new book is bought for the library.

The book borrowing is now recorded by creating a new table – tblBorrowing – with the following fields.

| UPI | book number | borrow date | return date |
|---|---|---|---|

There are now three tables, but they are linked. The primary key fields from the Learner and Book tables are both in the Borrowing table.

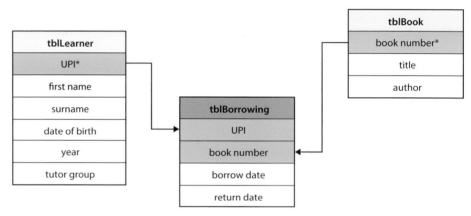

**Figure 3.17** An example of a relational database

The primary key fields in tblLearner and tblBook are indicated with asterisks.

tblLearner and tblBook are linked to tblBorrowing because their key fields are included in it. tblBorrowing is said to be a link table.

When a key field from one table is included in another it is called a **foreign key**.

By linking the tables we have structured the data to create a **relational database**.

Whenever a learner borrows a book, their UPI, the book number and the borrowing and return dates are entered into a new record in the Borrowing table.

This allows the librarian to create a search or query, linking the three tables, to find overdue books and the learners who have borrowed them.

## Key terms

**Foreign key**: a field in one table that uniquely identifies records in another table (i.e. it is a primary key in another table).

**Relational database**: a database that allows data elements in one table to be related to any piece of data in another table as long as both tables contain a common element.

If a book is overdue, all the librarian has to do is identify the learner from their UPI by looking in the Learner table and the book from its book number by looking in the Book table. They can send an overdue letter to the learner stating the book borrowed and when it should have been returned. They can also work out the fine.

## Compound keys

A key field has not been identified for tblBorrowing.

| tblBorrowing |
| --- |
| UPI |
| book number |
| borrow date |
| return date |

If the UPI is chosen as the unique identifier, then each learner will only be allowed one record in the table. They could only ever borrow one book.

If 'book number' is chosen, then each book will only be allowed to be borrowed once. That would be a waste of money.

This problem can be solved by having a **compound key**.

| tblBorrowing |
| --- |
| UPI* |
| book number* |
| borrow date |
| return date |

In tblBorrowing both UPI and book number could be combined into a compound key. So learners will be able to borrow more books because their book number fields will be different and books can appear more times in tblBorrowing as long as they are combined with a different UPI.

**Key term**

**Compound key**: a key that consists of two or more fields used to identify a record uniquely.

There is still a problem. What if a learner wants to reread a book? The database will not allow this as the UPI and book number fields will contain the same data as in the previous record.

| tblBorrowing |
| --- |
| UPI* |
| book number* |
| borrow date* |
| return date |

This is solved by expanding the compound key to include the 'borrow date' field. Now a learner can borrow a book again as long as it is on a different day.

An efficient database has been created by carefully structuring the data storage.

## Table relationships

Each learner appears only once in tblLearner, but can appear many times in tblBorrowing.

Each book appears only once in tblBook, but also can appear many times in tblBorrowing.

There are therefore 'one-to-many' relationships between the Learner and Book tables and the Borrowing table.

This is shown as follows.

**Figure 3.18** A one-to-many table relationship

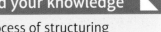

Extend your knowledge

The process of structuring the data to create relational databases is called normalisation. Find out about first, second and third normal forms.

# Data

## Activity 19 ?

Catherine is creating a database. She wants to store details of all her books and also information about their authors.

She has created the following table:

| BOOKS |
| --- |
| Book_ID* |
| Title |
| Publisher |
| Date_Published |
| Author_Surname |
| Author_First_name |
| Author_DOB |
| Author_Nationality |

When she starts to enter data, she creates records as shown below.

| Book_ID | Title | Publisher | Date_Published | Author_Surname | Author_First_name | Author_DOB | Author_Nationality |
| --- | --- | --- | --- | --- | --- | --- | --- |
| 1 | Harry Potter and the Philosopher's Stone | Bloomsbury | 1997 | Rowling | J K | 31/07/1965 | British |
| 2 | Harry Potter and the Chamber of Secrets | Bloomsbury | 1998 | Rowling | J K | 31/07/1965 | British |
| 3 | Harry Potter and the Prisoner of Azkaban | Bloomsbury | 1999 | Rowling | J K | 31/07/1965 | British |

1   Explain what is meant by:

   a   data redundancy

   b   data inconsistency.

2   Restructure Catherine's database design to remove the problems listed in Question 1.

## Unstructured data

Most of the data in existence today is not stored in structured databases. It is unstructured. In other words, it has no pre-defined structure.

Sources of unstructured data include things such as emails, word-processing documents, Microsoft® PowerPoint® presentations, images, spreadsheets, uploads to social networking websites and sensors.

Not surprisingly, unstructured data is growing significantly faster than structured data. The amount of unstructured data doubles roughly every three months. This creates major challenges for organisations – how do they store such vast quantities of data and how do they extract useful information from it?

Unstructured data is a rich source of valuable information that can help organisations make better decisions and give them a competitive edge. However, extracting information from unstructured data is much more difficult than searching a structured database. To overcome this challenge, a number of powerful data mining tools have been developed. Some are capable of analysing text and natural language to identify a person's likes and dislikes, feelings and priorities. Others use geospatial data from satellites, GPS systems and sensor networks to analyse trends and make predictions – areas where the population is set to grow, potential crime hotspots, regions at risk from natural disasters etc. Business analytic tools are used to identify customer preferences, emerging markets, consumer trends etc.

### Activity 20 ?

XtraSave supermarket allows customers to order online and have their orders delivered.

XtraSave would like to be able to print out reports showing the following details for each order:

- the name and postcode of the customer
- the date of the order
- the items that were ordered
- the name of the delivery driver.

It wants to avoid data redundancy as customer name and postcode, items ordered and the delivery driver name will need to be in more than one order and they do not want to have to input the customer, item and delivery details more than once.

Design the table structure required, indicating the key fields, and show how the tables are linked.

## Exam-style questions

A sports centre uses a database to store details of their members.

MEMBER, SPORT and TEAM are three of the tables used in the database.

1 The data for the first three members in the MEMBERS table is shown below.

| MemberNumber | Surname | FirstName | DOB | SportCode | TeamCode |
|---|---|---|---|---|---|
| 00033 | Abbot | Catherine | 13/1/1980 | HCK | HCK_A |
| 00045 | Ali | Mohammed | 10/10/1995 | FBL | FBL_C |
| 00069 | Anderson | Patricia | 6/6/1994 | HCK | HCK_C |

    a State the field that is used for the primary key in the MEMBER table. **(1 mark)**

    b Explain why your chosen field is most likely to be used as the primary key. **(2 marks)**

2 The database also contains a SPORT and TEAM table.

    Explain why SportCode and TeamCode have been included in the MEMBER table. **(2 marks)**

# Data

## Exam tips

1 You should explain what is meant by a primary key and why the field you choose is the only one that could contain unique data.
2 You should explain how relational databases function and how tables can be linked using foreign keys so that data does not have to be duplicated.

## Summary

- A database is an organised store of data.
- An entity is something with an independent existence that is uniquely identified and about which data can be stored.
- A table is a collection of rows and columns that are used to store data in a structured and organised manner.
- A field is one item of information in a database table.
- A record consists of all the fields about an individual entry in a database (e.g. all the details about one learner in a table).
- The primary key uniquely identifies each record in the table. It is usually a field that is guaranteed to hold unique information for each record.
- A relational database allows data elements in one table to be related to any piece of data in another table as long as both tables contain a common element.
- Massive amounts of unstructured data are produced every day. Unstructured data is information that isn't organised in a pre-defined structure. Examples include tweets, photos, emails and output from sensors. Organisations use powerful analytic software tools to extract valuable information from unstructured data.

## Checkpoint

### Strengthen

**S1** Describe the property needed by a field if it is selected as the primary key.
**S2** Explain why the key field from one table may be included in another table.
**S3** Explain how unstructured data differs from structured data.

### Challenge

**C1** Explain how relational databases minimise data redundancy and data inconsistency.
**C2** Explain what is meant by the term 'big data' and why the effective use of big data gives organisations a competitive advantage.

How confident do you feel about your answers to these questions? If you're not sure you answered them well, try the following activities again:

- For S1 have a look at the definition on page 132.
- For S2 have a look at page 134.
- For S3 have a look at page 137.

# Chapter 4

# Computers

# Computers

## 4.1 Machines and computational modelling

### The input-process-output model

How many computers do you have in your house? There are probably a lot more than you think. Let's find out why.

How many of these things do you think of as computers?

### Key terms

**Input**: to enter data into a computer.

**Process**: to change the meaning or format of some data.

**Output**: to display or output data that has been processed (or has been stored).

You might be surprised to know that every device shown above contains an embedded computer. A computer is a machine that takes some kind of **input** from its surroundings, **processes** the input according to given rules, and provides some kind of **output**.

**Figure 4.1** A simple input-process-output diagram

You are probably familiar with a desktop computer: the keyboard provides input and the screen provides output (which depends on what you type). In a similar way, the embedded computer in a washing machine has controls that provide input and a motor and heater as outputs; how fast they spin and how much heat they produce depends on the input setting.

### Activity 1 ?

1   Name any other inputs and outputs for
    **a**   a desktop computer
    **b**   a washing machine.
2   Sid is a central heating installer. Research the computing devices he might use in his job.
3   Discuss in a group the inputs and outputs for the devices shown on the previous page. Think of some categories that you could use to group the input and output devices you come up with, for example pointing device or audio input device.

### Exam-style question

List **three** outputs and **three** inputs of a smartphone.
**(6 marks)**

### Exam tip

A touch screen is an input and output device so could appear twice in your answer.

The clever bit in computer science is the activity that goes on between the inputs and outputs – the processing. Processing means performing a series of actions on the inputs according to a given set of rules. You might have met this idea in maths already if you have studied 'function machines'. You might also have processed ingredients according to a recipe to make a cake; or put together steps according to a choreography to make a dance; or musical notes in harmonic combinations to make a song.

In Chapter 1 (page 2) an algorithm was defined as a precise method for solving a problem, consisting of a sequence of step-by-step instructions. In order for processing to produce meaningful results it has to follow an algorithm. So you might also think of an algorithm as the sequence of steps that is used to process the input to produce the output.

**Figure 4.2** A simple maths function

If you try to follow a more complicated function machine than this one you will probably need a notepad to keep track of your working. In a similar way, anything beyond the simplest algorithm needs temporary storage or memory. We should change our diagram of a computer to include this.

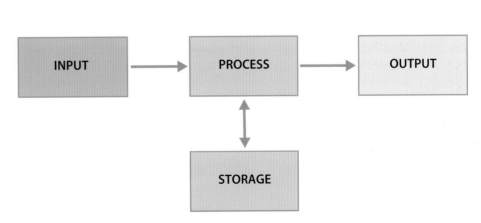

**Figure 4.3** A simple function machine with storage

# Computers

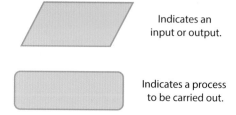

Indicates an input or output.

Indicates a process to be carried out.

**Figure 4.4** Flowchart symbols for input/output and process

As your algorithms become more complicated it can be useful to show the steps in a flowchart. These are the flowchart symbols that you met in Chapter 1 (page 3).

## Summary

- Although computers come in all sorts of shapes and sizes they all do principally the same thing. They take in inputs, process them according to a given set of rules, and generate outputs.

- Algorithms expressed in program code specify the processes a computer carries out.

# 4.2 Hardware

## Stored programs: the von Neumann model

You probably have a calculator app on your smartphone, but your calculator almost certainly can't play Candy Crush.

Your calculator is designed to do just one job – sums. Your smartphone on the other hand is a general-purpose computer – it can be programmed to do a number of different jobs, from sums to web browsing to games.

The first computers, like your calculator, had to be redesigned or at least rewired to do a different job. The idea of a general-purpose computer developed in the 1930s and 1940s through the work of Alan Turing and John von Neumann who proposed that the instructions for the processing could be held in storage with the input data.

# Computers

A computer in which the processing instructions are stored in memory with the data is called a stored-program computer or a **von Neumann architecture** computer.

You will remember from Chapter 3 that all types of data (including pictures and sounds) are stored in memory as binary numbers. In the same way, the processing instructions are written as binary numbers. You will learn more about this in section 4.5 on page 167.

In a von Neumann architecture computer the hardware device that does the processing is called the **central processing unit (CPU)** and the storage is called **main memory/random-access memory (RAM)**. They are connected to each other, and to the input and output (I/O) devices, by a group of connecting wires called a **bus**.

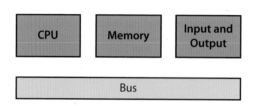

**Figure 4.5** Buses used in a computer

When a computer is turned on, the CPU fetches an instruction from the memory, carries out the instruction it receives, and then fetches the next and so on. This sequence is called the **fetch-decode-execute** cycle and it carries on until the power is turned off.

## Hardware components of a computer system
### RAM and ROM

If you have ever bought a desktop or laptop computer you will have seen the main memory referred to as random-access memory (RAM). This is the temporary store that the CPU uses for data and instructions (programs).

Remember that both data and instructions are just binary numbers, usually in bytes (8 bits). RAM is typically measured in gigabytes (GB). See section 3.3 (page 117).

When the CPU saves data into memory this is called **writing**: the CPU uses the bus to tell the memory what data to save and where in memory to save it. The reverse process is called **reading** and the CPU must specify which part of memory to read from. Each memory location has a unique **memory address**, in the same way that your home is identified by an address. You can think of memory like a series of letter boxes each with space for one byte of data. The memory addresses are just numbers, starting from zero, labelling each mailbox.

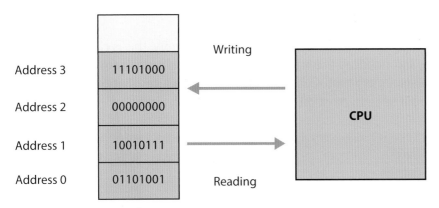

| | | Writing | |
|---|---|---|---|
| Address 3 | 11101000 | | |
| Address 2 | 00000000 | | CPU |
| Address 1 | 10010111 | | |
| Address 0 | 01101001 | Reading | |

**Figure 4.6** Memory addressing

RAM is described as **volatile** which means that its contents are lost when the power is turned off. Because of this, computers also need **non-volatile** memory to store any programs that must run when the computer is first turned on – this memory is called **read-only memory (ROM)**. Programs permanently stored in ROM are known as firmware. Typically these programs are small and carry out specific tasks, such as initialising the hardware components and starting the operating system when a computer is switched on. You might have heard of these programs being called the BIOS (short for Basic Input/Output System) or UEFI (short for Unified Extensible Firmware Interface). Nowadays, UEFI has replaced BIOS as the standard firmware used in desktop computers.

The photograph below shows the main circuit board of a 1980s computer (the Sinclair ZX81). The ZX81 had either one or two RAM chips. Two are shown in the diagram along with three other chips: CPU, ROM and a fourth chip that connects the input and output devices. You can also see groups of parallel silver 'tracks'; these are the buses (the wires connecting the chips together).

The photograph on the right shows a modern-day computer (the Raspberry Pi). The chip in the centre contains both the CPU and RAM as well as handling some of the I/O, such as the screen. The role of the ROM is replaced by a plug-in memory card (not shown). The smaller chip to the right handles the slower I/O devices such as USB (Universal Serial Bus). Buses can still be seen although a bit less clearly.

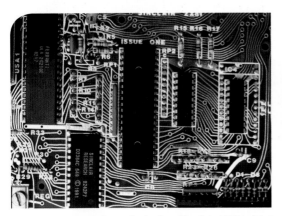

Computer circuit boards: Left – Sinclair ZX81; Right – Raspberry Pi

## Cache memory

Most computers require a third kind of main memory: this is called **cache** memory (pronounced like 'cash'). Cache memory is a small amount of fast, expensive memory that is used in-between two devices that communicate at different speeds, most often the CPU and RAM.

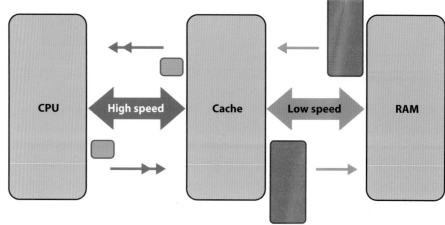

**Figure 4.7** Diagram of cache memory

In a CPU cache, frequently used code or data is loaded in chunks from the slower RAM into the cache. The CPU accesses the cache memory at its own, faster speed. This means the CPU isn't slowed down by having to wait for data from RAM.

### Extend your knowledge

In computers up to around the 1980s CPUs and RAM worked at the same speed as one another, but CPU technology developed much faster than RAM. This meant that the RAM in newer computers could no longer keep up with the demands of the CPU, causing a bottleneck that limited the performance of those computers. To solve the problem, engineers introduced cache memory, but this created a new challenge. If the data the CPU needs is not already in the cache (called a cache miss), then the CPU has to wait for the cache to reload with the correct data. A lot of research has gone into ways of predicting which chunk of RAM to load into the cache at any time to reduce cache misses.

### Extend your knowledge

Most I/O devices have memory between themselves and the main system because they communicate at different speeds; this is often called a buffer (e.g. disk buffer, print buffer or frame buffer (for graphics)). Data is transferred at high speed between a processor and this memory. The CPU can then continue with other tasks while the I/O device takes data from its buffer at a slower rate.

## Activity 9 ?

1  What is cache memory used for?

2  Describe the difference between RAM and ROM. Suggest a use for ROM.

3  Make a cartoon strip or storyboard showing the fetch-decode-execute cycle.

4  Look back at the photographs and descriptions of the ZX81 and Raspberry Pi. Working with a partner, identify the similarities and differences between them. After 35 years, what has changed and what is the same?

## Fetch-decode-execute: in detail

There are many different kinds of CPU, but they share some features in common. To understand the fetch-decode-execute cycle in more detail you need to know a bit more about what goes on inside the CPU.

The part of the CPU that does calculations and logic operations is called the **arithmetic/logic unit (ALU)**.

Inside the CPU are a number of memory locations called **registers**. These are extremely fast to access but there are usually only a relatively small number of them. Some registers play a specific role in the fetch-decode-execute cycle, for example holding a memory address, an instruction or a piece of data, while others are general purpose. Some of the registers with a specific role that are found in most computers include the following.

### Common registers

**Accumulator**: holds the results of calculations performed by the ALU. All input and output from the CPU passes through the accumulator.

**Program counter**: holds the memory address of the next instruction to be fetched.

**Current instruction**: holds the instruction currently being executed.

### Key terms

**Arithmetic/logic unit (ALU)**: the part of the CPU that performs calculations and logic operations.

**Register**: a storage location inside the CPU used to hold an instruction, an address or other single item of data.

**Control unit**: the part of the CPU that organises the actions of the other parts of the CPU.

**Clock**: an electronic device inside a CPU that 'ticks' at regular intervals and is used to synchronise the actions of the other parts of the CPU.

The steps in the cycle are controlled by a **control unit** and synchronised by an electronic **clock**. You have probably seen the advertised clock speeds of CPUs; for example, a 2.2 GHz CPU means that its clock 'ticks' 2200 million times per second.

**ON (1)**

**OFF (0)**

**Figure 4.8** Clock signal

The bus that connects the CPU to other devices in the computer is split into three parts: the address bus, the data bus and the control bus. The address bus carries memory addresses between the CPU and memory to identify uniquely a memory location; the data bus carries the value to be read from or written to memory; and the control bus carries the signals that, for example, determine whether to read or write the data, and when to do so.

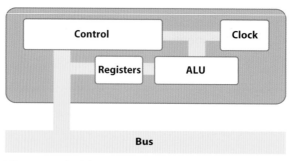

**Figure 4.9** Inside a CPU

The number of connections on a bus is called the **bus width**. Since each connection represents a binary digit, a 1 or a 0, a greater bus width means larger number values can be communicated. For example, an eight-bit address bus can send values from 00000000 (0) to 11111111 (255), only 256 possible addresses. By contrast, a 32-bit computer can address up to 4 GB of RAM.

Now that you know a little more about the parts of a CPU you can understand in more detail what happens at each step of the fetch-decode-execute cycle.

**Fetch-decode-execute cycle**

**Fetch**
The CPU control unit places the memory address of the next instruction on the address bus. It also sends a signal on the control bus requesting to read from memory.

The memory receives the signal and looks up that memory location. The data in memory is copied on to the data bus. The CPU copies this into a special register.

**Decode**
The control unit analyses the contents of the register and sends signals to the other parts of the CPU telling them what to do (e.g. add numbers, store data back into memory).

**Execute**
The instruction is completed by the CPU.

**Extend your knowledge**

You are probably wondering how you get computer games just from copying, adding and storing binary numbers. First, remember that the I/O devices are also connected to the bus and they have their own addresses; storing numbers in their addresses can make pixels appear on a screen or sounds come from a speaker. Second, remember that modern CPUs can do billions of these simple instructions per second. What appears to be very complex behaviour is actually just a very large number of very simple operations.

## Secondary storage

In most situations you need to be able to store your data and programs after the power is turned off. You have learned that RAM is volatile so most computers need to be able to copy the contents of their RAM to another kind of storage that is not volatile – a type that doesn't lose its contents when there is no power. This more permanent storage is called **secondary storage**. Secondary storage is non-volatile and, compared to RAM, is slower to access, cheaper and has much higher storage capacity. Typical capacities are now in the terabytes, i.e. millions of megabytes.

You remember that all data is stored as binary: 1s and 0s. There are three physical ways of recording 1s and 0s that do not require power.

**Magnetic storage** uses the fact that magnets have north and south poles. By magnetising something, the north and south poles can represent the 1s and 0s of your data. This is used in hard disks and magnetic tape storage.

**Optical storage** is used by CDs and DVDs. Shinier or more reflective parts of the disk represent the 1s or 0s.

**Solid-state storage** or 'flash' memory (such as USB memory sticks or SD cards) represents the 1s and 0s by little pools of trapped electrons on a microchip.

### Magnetic secondary storage – hard disks

Inside a hard disk drive is a stack of disks called platters with a magnetic coating on each surface. Tiny magnetic recording heads on the end of an arm float a millionth of a centimetre above the disk spinning at 110 km/h underneath.

Data is recorded on each disk along circular tracks, each split into smaller parts called sectors.

When data is read:

1   The arm moves across to be above the right track.

2   The required sector comes around under the head.

3   The magnetised surface induces a tiny current in the head.

4   The disk controller translates this into 1s and 0s.

Because of these steps, data does not come from the disk immediately. Each step takes some time. The time for step 1 is called the seek time; for step 2 it is called the latency.

> **Key terms**
>
> **Secondary storage**: any kind of permanent storage to which the contents of ROM/RAM are copied (usually a hard disk, optical or solid-state device).
>
> **Magnetic storage**: secondary storage that works by magnetising parts of a substance as north and south poles to represent binary 1s and 0s.
>
> **Optical storage**: secondary storage that works using differences in light reflection from a material.
>
> **Solid-state storage**: secondary storage that works by storing charge (electrons).

# Computers

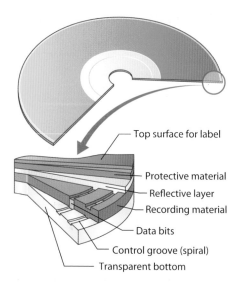

- Top surface for label
- Protective material
- Reflective layer
- Recording material
- Data bits
- Control groove (spiral)
- Transparent bottom

**Figure 4.10** The structure of a DVD

## Optical secondary storage – DVDs

A CD, DVD or Blu-Ray™ disc is made of several layers as shown in Figure 4.10. Data is written along a single track that spirals out from the centre of the disc.

The player uses two lasers: one to write data on to the disc and the other to read data.

When writing, one laser heats the recording material, which creates non-reflective depressions on the surface of the disc, called pits. This is slow because the heating and cooling of the surface takes a little time for each bit of data.

If a CD is manufactured ready written, it has pits in the recording layer that are less reflective than the flat parts, called lands.

When reading, the laser reflects differently off the surface and this is detected by a light sensor.

The spiral track is longer on the outside so when reading data from the outside edge the disc has to reduce its rotation speed so that the data passes under the laser at a constant speed.

When data is read:

1 The disc spins in the drive to ensure all data can be read.
2 The tracking mechanism moves the laser into the correct position over the disc.
3 The laser shines on to the disc and is reflected back on to a light sensor.
4 Signals from the sensor are translated into 1s and 0s.

## Electrical secondary storage – flash drives

Solid-state storage uses chips, called NAND flash, comprised of special kinds of transistors that can trap electrons in a 'pool'. Electrons in a pool represent the 0s of the data, while empty pools represent 1s.

Because billions of transistors will fit on a chip, solid-state devices are small and have high capacity, often several gigabytes, as you will know from the memory sticks you carry around in your pocket. They also give much faster access to read data than hard disks.

When data is read from the chip:

1 Control signals identify which bit is to be read out and apply a small voltage.
2 If the electron pool is empty the transistor turns on and a 1 is read out.
3 If the electron pool is full the transistor doesn't turn on and a 0 is read out.
4 The control signals are changed to read other bits.
5 When data is written to the chip, control signals identify which bit is to be written and apply a higher voltage.
6 This pulls electrons into the pools of those transistors, recording the 1s and 0s.

Erasing data also requires higher voltages to remove electrons from the pools. Because of this, both erasing and writing cause the transistor to break down slowly; so flash drives can only be rewritten perhaps 1 million times before eventually failing.

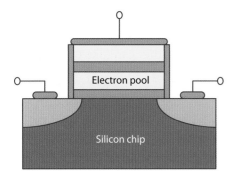

**Figure 4.11** Flash drive

Both magnetic hard disks and solid-state flash memory are developing rapidly and will continue to increase in capacity and decrease in size for several years. The largest computer companies are currently researching some brand new technologies that might become important in the future. For example, HP is experimenting with a new type of electrical component called a memristor to create super-fast, high capacity, non-volatile memory chips. IBM is developing race track memory – a type of magnetic storage that stores information as magnetic patterns on tiny wires, providing much faster data access speeds than current hard drives or flash disk technologies are capable of. You might also have heard of quantum computing. Quantum computers store data as qubits. Qubits can be individual atoms and each one is capable of storing (and processing) more than one bit at once.

---

### Activity 11 ?

1   What is the purpose of secondary storage?
2   Name one kind of magnetic storage and one kind of solid-state storage.
3   Monty runs his own gardening business. Explain which kind of secondary storage you would advise Monty to use for:
    a   storing his garden design software
    b   taking garden designs to show potential customers
    c   backing-up all his financial records for seven years.
4   Produce a presentation about future storage: you can start your research by searching online for the keywords in the text (e.g. memristor, qubit).
5   If you have an old hard disk you no longer need, try taking it apart to look at some of the components you have learned about. Your tutor might have one to show you; you could also ask your school's IT technician.

---

## Cloud storage

Sometimes it can be useful to have your secondary storage in a different place from your computer. For example, you might want to have a back-up copy of your data in a secure location or share your data with users of other computers; or you might want to be able to access your data when you are not sitting at your usual computer.

In Chapter 5 you will learn more about how networks can be used to share computing resources. Computers that share their secondary storage across a network are called file servers. You are probably used to using the secondary storage on a server on your school network (your home drive or a learner shared area). Some hard disk drives are able to connect directly to a network (called NAS or network-attached storage). Others connect to several servers

# Computers

using their own storage area network or SAN. This type of arrangement is useful when it's important not to lose access to your data, for example in a banking system. If one server or hard disk fails, another can take over its job without users of the system even noticing.

Sometimes storage is accessed via the internet using internet services such as Dropbox or Google® Drive. In this situation it is usually called **cloud storage**. This is an example of **virtualisation**: you seem to have access to a single, virtual hard drive when in fact your storage might be spread across several servers around the world, with software dealing with the details of where each part of each file is actually stored.

Storing data on servers accessed via the internet has the advantages that

- you can access the data from anywhere on many devices using a web browser.
- the data is securely backed up by the company providing the storage service.
- you don't need to transfer your data if you get a new computer.

Some people will be concerned about security: you might, for example, have read about high-profile cases of private photographs being accessed and released on the internet. Other people might be uncomfortable with not being able to have their data 'in their hand' and worried about losing access if they lost their internet connection. See section 5.2, page 193, for more on cloud security.

## Key terms

**Cloud storage**: secondary storage, often belonging to a third party, that is accessed via a network, usually the internet, and so is not in the same physical place as the machine's RAM/ROM. Files stored 'in the cloud' can be accessed from anywhere via an internet connection.

**Virtualisation**: any process that hides the true physical nature of a computing resource, making it look different, usually to simplify the way it is accessed.

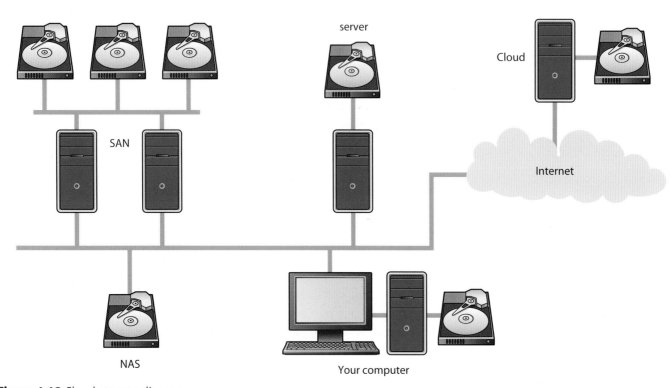

**Figure 4.12** Cloud storage diagram

# Embedded systems

An embedded computer system is one that is designed to do a specific job, usually as part of a bigger system that might have other electrical or mechanical parts, such as a washing machine. This makes them distinct from general-purpose computers like the PC or laptop you use every day. Embedded systems are all around us in every part of daily life, for example in your cable or satellite TV box, your car, games console, traffic lights, toaster or toys. They might be so simple that you don't even think of them as computers.

Embedded computers are often cheap, low-power devices using simple technology and limited memory. They might run just one program, which is very rarely updated, and so is stored permanently in firmware (ROM or flash memory). They often use sensors of some kind.

> ## Activity 12 ?
>
> Find out about the storage systems used on your school network. Research, for example, what 'drives' are available in My Computer. Does your school use a SAN or NAS? Where are the servers located? How does this compare to using a service such as Google Drive?
>
> Write a short report giving the advantages and disadvantages of different systems.

> ## Activity 13 ?
>
> 1 Modern cars contain an engine management system. This is an example of an embedded computer system.
>    a Suggest two inputs to and two outputs from this system.
>    b Explain one function of the engine management system.
> 2 Make a table listing five other embedded systems you might encounter in your daily life. You could look back to page 140 at the beginning of this chapter to get some initial ideas.

In recent years wireless network technology, the internet and embedded systems have come together (converged) so that many devices can now communicate and be accessed and controlled remotely via the internet. This has become known as the 'internet of things'. For example:

- your printer in school might automatically order new toner when it is getting low;

- your electricity meter might automatically send readings to the supplier via the internet;

- you might be able to control your central heating from your smartphone.

Imagine a future where your fridge knows when you're running out of milk and sends you a text telling you to pick up some more on the way home.

# Computers

## Exam-style questions

1 State what is meant by the term volatile memory. **(1 mark)**

2 Explain why having cache memory can improve the performance of the CPU. **(2 marks)**

3 List the steps in the fetch part of the fetch-decode-execute cycle. **(4 marks)**

## Exam tip

In Question 2, remember that 'explain' means you have to give a reason as well as your answer.

## Activity 14

1 Write a computer program that simulates a traffic light control system. It must cycle through the normal sequence of lights, printing out the current state. Your tutor might give you the opportunity to use your program to control a real light output.

2 Draw a flowchart showing the processing required by a chip-and-PIN credit card reader. This is used when you pay for something in a shop: it collects data about the purchases from the till, gets your card details, checks your PIN, sends encrypted data to the bank and waits for a reply; it might print a receipt if the transaction is allowed and informs the till of the result.

## Summary

- von Neumann computers process data using a stored program.
- A CPU runs a program by accessing main memory using the fetch-decode-execute cycle.
- Main memory can be volatile RAM or non-volatile ROM.
- Cache memory is used between devices that communicate at different speeds.
- CPU, memory and I/O devices are connected using a bus.
- Inside the CPU, registers provide storage and the ALU performs calculations.
- Secondary storage can be magnetic, optical or solid state.
- Secondary storage can be located away from your computer in the cloud.
- Embedded systems are cheap, low-power computers that are dedicated to a specific task.

## Checkpoint

### Strengthen

**S1** Describe in detail the fetch-decode-execute cycle. Include the roles of the memory, buses and special registers.

**S2** Describe the advantages and disadvantages of different kinds of secondary storage.

**S3** Explain what is meant by the term internet of things.

### Challenge

**C1** Describe the operation of a von Neumann architecture computer.

**C2** Compare the features of CPU registers, cache memory and RAM.

**C3** Explain the purpose of secondary storage and justify an example of a situation where optical storage is the best choice.

**C4** Evaluate the use of embedded systems to produce 'driverless cars'.

How confident are you in your answers to these questions? If you are not sure that you answered them well, go back and review the fetch-decode-execute section on pages 147–148. Try to explain this to a family member at home; this will help you to understand it yourself.

# 4.3 Logic

## Learning outcomes

By the end of this section you should be able to:

- construct truth tables for a given logic statement (AND, OR, NOT).
- produce logic statements for a given problem.

## Truth tables

You learned in Chapter 1 (page 9) about selection – determining which parts of a program run depending on certain conditions – usually expressed using IF statements.

```
IF health <= 0 THEN
   SET game_over TO true
END IF
```

In general, this kind of statement has the form:

```
IF CONDITION THEN COMMANDS
```

When this code is translated the logic statement or condition is calculated. If the result is TRUE then the commands will run.

Here is a more complicated condition.

```
IF health <= 0 AND lives = 0 THEN
   SET game_over TO true
END IF
```

You can probably work out from this code when the game is over because you will have played games and understand what 'health' and 'lives' mean. But how does a computer do this? A computer needs to be able to calculate AND to work out if the condition is TRUE or FALSE.

In the example the game is only over if both parts of the condition are true. We can show all the possibilities for this condition in a table.

This kind of table is called a **truth table**. It is the truth table for the AND operator. The outcome is only true if both of the conditions are true. (Usually you will see a 'Yes' written as a '1' and a 'No' written as a '0'.)

Perhaps the game doesn't have lives and we only want to end the game if you run out of 'health' or you pass the winning score of 1 million.

```
IF health <= 0 OR score > 1000000 THEN
   SET game_over TO true
END IF
```

Here are the possibilities – this time it is the truth table for the OR operator.

In this case the outcome is true if either of the conditions is true.

> **Key term**
>
> **Truth table**: a table showing all possible combinations of the inputs and outputs of an operator.

| health <= 0 | lives = 0 | Game over? |
|---|---|---|
| No | No | No |
| No | Yes | No |
| Yes | No | No |
| Yes | Yes | Yes |

| Health <= 0 | score > 1000000 | Game over? |
|---|---|---|
| 0 | 0 | 0 |
| 0 | 1 | 1 |
| 1 | 0 | 1 |
| 1 | 1 | 1 |

# Computers

There is one more logical operator (or **Boolean** operator) called NOT. This operator just swaps 1s and 0s. Notice that unlike AND and OR, NOT has only one input.

| Input | Output |
|-------|--------|
| 0 | 1 |
| 1 | 0 |

We could use this in our 'game over' example as follows.

```
IF (NOT god_mode AND health <= 0) OR score > 1000000 THEN
    SET game_over TO true
END IF
```

We can list all the possible combinations in a truth table as below. (Like in maths, brackets are evaluated first.)

| god_mode | NOT god_mode | health <= 0 | NOT god_mode AND health <= 0 | score > 1000000 | game over? |
|----------|--------------|-------------|------------------------------|-----------------|------------|
| 0 | 1 | 0 | 0 | 0 | 0 |
| 0 | 1 | 0 | 0 | 1 | 1 |
| 0 | 1 | 1 | 1 | 0 | 1 |
| 0 | 1 | 1 | 1 | 1 | 1 |
| 1 | 0 | 0 | 0 | 0 | 0 |
| 1 | 0 | 0 | 0 | 1 | 1 |
| 1 | 0 | 1 | 0 | 0 | 0 |
| 1 | 0 | 1 | 0 | 1 | 1 |

The three logic operations AND, OR and NOT are very easy to build as electronic circuits known as **logic circuits**.

## Activity 15

1. Write, in words, the condition for the game to be over in the final example in the table. (You will see why Boolean logic is clearer and easier to use than English when the situation gets complicated.)

2. State which part of the CPU works out the logic for conditions.

3. Write a computer program that asks for your year group, grade and target and then prints out whether you are invited to revision class or not. Start by assuming revision classes are only for Year 11 students whose grade is below target, then you can invent your own criteria for invitations to revision class.

4. Write the truth table for the statement below. This time there are three parts to the condition. Remember: as in maths, brackets are worked out first.

```
IF year = 11 AND (grade < target OR target > 7) THEN
    SET revision_class TO true
END IF
```

# Writing logic statements

When you write programs you will often have to work out the correct logic statements for a given situation so that the right code runs. Mistakes in the logic (logic errors) are a frequent cause of bugs so it is important to check both that the logic is right and that the code matches the logic you have worked out.

## Worked example

Monty has decided to expand his gardening business to give online advice. He is writing a web page that advises customers which fertiliser to buy from his online shop. The web page will ask customers about their plants and then give relevant advice using these rules:

- If plants have yellow leaves mainly near the soil then they need a nitrogen fertiliser.
- If plants have brown leaves that are small then they need a phosphorous fertiliser.

To program this, you first need to work out what are the important features in the rules – these will be your variables. In this case, the colour of the leaves is important. We can write the rules in pseudo-code like this.

```
SET advice TO 'nothing needed'
IF colour = 'yellow' THEN
   SET advice TO 'nitrogen'
ELSE
   IF colour = 'brown' THEN
      SET advice TO 'phosphorous'
   END IF
END IF
```

Notice that we started off by assuming the plants were growing normally and only changed the advice if certain conditions were met.

Monty points out that if leaves go brown, but are normal sized, then the customer needs potassium fertiliser – now the size of the leaf is also important.

```
SET advice TO 'nothing needed'
IF colour = 'yellow' THEN
   SET advice TO 'nitrogen'
ELSE
   IF colour = 'brown' AND size = 'small' THEN
      SET advice TO 'phosphorous'
   ELSE
      IF colour = 'brown' AND size = 'normal' THEN
         SET advice TO 'potassium'
      END IF
   END IF
END IF
```

# Computers

## Activity 16 ?

1 Add the following rules to Monty's website logic on page 157.

- If plants have cracked or misshapen leaves then they need a calcium fertiliser.

- If plants have leaves that are yellow mainly on the tips then they need a magnesium fertiliser.

2 Why is Monty's advice an example of abstraction?

## Activity 17 ?

1 Explain why this code would not work if the last two lines were swapped around.

2 How can you change the conditions so that it works with the code either way round?

## Top tip

Note that we have used brackets in this example. You have learned about BIDMAS in your maths lessons and in Chapter 1 (page 25). It tells you the order to do the sums. It is the same with logic operators: brackets go first, then NOT, then AND and finally OR. This is called **operator precedence**.

## Key term

**Operator precedence**: the order in which you apply the operators (including logical operators) in a mathematical equation.

## Worked example

Lisa has built her own programmable alarm clock. She wants to program the alarm to wake her up at the correct time depending on the day. She gets up

- at 7.30 a.m. if it is a school day.
- at 9.00 a.m. if it is the weekend or a school holiday, except on Saturdays in term time when she gets up at 8.00 a.m. to play hockey.

Let's work out the important features of these rules. The alarm times depend on whether it's term time or holidays and also on the day of the week; so term time and day will be the variables for your conditions.

```
SET alarm TO '7:30 am'
IF term_time = false OR (day = 'Saturday' OR day =
'Sunday') THEN
   SET alarm TO '9:00 am'
ELSE
   IF term_time = true AND day = 'Saturday' THEN
      SET alarm TO '8:00 am'
   END IF
END IF
```

## Activity 18 ?

1 Work out what happens for the following statement.

```
IF gender = 'female' AND (subject = 'computer science'
OR subject = 'physics') THEN
   SEND "Superstar!" TO DISPLAY
END IF
```

a For a girl studying French.

b For a girl studying computer science.

c For a boy studying physics.

2 Which answer would be different if the programmer had forgotten the brackets?

## Exam-style questions

1   Edward is developing a logic circuit for an automatic door system.
    - The output from the sensor on the street (S) is 1 when someone approaches the door from outside.
    - The output from the sensor in the building (B) is 1 when someone approaches the door from inside.
    - The opening mechanism works only if the manual switch (M) is off (0).

    Write a suitable IF statement in pseudo-code to represent this logic.
    **(2 marks)**

2   Write pseudo-code representing the logic for a cinema ticket pricing application. **(3 marks)**
    - Standard pricing is £5.
    - Children under 4 are free.
    - Children under 16 and people over 65 are half price.

### Exam tip

The operator precedence for NOT, AND and OR are likely to be tested in the exam question, so you need to know it.

This means you should always check carefully whether you need brackets.

## Summary

- AND, OR and NOT are called logical or Boolean operators.
- They are used in selection statements such as IF.
- A truth table shows all possible combinations of inputs and the output produced.
- The order of precedence is: brackets, NOT, AND, OR.

## Checkpoint

### Strengthen

**S1**  Construct a truth table for the AND operator.

**S2**  Write a logic statement for the operation of headlamps on a car – the headlamps come on if the light sensor reading is dark or if the headlamp switch is turned on.

**S3**  Produce a revision summary of this chapter.

### Challenge

**C1**  Construct a truth table for the expression P = (A AND B) OR C.

**C2**  What combination of logic operations would produce an output of 1 only if the two inputs were different?

How confident are you in your answers to these questions? If you are not sure that you answered them well, go back and review the examples on pages 157–158.

## 4.4 Software

### Learning outcomes

By the end of this section you should be able to:

- describe what an operating system is and how it manages files, processes, hardware and the user interface.
- describe the purpose and functions of utility software (managing, repairing and converting files; compression; defragmentation; backing up; anti-virus, anti-spyware).
- describe how software can be used to simulate and model aspects of the real world.

### Key terms

**Software**: the set of programs run by a computer system.

**Application software**: software that performs a task that would otherwise be done by hand, perhaps with pen and paper.

**Operating system**: software designed for particular hardware and which manages other programs' access to the hardware.

**Utility software**: software that does a useful job for the user that is not essential to the operating system and not the reason for using a computer in the first place.

Computer systems consist of both hardware and **software**. Software is the set of programs that run on a computer system. You can usefully divide software into two types. The first type is what you normally think of as programs, those that do a job for us that would otherwise have to be done by hand, such as payroll calculations. This is **application software**. The other kind of software is there to help us use the computer and the application programs, such as providing the user interface and tools to manage the hardware. This is system software and it is usually divided into **operating systems** and **utility software**.

### Operating systems

The operating system (OS) is usually loaded when the computer starts up. You will probably already know several operating systems, for example Microsoft® Windows®, Linux, Android, iOS etc.

Why do you need this software? Unlike embedded systems, a general-purpose computer can be used to do a range of jobs. Software written for general-purpose computers needs to be able to run on a range of different hardware, for example your favourite web browser runs on your laptop or desktop computer and also on your mobile phone or tablet. One of the jobs of an operating system is to manage whatever input and output devices the computer has. A programmer writing an application uses simple commands, say OpenFile, and the operating system deals with exactly how to open a file. This will depend on what sort of secondary storage the file happens to be on. You might have realised this is yet another example of abstraction.

This system means applications have to be written for a particular operating system but will work on any hardware. You will probably already be familiar with this idea because you know, for example, that Android apps run on any Android device. Many different models of smartphone or tablet will run the app, but the same apps won't run on your friend's iOS phone.

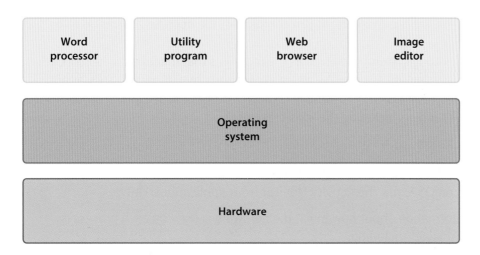

**Figure 4.13** The operating system sits between the hardware and the programs

Managing files and the directory structure, and input/output in general, is one of the important jobs of the operating system. An operating system also shares access to the hardware among the different programs that are running (and on some operating systems among the different users who are logged on to the computer). Two important pieces of hardware that have to be shared are the CPU and RAM.

- In section 4.2 you learned that a von Neumann system does only one thing at a time. When you have several applications open they can't really be running simultaneously. The operating system keeps up this illusion by allowing each program to use the CPU for a short time before switching to the next program. This is called **scheduling**.

- It is possible to load many applications all at the same time and each uses some memory. What if you keep loading applications until RAM is full? In this case the operating system creates another illusion, by moving programs from RAM to disk and back again when needed. This is called **paging**, swapping or virtual memory. You might notice this as a lot of disk activity and your computer running more slowly when lots of applications are open.

# Computers

## Exam-style questions

One of the functions of an operating system is scheduling.

1 Describe the purpose of scheduling. **(2 marks)**
2 Give **three** other functions of an operating system. **(3 marks)**

## Exam tip

The command word in Question **1** is 'describe' and two marks are allocated to the question, so make sure you make two distinct points in your answer.

## Key terms

**Concurrent**: processes that run apparently at the same time are described as being concurrent.

**Authentication**: the process of proving to a computer system who you are (e.g. using a username and password).

**User interface**: the way the user interacts with the operating system

As well as the applications you are running, the operating system is also running other programs in the background. They include various parts of the operating system itself such as the programs that manage the network, the scheduler and also any hardware drivers and utility programs such as anti-virus. Each task that is running is called a process. To see all the processes that are running, including the invisible ones

- on Microsoft® Windows®, press CTRL-ALT-DEL and choose Task Manager.
- on Linux, type ps aux at the command prompt.
- on OS X, run the Activity Monitor from Applications/Utilities.

Information about how much the hardware is used by each process is displayed, including.

- the proportion of the CPU time spent on this process.
- the amount of memory used by this process.
- the amount of available memory (real memory and virtual memory, VM).

These processes are running one at a time, being given their share of the CPU time by the scheduler. They are all running alongside one another, but not really at the same time, so we say they are running **concurrently**. An operating system that allows processes to run concurrently is called a multi-tasking operating system. Almost all modern operating systems are multi-tasking.

As well as allowing multi-tasking, some operating systems allow different users to use the hardware. In some cases only one user can use the hardware at once (single user), whereas in others several users can be sharing the hardware (multi-user). Your smartphone is an example of a single user system, whereas your school network servers will be running a multi-user operating system so that many of you can log on at the same time. In a multi-user system, each user has to identify themselves (with a username, fingerprint etc.) and provide a password (or other log in) to prove they are who they say they are – this is called **authentication**. Authority to use the facilities of the computer system is based on who you are, for example learner users might not be able to print, whereas tutor users can. In such systems there is usually also a super-user (sometimes called administrator or root) who can access all resources and also control the access rights of other users.

The operating system also provides and runs the **user interface**. Sometimes this is a graphical user interface (GUI) with windows, icons, menus and pointers (WIMP) like Microsoft® Windows® or MacOS, or sometimes it is just a text, command-line interface (CLI) like MS DOS.

The choice of user interface depends on the applications a computer is expected to run. An embedded system might not have an operating system as such, and therefore does not have a user interface. A computer acting as a web server might only need a command-line interface because it is intended only ever to be managed by technicians. A computer used for video-editing will almost certainly need a graphical user interface.

## Did you know?

In common with many school subjects, as you learn more about computer science you will discover that some details were missed out so that you could understand the key ideas first. At least in computer science you are used to this idea of abstraction. One such detail is the idea of a driver. The driver for a device is the software that really communicates with the I/O device on the computer's bus. It transfers data between the hardware device and the operating system in an agreed format – also known as the application programming interface (API). To find out more about drivers and operating systems search online for 'NDIS' – this is the API that is used for Microsoft® Windows® network drivers – or 'ALSA', the API for sound drivers on Linux.

An API is yet another example of abstraction. A software developer deals with the essential tasks like OpenFile, but the detail of how data is taken from secondary storage is hidden, managed by the operating system.

## Activity 19

1  Run/open the program that lists the running processes on an operating system you are familiar with. Make a table listing the application software, utility software and operating system processes that are running.

2  There are several different algorithms that operating systems can use for scheduling. The one described on page 161 is called round-robin scheduling. Research and describe at least one other method used for scheduling.

3  Take one of the programs you have already written and add a feature to save or load data using the operating system API.

## Utility software

Utility software is software that does a useful job for the user. It is
- inessential to the operating system, and
- not the reason for using a computer in the first place (that is, it is not application software).

Utility software, sometimes called tools, can be split into three areas:
- basic tools;
- file management;
- security.

### Basic tools

Basic tools include things like a simple text editor (e.g. Notepad or nano), calculator, command prompt, hex editor and software for accessibility such as for producing large print. They are usually included as part of the operating system.

# Computers

## File management tools

No matter how much storage you have, somehow you always manage to fill up the space with files. This brings problems such as not being able to find your favourite photos, losing files if there is a fault and things simply running slower on your computer.

File management tools include software to keep your data secure by making a **back-up** copy of your files in another location. Some programs can recover files that have been deleted or repair files that might have become corrupted.

Another useful file management tool is for converting files between different formats. This is especially useful for multimedia files where there are a large number of common formats (e.g. jpg, gif, png).

Another important file management tool is a **defragmenter** which is used to speed up access to data stored on magnetic hard disk drives. Files are not stored on disk in one large chunk. They are stored in smaller pieces called sectors or clusters and a single file's clusters can be spread across the disk. Accessing these fragmented files can be slow, so a defragmenter moves the bits of files around so they are closer together, speeding up disk access (at least in theory). Note that, unlike magnetic disk drives, solid state/flash drives do not require defragmentation as access times are the same across the entire volume.

You can also use a file management tool to compress the files you don't use very often. This frees up space on the disk but those compressed files are then slower to access as they have to be uncompressed to open them.

## Security tools

Security tools include anti-**virus** and anti-**spyware** software. Computer viruses and spyware can be used to capture private information, to introduce a process on your computer to do a job for the attacker such as send out spam email, or to crash an important machine such as a web server. Some are simply written to annoy users. Such software is called a virus because it copies itself and spreads: anti-virus tools try to identify code that copies itself and prevent those processes from running.

**Firewall** software controls your connection to a network, deciding which network data can flow to and from your computer. This can help to prevent infection by viruses.

Encryption software is used to make files unreadable without a password. Data on your tutor's laptop might be encrypted so that it is not understandable if the laptop is stolen.

# Simulation and modelling

In Chapter 1 you learned about how you can use abstraction to model the real world. By now you will be getting used to the idea of abstraction as a central part of computer science. It means hiding complexity, only exposing the key or important features of a situation and leaving out the details.

One important application for computer science is the ability to do experiments that can't or shouldn't be done in the real world. For example,

- you can't increase the average temperature of the Earth to see what happens to our weather;
- you shouldn't stop one of a pair of twins from exercising to see if it causes depression.

You can, however, write a computer program to model or simulate these situations and see what results you obtain. Scientists, engineers, economists and other experts can ask **'what if?' questions** using computer models, for example, what if the bridge were twice as long?

There are two big problems with this approach.

- The model or simulation includes assumptions. It is not reality so the answers might not be right.
- The real world is far too complicated to allow for every possible factor in your model, so you have to use abstraction to simplify it. This makes it even less likely that you will get a totally right answer.

Nevertheless, computer models can reveal some interesting things about how the world works or about how humans work with machines.

## Examples of computer models

A flight simulator allows pilots to train to fly aircraft safely. They can make mistakes in the simulator without endangering their own lives or the lives of passengers. Commercial flight simulators use a moveable cabin and real flight controls so pilots can see, hear and feel things just as if they were flying a real aircraft.

If you ever watch the weather forecast you will sometimes hear the presenter talking about their computer and sometimes even about computer models. The atmospheric models used to forecast the weather are some of the most complex pieces of software that exist. They split the atmosphere up into small pieces and keep track of the temperature, pressure, humidity and other factors in each piece. They start the model with real measurements, then they let it calculate the effect each piece of atmosphere has on its neighbours and see how the weather patterns develop.

Another example of a computer model is used for earthquake prediction. Unlike the previous examples, we don't know the mathematics behind how earthquakes work. Models like these have to use information from past examples and probability to come up with best guesses as to what might happen and when. Some common techniques used in such models are **heuristics**, **Monte Carlo methods** and **neural networks**. There is a whole field of computer science devoted to finding patterns in data and using them to predict the future: this is machine learning.

---

## Key terms

**'What if?' question**: running a computer model with a given set of inputs to see what the model produces as an output or prediction.

**Heuristic**: a type of algorithm capable of finding a solution to a problem quickly and easily, by using a combination of trial and error and educated guesswork to cut corners and eliminate less likely alternatives. Heuristic algorithms don't always find the best solution but they will usually find one that works.

**Monte Carlo methods**: carrying out a statistical analysis of a number of random samples in order to obtain approximate solutions to a problem. The larger the number of samples used, the more accurate the result is likely to be.

**Neural networks**: processing information in a similar way to human brains and learning and adapting over time. This makes them useful tools for solving pattern recognition problems, such as facial recognition, medical diagnosis and quality control, which computers are normally not very good at.

# Computers

1   Using a programming language that you are learning,
    a   write a simulation of rolling a die. The die must come up with 1 to 6 with equal probability.
    b   adapt your program so that the die is biased to give 6 more often than it should.

2   In a group, research techniques used in machine learning and illustrate your findings using presentation software. Bring your talks together and present them back to the class.

## Summary

- An operating system (OS) is software that
  - o  manages a hardware device;
  - o  manages users' access to the I/O devices, including files on secondary storage;
  - o  provides the user interface;
  - o  shares the computing resources such as CPU and memory between processes.
- Processes are tasks running on the computer, including application programs.
- Utility software does useful jobs for the user, such as file management.
- Computer modelling enables experts to ask 'what if?' questions without affecting the real world.
- Computer models are very useful, but contain assumptions and simplifications so you can't rely completely on their results.

## Checkpoint

### Strengthen

**S1**   Name one operating system and list the main functions it performs.

**S2**   Describe the differences between command-line and graphical user interfaces.

**S3**   Explain why anti-virus software is utility software.

**S4**   Computer models suggest that if we continue burning fossil fuels at the current rate, average sea levels will rise 25 cm by 2050. Discuss the advantages and disadvantages of using a computer model for this problem.

### Challenge

**C1**   State what is meant by a process and explain the purpose of scheduling.

**C2**   Suggest why some users might prefer a command-line interface to a graphical one.

**C3**   Write a program to model the populations of rabbits and foxes in a habitat. Use the following information to help you.
     Foxes eat rabbits
     Foxes die of starvation if they don't eat enough rabbits
     Rabbits and foxes both reproduce, but rabbits reproduce faster
     Rabbits and foxes both die of other causes

How confident are you in your answers to these questions? If you are not sure that you answered them well, make a revision resource by researching operating systems, utility software and computer models online before attempting the questions again.

# 4.5 Programming languages

## Learning outcomes

By the end of this section you should be able to:

- explain what is meant by high-level and low-level programming languages, and describe their suitability for a particular task.
- explain what is meant by a compiler and an interpreter and give the advantages and disadvantages of each.

## Low-level programming language

You learned in section 4.2 that a von Neumann architecture computer uses the stored program concept. The instructions that the computer carries out, the program, are stored in memory just like any other kind of data. This means that programs are also just binary numbers – that's all you can store in memory, after all. So how can binary numbers represent a program?

One other thing you learned in section 4.2 is that the CPU can only do a few very simple things. It only 'understands' a few very simple instructions. Complex things like playing games emerge from having a really large number of those simple things happening very fast. Those few simple instructions that a CPU knows how to do are called the **instruction set** for that type of CPU. Each instruction is given a binary code and it is these codes that make up your programs. The binary codes representing a program are called **machine code**.

A machine code program would look something like the diagram below – you can probably see why programming in machine code would be completely impractical.

```
0110100100100101010101011111010101100101011010110101010
```

**Figure 4.14** An example of a machine code program

Not only would it be incredibly difficult to work out the sequence of 1s and 0s you need, but also your program would only work on that kind of CPU because different CPUs have different instruction sets. Instead, you need a **translator** which converts your programs into the CPU's machine code language.

Translators are also programs. Their input is the text of your program – this is called your **source code**. Their output is machine code which the CPU can run (execute).

The simplest translator is called an assembler. It converts **assembly language** to machine code. Assembly language is called a **low-level programming language**. This is because the programmer is working at the lowest level of

### Key terms

**Instruction set**: the list of all possible commands a particular CPU knows how to carry out.

**Machine code**: the binary codes representing each of the instructions in the instruction set.

**Translator**: a program that converts source code into machine code.

**Source code**: the text of the program that a programmer writes.

**Assembly language**: a low-level language written using mnemonics.

**Low-level programming language**: a programming language that is closely related to the CPU's machine code.

# Computers

detail, the level of the CPU hardware itself. Each instruction in assembly language is the same as a machine code instruction.

Assembly language is a bit easier to work with than machine code because each instruction is written as a short, memorable keyword called a **mnemonic**. For example, the instruction for the CPU to add numbers together might be 01101001 in machine code, but is just ADD in assembly language. The assembler replaces each mnemonic with the appropriate binary machine code and data.

```
LDR R3, [R1]
MQV R2, #0
CMP R3, R0
MOVGT R2, #1
```

An example of assembly code

**Did you know?**

The 1980s space-trading game Elite, which featured 3D graphics and a galaxy of hundreds of planets to explore, was written entirely in assembly language and occupied just 22 KB. To see what an amazing feat of programming that was, look at the file size of a modern 3D graphics game. To learn more you could play an authentic version of the game on an emulator – search online for 'BeebEm'.

Writing programs in assembly language is challenging for three reasons.

- A very limited range of instructions is available. Every task, even the simplest, has to be built up from the smallest steps – some older CPUs could not even multiply numbers.

- You have to manage all your data. There are no strings, integers or real numbers, just binary, so you have to decide how to represent your data. You also have to decide and manage where it is stored in memory.

- Debugging is very difficult. When the assembled program runs, any bugs usually just make the machine crash and you have to reboot to try again.

Nowadays almost no programs are written in assembly language. The exceptions are some hardware drivers and programs designed to run on embedded systems that you learned about in section 4.2. This is because writing in the CPU's home language can be useful if you want your program to be very small and very fast or to directly control the I/O hardware.

**Extend your knowledge**

Research the Little Man Computer simulation. Make a list of the machine code instructions that Little Man Computer 'understands'.

# High-level languages

It is much more common to write software in high-level programming languages such as Python, C, Java or Visual Basic. For these programs to run on the CPU the source code has to be translated into machine code. This can be done

- all at once, and the finished machine code program saved and run later;
- one line at a time.

## Compilers and interpreters

A translator that translates the whole program in one go is called a **compiler** and one that translates and runs your program one line at a time is called an **interpreter**.

A compiler converts high-level language to machine code and saves the output as a machine code program, sometimes called **object code**. This usually has the .exe file extension, short for 'executable', because the machine code can be executed or run.

An interpreter translates your source code one line at a time and runs it there and then. There is no object code file, only your original source code.

**Key terms**

**Compiler**: a translator that converts high-level language source code into object code, often machine code. The source code is translated all at once and saved to be executed later.

**Interpreter**: a translator that converts high-level language source code into object code, often machine code. The source code is translated and executed one line at a time.

**Object code**: the translated source code. Often this will be machine code, but might also be an intermediate code, which has to be further translated before it can be executed.

**Using compilers or interpreters – a comparison**

| Interpreter | Compiler |
|---|---|
| Every computer that will run your program needs the interpreter software installed. | The output from a compiler will run on its own on any similar computer. |
| Interpreters find errors when they happen and can often tell you what has gone wrong. | A compiler cannot produce any object code unless the whole program is correct – they tend to report a lot of errors initially, making it harder to debug your program. |
| Programs tend to run slower using an interpreter because the interpreter has to translate the source code while the program is running. | It can be easier to protect your code from being altered or copied if it has been compiled because you only give people the object code (machine code), which is hard to understand. |

**Activity 23**

Implement one of the algorithms you designed in Chapter 1 in a graphical programming language, such as Scratch, and a textual language, such as Python.

Which language did you find most intuitive, which was easiest to use? Which one would you recommend for someone starting to program?

# Computers

## Exam-style questions

Manjit is using a high-level programming language to develop a computer game for children.

1  Explain why the program code she writes will need to be translated before it can be executed by a computer. **(2 marks)**

2  Compare using a compiler with using an interpreter to translate the code. **(4 marks)**

## Exam tip

The command word in Question **2** is 'compare', so you need to talk about similarities and differences between a compiler and an interpreter. Make sure your answer relates to both.

## Summary

- CPUs can only run programs written in machine code.
- A translator is a program that converts source code into machine code.
- Humans program computers mostly using a range of high-level languages, but sometimes in assembly language (a low-level language).
- Compilers and interpreters are types of translator, each having their own advantages and disadvantages.

## Checkpoint

### Strengthen

**S1**  Explain what is meant by machine code.

**S2**  What is the job of a translator?

**S3**  Momina is a C programmer and uses a compiler. Denis is a Python programmer and uses an interpreter. What challenges will Momina face in developing software compared with Denis?

### Challenge

**C1**  Explain the difference between high-level and low-level programming languages.

**C2**  Evaluate the choice of translator between compilers and interpreters.

How confident are you in your answers to these questions? If you are not sure that you answered them well, you could review the chapter by searching online.

# Chapter 5

## Communication and the internet

# Communication and the internet

## 5.1 Networks

## Computer networks and their use

### Computer networks

A **network** is a collection of two or more computers that are connected together for the purpose of sharing resources and data. All types of computer (e.g. desktops, laptops, tablets, e-readers, gaming systems, shop tills and even internet-enabled fridges) can be linked in networks.

Many networks include servers. A server is a powerful computer that provides the network with a service, such as storing files or sending/receiving emails. A small network might have one server, whereas a large business network could have tens or hundreds of servers.

### Why are networks used?

A network can support multiple users accessing multiple services simultaneously.

Almost all organisations (small or large), including schools, have a computer network that provides multiple services to its users. The network allows multiple users:

- to read/write personal files on a central server – this provides extra storage space to that on a single computer and also gives a back-up facility;
- to access shared files among several users;
- to download data or updates to computer programs;
- to send data to a shared printer;
- to access the internet;
- to communicate with each other – perhaps through email or video, or to play interactive games.

## Different types of network

### LAN and WAN

A **local area network (LAN)** is a network that covers a relatively small geographical area. This is often a single site, such as a home, a hospital or a factory.

The hardware (e.g. cables, routers, etc.) that connects the computers, servers and other hardware devices are usually owned by the organisation that the network belongs to.

Many people have a **wireless local area network (WLAN)** at home. A wireless router allows all the computer devices in a household to access the internet and share devices such as printers and external hard drives.

A **wide area network (WAN)** covers a large geographical area, usually across several sites of an organisation. Each site has one or more LANs, and they are all connected together to make a WAN. The WAN allows employees on different sites to communicate and share data.

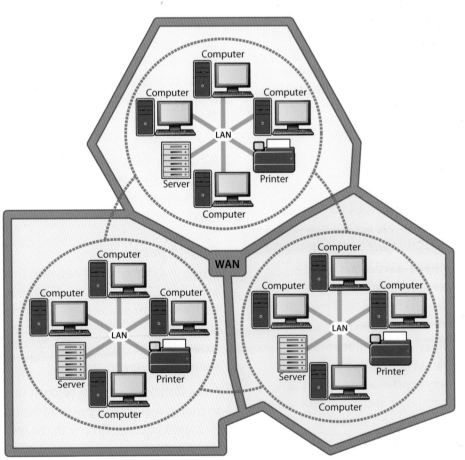

**Figure 5.1** LANs may be connected together to form a WAN

# Communication and the internet

## Exam-style question ⦿

A bank wants to share data between its head office and its 400 branches. Explain why the bank would use a WAN rather than a LAN for this purpose.
**(2 marks)**

## Exam tip ⦿

This question tests your understanding of the differences between a LAN and a WAN. A good answer should explain the difference between a LAN and a WAN and then explain why the network used by the bank to share data between head office and the branches would need to be a WAN.

## Key terms ◥

**Client–server network**: a network that has at least one server to provide services to the client computers.

**Peer-to-peer network**: a network that doesn't have any centralised servers. Each computer in the network can act as client and server.

## Client–server and peer-to-peer networks

There are two main models relating to computer networks – client–server and peer-to-peer.

### Client–server

In a **client–server network** there is at least one server, which is a powerful computer that provides a service or services to the network. Individual computers (such as the ones in a typical school computer room) are referred to as the client computers. The server will authenticate the user (see section 5.2) and then give the user access to the files that he/she has been given permission to access.

The server provides services to the clients as required.

A client accesses data or files from a server using the following process:

1  A client will make a connection to the server using its address. The server will know the address of the client because this will be included in the request for a connection.

2  Once the connection has been made, the client will make a service request to the server.

3  If the request is valid, the server will send the requested data to the client using the address identified in step 1.

Sometimes additional steps, such as authentication, are needed, depending on what the client is trying to access. For example, when Chris wants to check his web-based email from his laptop he will use a web browser (the client) to access the website, which is hosted on a server. The website will serve a web page that asks for his username (his email address) and his password.

He will enter his username/password and then submit them to the server. If the details are correct he will be authenticated and the server serves back the web page that displays his emails and allows him to manage his email.

### Peer-to-peer

Unlike in a client–server network, there aren't any centralised servers in a **peer-to-peer network**. Each computer can act as both a client and a server. Each computer in a peer-to-peer network can provide a service, such as share some files or provide access to a printer. Each computer can also request services from any other computer that has been configured to provide that service.

Some instant messaging systems use a peer-to-peer service to allow users to chat in real time. There is no central server that you sign on to and your messages are sent directly to the recipient.

## Did you know?

Some peer-to-peer networks connect using the internet. These particular peer-to-peer networks are often used for sharing files, especially pirated movies, music and computer games. It is difficult to find out who is sharing files when they are distributed using peer-to-peer networks because no records of who downloaded what are normally kept.

There are also legal uses of internet-based peer-to-peer file sharing, for example some versions of Linux are only downloadable using peer-to-peer file sharing. The lack of records also benefits those people worried about privacy.

### Network topologies

There are several different ways that the connections between networked devices can be arranged. The arrangement of these connections is referred to as the **network topology**.

There are four main network topologies – bus, ring, star and mesh.

## Activity 2 ?

1 Create a table comparing a client–server network with a peer-to-peer network. Use one column for the client–server network and another for the peer-to-peer network.

2 Research why internet-based peer-to-peer networks are a popular way of distributing pirated material such as movies or music. Present your findings as a short report.

## Key term

**Network topology**: describes how the devices on a network are connected together.

### *Bus*

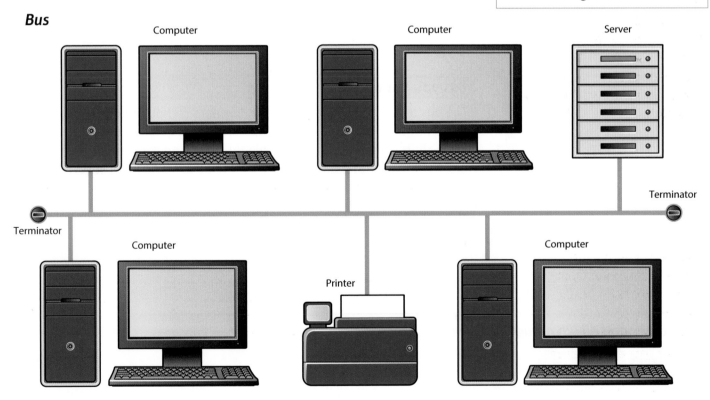

**Figure 5.2** Bus network topology

A bus network consists of a single cable to which each networked device is connected. Messages are sent along the cable in the form of electronic signals. At each end of the cable is a terminator.

The purpose of a terminator is to absorb signals that have reached the end of the cable, preventing them from bouncing back and causing interference.

As a bus network only has one cable (the bus), only one message can be sent at any one time. A bus network needs a system to deal with multiple devices sending a message at the same time. The most common method is called Carrier Sense Multiple Access with Collision Detection (which is shortened to CSMA/CD). A collision occurs when two or more network devices send a message at the same time, making all the messages unreadable.

A simplified CSMA/CD sending algorithm works like this.

| | |
|---|---|
| **1** | Check if bus is busy. |
| **2** | If not busy then send message, else go to step 1. |
| **3** | Listen to see if message received correctly. |
| **4** | If message not received correctly then go to step 5, else go back to listening for messages. |
| **5** | Wait random amount of time, go to step 1 to retry sending message. |

Making each device wait a random amount of time (a small number of milliseconds) before checking whether it is safe to send prevents the competing senders from repeatedly sending at the same time.

### Did you know?

The bus topology isn't widely used in business computer networks any more; however, it is used in many modern cars and some aircraft to allow all the different systems within the vehicle to communicate. The most well-known standard is called CAN (Controller Area Network) bus.

### Top tip

Algorithms can be represented in many different ways. Improve your skills and understanding by drawing a flowchart (see section 1.1 of Chapter 1, page 3) that shows how the CSMA/CD algorithm works.

## Advantages and disadvantages of the bus topology

| Advantages | Disadvantages |
|---|---|
| Relatively cheap to install since only one cable is needed | Whole network will fail if the cable is cut or damaged |
| Easy to add extra network devices | Can be difficult to identify where a fault is on the cable |
| | The more devices that are added to a bus network the slower they run. This is due to only one message being able to be sent at once and because more collisons happen |
| | All data sent is received by all devices on the network; this is a security risk |

## Ring

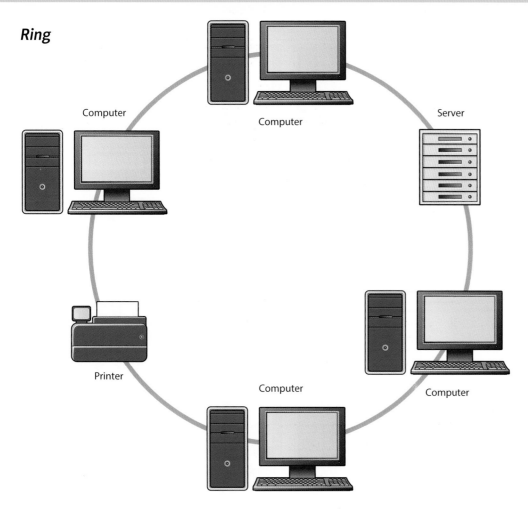

**Figure 5.3** Ring network topology

A ring network is a network in which the cable connects one network device to another in a closed loop, or ring. Each network device has what can be thought of as an 'in' and an 'out' connection.

Messages sent on a ring network all travel in the same direction and, unlike a bus network, there are no collisions. Data is passed from one device to the next around the ring until it reaches its destination.

### Advantages and disadvantages of the ring topology

| Advantages | Disadvantages |
|---|---|
| Adding extra devices does not affect the performance of the network | Whole network will fail if the cable is cut or damaged or a device on the network fails |
| Easy to add extra network devices | Because all the devices in the network are connected in a closed loop, adding or removing a device involves shutting down the network temporarily |
| | Can be difficult to identify where a fault is on the network |
| | More expensive to install than a bus network as it requires more cable to complete the ring |

# Communication and the internet

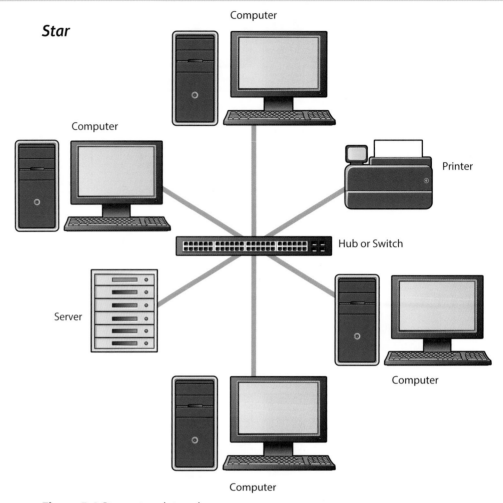

**Figure 5.4** Star network topology

In a star topology each network device is connected to a central point. This central point will be either a hub or a switch. A central hub receives and directs messages to the correct recipients. The star topology is the most widely used, but it does require a lot of cabling because each device is connected to the central point.

## Advantages and disadvantages of the star topology

| Advantages | Disadvantages |
| --- | --- |
| A damaged cable will not stop the whole network from working, just the network device connected to it | If the hub or switch fails then the whole network will fail |
| If a switch is used, then the network is efficient as messages are only sent to devices needing them. This also adds to security as not all devices will see a message | Expensive to install due to amount of cable needed and the hub or switch |
| Easy to locate faults because they will normally only involve one device | |
| A new device can be added or removed without having to close the network down | |

## Mesh

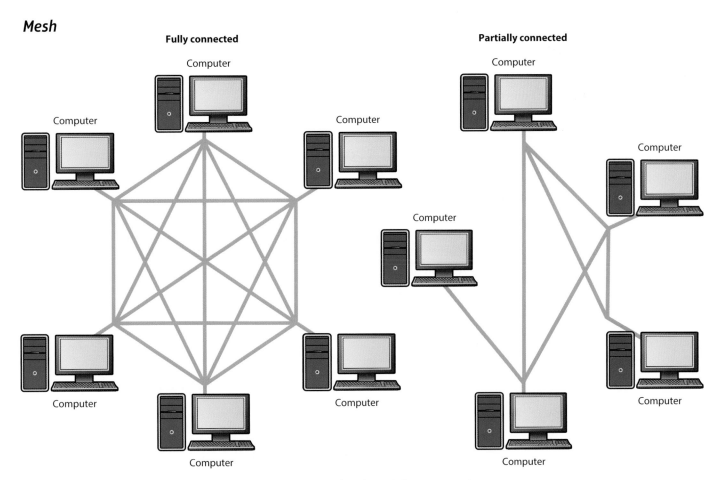

**Figure 5.5** Mesh network topology showing fully connected and partially connected types

There are two main types of mesh topology – fully connected and partially connected. In a fully connected mesh network every network device is connected to every other network device. In a partially connected mesh network some network devices may be connected to multiple other devices, but others might only be connected to one other device. Each device in a mesh network will pass messages on to other devices within the network.

Mesh networks can be wired or wireless. In a wired network the number of connections needed for a fully connected network soon becomes very expensive and difficult to implement as the number of network devices increases. Wireless mesh networks don't have the same problems.

Mesh networks are very fault tolerant. If a device or connection fails, messages are simply routed around it. In a fully connected mesh network a large number of failures could happen and the rest of the network devices would still be able to communicate. The ability of a partially connected mesh network to carry on working correctly will depend on how many connections to each device are available.

The largest mesh network of all is the **internet**.

Mesh networks are used to communicate between sensors in the 'internet of things', especially if the devices are mobile, because the optimum network paths can be used no matter where a sensor is located.

> **Key term**
>
> **Internet**: a worldwide system of interconnected networks that enables information to be exchanged and shared.

# Communication and the internet

*Advantages and disadvantages of the mesh topology*

| Advantages | Disadvantages |
|---|---|
| Very fault tolerant, especially in the case of a fully connected mesh network – if one device fails, messages can be rerouted | Difficult and expensive to install wired mesh networks |
| Very high performance because each network device is likely to be connected to multiple other devices | Can be difficult to manage due to number of connections within the network |
| In a wireless mesh network each node extends the range of the network | |

## Exam-style question

A small business has a network consisting of three computers, one printer and a server. The network uses a star topology. Draw a diagram of the network and label all parts. **(4 marks)**

## Exam tip

- This question tests your knowledge of network topologies and the components within them.
- A good answer will show the network cables in the correct layout, any required network hardware and the correct items connected to the network. The diagram will need to be labelled to show what each item is.

## Activity 3

1  Close this book and draw an annotated diagram for each of the following topologies: ring, star, bus and mesh.
2  From memory, list the advantages and disadvantages for each network topology you drew in Question 1.
3  Research which of the four network topologies in Question 1 would be most suitable for providing local access to the internet in a country that doesn't have reliable wired communication links. Write a paragraph explaining your decision and how the system could work.

## Communication media

There are many different ways that computers can be connected together to form a network. Networks are classified as either wired or wireless according to the transmission or **communication media** used.

### Wired

Wired connection methods involve a physical connection between the computer and the network. Most wired connections are made of copper wire but they could also be fibre-optic cable, which is made of either glass or plastic. Copper wire carries electrical signals, whereas fibre-optic cable carries light signals. Fibre-optic cables transmit data far faster and allow signals to travel over greater distances than copper wire.

## *Wireless*

Wireless connectivity does not require a physical connection between devices. Most wireless connections transmit and receive radio signals, but other connection methods such as infra-red light or microwaves can be used over limited distances.

Important methods of wireless communication are the mobile phone network, Bluetooth® and Wi-Fi®.

### Extend your knowledge

The internet of things is a term that covers the growing range of physical items that can be connected to the internet. These physical items (the 'things') can report details about themselves and be controlled over the internet. So your central heating could report the temperature of your house and allow you to adjust the thermostat from any internet-connected device, including your mobile phone.

ZigBee is an open-source **protocol** for allowing devices to be controlled by using low-power digital radio transmitters/receivers that are embedded within the device.

## Wired or wireless connectivity?

There are advantages and disadvantages to both wired and wireless connection methods.

### Did you know?

Many TV remote controls use infra-red light to send signals to control the volume or change the channel.

### Key terms

**Protocol**: a set of rules that govern how communications on a network should be formatted and what data they should include.

**Eavesdrop**: having unauthorised sight of data being sent from one computer to another over a network. This is covered more fully in the later section on technical weaknesses (section 5.2, page 189).

| Advantages | Disadvantages |
|---|---|
| **Wired connectivity** | |
| Faster than wireless connectivity | Expensive to install and reconfigure |
| Not easy to intercept or **eavesdrop** on data | Requires many cables at a premises |
| Less susceptible to interference than wireless connectivity | |
| **Wireless connectivity** | |
| No need for a cable to connect devices or to the internet | Data transmission speeds can be slower than wired connectivity |
| Allows users to use their own device | Interference from other wireless devices can adversely affect performance |
| A wider range of devices can communicate with each other/a network because it is not dependent on having the correct cable | Walls and other physical objects can adversely affect performance |
| | Data needs to be encrypted (see section 3.4) to prevent eavesdropping or interception |

# Communication and the internet

## Network data speed

Being able to measure the speed of a network allows you to:

- determine whether an equipment upgrade is necessary;

- estimate how long it will take to download a file;

- determine whether actual performance lives up to the promises made by the service provider.

The speed that data can be transmitted through a communications medium is measured in bits per second (this can shortened to bps, b/s or bit/s). Modern high-speed networks can transmit billions of bits per second.

| Unit | Abbreviation | bits per second |
|---|---|---|
| bits per second | bps | 1 |
| kilobits per second | kbps | 1,000 |
| megabits per second | Mbps | 1,000,000 |
| gigabits per second | Gbps | 1,000,000,000 |

Although the units listed above have similar names to the units used to measure storage (such as the capacity of a hard drive or the amount of RAM a computer has), they are different and you should make sure not to confuse them.

For example, you might measure storage in kilobytes (see Chapter 3, section 3.3, page 117); however, you measure the speed of a network connection in kilobits per second.

## Calculating the time needed to transmit a file

### Worked example

If you have a network connection of 12 Mbps and you want to download a 50 MB file, how long would it take?

To find out:

**1** Convert the file size from megabytes to bits.

50 MB × 1024 × 1024 × 8 = 419,430,400 bits

**2** Convert the transmission speed from Mbps to bits per second.

12 × 1000 × 1000 = 12,000,000 bps

**3** Divide bits by bits per second

419,430,400/12,000,000

Time = 34.95 seconds

These times are only theoretical as transmission speeds are not constant and other factors affect the speed of data transmission.

The amount of data that can be carried from one point to another on a network in a given period of time is referred to as its **bandwidth**. Bandwidth

### Key term

**Bandwidth**: the amount of data that can be carried on a network in a given period of time.

is usually expressed as bits per second (bps). Another important factor is the latency of the network connection. Latency refers to any kind of delay that data travelling through a network might encounter. A low latency network connection is one where any delays are small and a high latency network is one where data suffers from long delays.

## Protocols

In relation to computer systems and networks a protocol is a set of rules that determine how communications between devices are formatted and how these communications will be sent/received.

Without protocols different computers and other hardware wouldn't be able to communicate with each other because they would essentially be speaking different languages.

A protocol might contain details of:

- how each computer will be identified (its address);

- what route the data will take to get to its destination (routing information);

- how errors will be detected and dealt with (error checking);

- whether each part of a message should be acknowledged as received correctly;

- what to do if data isn't received correctly;

- how the data is to be formatted;

- how the data is to be sequenced (i.e. does it need to be sent in order or can it be put in its correct order later?);

- how the speed of the sender and receiver can be synchronised.

# Communication and the internet

There are many different protocols for different purposes. The main ones in use relating to networks and the internet are detailed below.

## Email protocols

Emails are sent and received using a set of standard protocols. This means that when you send an email it doesn't matter what email provider the recipient uses or what type of computer system they have.

There are three main email protocols in use.

| Protocol | Description |
|----------|-------------|
| **SMTP** | Simple Mail Transfer Protocol. This protocol is used when sending email through the internet. It details the format that messages are sent in, what commands email servers should understand and how they should respond to them. |
| **POP3** | Post Office Protocol, Version 3. POP3 is the current version of the Post Office Protocol that is used for retrieving email from an email server. Normally email clients using POP3 will connect to the mail server, download any messages and then delete the messages from the server. |
| **IMAP** | Internet Message Access Protocol. IMAP allows emails to be accessed using multiple email clients. For example, you might access your email using an email client on your computer, your tablet and your mobile phone. IMAP leaves messages on the server until you delete them. This means that no matter which email client you use, you should see an up-to-date list of your email messages. |

## Network protocols

### Ethernet

Ethernet is a family of protocols that are used in wired LANs. They cover everything from the physical parts of a network, such as type of cable or optical fibre and type of connector to be used, to the logical parts, such as how data is sent, checked for errors and the speed that data can be transmitted.

### Wi-Fi

Wi-Fi is a digital communications protocol that sets out how data is transmitted on wireless LANs. Wi-Fi is a trademarked term that is owned by Wi-Fi Alliance.

## TCP

The Transmission Control Protocol provides a reliable connection between computers. In this context 'reliable' means that the receiving computer can be certain that it has received all the data it should have (none of it is missing) and the data received is identical to the data sent (the data is correct).

TCP does this by:

- specifying that the receiving computer sends acknowledgements that each section of the data sent has been received;

- using **checksums** to ensure that the data received is accurate;

- allowing the receiving computer to tell the sending computer to slow down transmission, so the receiving computer has time to process the received data (this is called flow control);

- ensuring that data sent up to the application layer (see below) contains no duplicates and is in the correct order.

TCP is used when you access web pages, send/receive email or upload/download files.

## TCP/IP

TCP/IP stands for Transmission Control Protocol/Internet Protocol. TCP/IP is a protocol stack, which means that it is a collection of protocols that work together. It is named after the two most important protocols used in the stack.

These protocols work in a hierarchical set of layers, where each layer deals with a particular function of the network. Each layer will pass information up and down the protocol stack as it is processed.

The TCP/IP protocol stack has four layers. Data passes down the stack when sending, and back up when receiving.

| Layer | Description |
|---|---|
| Application | This is the top layer of the stack. It is the layer which interacts with the user to provide access to services and data that is sent/received over a network. Examples of protocols that work at this layer are HTTP, FTP and email protocols. |
| Transport | This layer manages end-to-end communication over a network. There are two main protocols that operate at this layer – TCP and UDP. (You only need to know about TCP for GCSE Computer Science.) |
| Internet | This layer deals with sending data across multiple networks (possibly the internet), from the source network to the destination network. This is known as routing and is the role of the Internet Protocol (IP). |
| Link | This layer controls the transmission and reception of packets of data to/from a local network. |

> **Key term**
>
> **Checksum**: an error detection technique. A mathematical formula is applied to the data and the resulting numerical value is transmitted with the data. The recipient computer applies the same formula to the received data and then compares the checksum sent with the data to the calculated checksum. If the checksums don't match the data is likely to have been corrupted and the recipient computer requests the data again.

> **Did you know?**
>
> You will sometimes see *TCP/IP* described as protocol suite rather than a protocol stack. These two terms are often used interchangeably, but some sources state that the suite is the definition of the protocols and that stack is the software implementation of the protocols.

> **Top tip**
>
> Remembering a list of items where the order is important (such as the TCP/IP layers) can be difficult. Why not try using a mnemonic like '**Another Truck Is Late**', where the initial letter of each word matches the initial letter of the layer name?

# Communication and the internet

## Key terms

**Packet**: a small quantity of data being sent through a network. The packet is labelled with the sender's address (source), the recipient's address (destination), how many packets are being transmitted and the position of this packet in the complete message.

**Web server**: powerful computer systems that store web pages and any multimedia that the pages might contain.

Data sent using TCP/IP is broken up into **packets**. Each packet of data consists of a small section of the data being sent along with a packet header.

A packet header contains details of:

* the sending computer;
* the recipient computer;
* how many packets the data has been split into;
* the number of this particular packet.

Once the recipient computer receives all the packets, it will use the information in the header to reconstruct the data into its original format.

A network that moves data in packets is called a packet switched network. (More details of how this works can be found in section 5.3.)

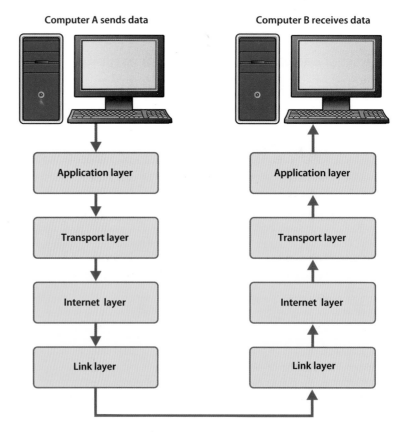

**Figure 5.6** Layers within the TCP/IP suite pass data down the stack when sending and back up the stack when receiving

## *HTTP*

The **H**yper**T**ext **T**ransfer **P**rotocol is used when sending and receiving data between web browsers and **web servers**. The HTTP protocol covers how data should be formatted, what commands the web server and web browser should understand and how they should react to each command.

For example, if you request a web page that doesn't exist on the web server, then the web server will send your web browser a 404 error message and your web browser will display this error and a short description of the error.

## Extend your knowledge

Another protocol that plays a major part in the TCP/IP protocol suite is called UDP. Research this and create a table explaining the differences between TCP and UDP.

### HTTPS

The HyperText Transfer Protocol Secure is the secure version of HTTP. This means that the data sent between your web browser and the web server is encrypted, which should prevent the data being sent/received from being read by a third party. HTTPS also helps the web browser and user to know that they are communicating with the intended web server rather than a fake that is trying to steal sensitive data, such as passwords or bank details.

### FTP

File Transfer Protocol is used to transfer files over a network that uses the TCP protocol (see above), such as the internet.

FTP is often used when sending web pages and other associated files that have been created on a web developer's computer to the web server. Once the files are on the web server, other computers connected to the internet will be able to view them.

## Internet protocols

### IP

At the internet layer, the Internet Protocol (IP) deals with:

- the addressing system to identify individual computers/servers on the network (usually the internet);

- splitting data into packets and adding the packet header with details such as the sender/receiver addresses.

Each device linked directly to the internet has a unique IP address assigned to it to allow data to be routed to it. There are two versions of the Internet Protocol (IP) in use: the earlier version is called IPv4 (Internet Protocol version 4) and the newer version is called IPv6. IPv6 has a number of improvements compared with IPv4. One of the major ones is that it has a larger address space than IPv4. Address space refers to the number of addresses available to assign to devices.

> **Activity 5**  ?
>
> When you use online banking your data will be transferred using HTTPS. Research why HTTPS is used rather than HTTP. What advantages does HTTPS give the bank customer and the bank itself? Create a poster summarising this information.

### Extend your knowledge

We are rapidly running out of IPv4 addresses, which is why IPv6 is being introduced.

IPv4 has 4,294,967,296 addresses, whereas IPv6 has 340,282,366,920,938,463,463,374,607,431,768,211,456 addresses.

The format of IP addresses differs between the versions.

- An IPv4 address consists of four sets of decimal numbers separated by a dot. Each decimal number can range from 0 to 255. A typical IPv4 address looks like this – 192.168.182.42

- An IPv6 address consists of eight blocks, separated by a colon. Each block is a 16-bit hexadecimal number (leading zeros can be removed). A typical IPv6 address looks like this – fd2a:1450:4013:c01:0:0:0:5e

**Source**: https://www.arin.net/knowledge/ipv4_ipv6.pdf

# Communication and the internet

## Activity 6 ?

Create a revision sheet that includes the following:

1 a definition of what a protocol is;

2 a table that includes the following protocols: SMTP, POP3, IMAP, Ethernet, Wi-Fi, HTTP, HTTPS and FTP along with a brief description of what each one is used for;

3 a diagram showing the TCP/IP protocol layers – you should annotate this to show what each layer does and which protocols run at each layer.

## Summary

- A network is a number of computers and other devices connected together to allow them to communicate and share data.
- A LAN covers a relatively small area. A WAN connects LANs together and spans a large geographical area.
- Client–server and peer-to-peer networks are two different network configurations. In a client–server network a central computer fulfils service requests from client computers, whereas in a peer-to-peer network each computer can act as a client and a server.
- Network devices can communicate using wired or wireless connections.
- A protocol is a set of rules governing communications on a network. They specify the format for communications and how they must be sent/received.
- There are many different protocols, each serving a different purpose.
- A network topology is how the connections between devices in a network are configured.

## Checkpoint

### Strengthen

**S1** What is the difference between a LAN and a WAN?

**S2** What are the advantages of wireless networks compared with wired networks?

**S3** What are the three major protocols used in sending and receiving email?

**S4** What is a protocol stack?

**S5** From memory, draw a diagram showing the bus, ring and star topologies.

### Challenge

**C1** Why might a chain of supermarkets use a WAN to connect all its stores?

**C2** Explain the advantages of a peer-to-peer network in terms of privacy when sharing files.

**C3** Most networks in use in schools and offices today are based on the star topology. Why do you think this topology is used?

**C4** IMAP is now used much more than POP3. Can you explain the link between this and the popularity of smartphones?

How confident do you feel about your answers to these questions? If you're not sure you answered them well, try drawing a concept map showing how the information in this section links together. Your concept map can have brief definitions on it and some people use colours/pictures to help them memorise the contents.

# 5.2 Network security

## Network security and its importance

**Network security** covers a wide range of activities that protect data from threats to its confidentiality, correctness (integrity) and availability.

**Confidentiality** – An organisation's computer system often holds data about its people (employees and customers), products or financial performance. It could not run efficiently, or sometimes at all, without a network and this data. It is important (and in the case of personal data, the law) that the network is not hacked so data is not intercepted or stolen by criminals or competitors who might use the data for illegal purposes or business advantage.

Some ways to protect data confidentiality include:

- ensuring only authorised users can access the parts of a network and its resources that they have a reason to require, such as its storage (data), printers or internet connection. For example, the managing director of a company is able to access the financial records, whereas a checkout employee is not (see also in the later section 'Other ways to secure a network').

- stopping misuse – even users who have been given permission to access a network might deliberately or accidentally access data they have not been given permission to read.

- encrypting data – if a criminal or other unauthorised person gains access to data and it is encrypted then they won't be able to read it without the encryption key.

**Correctness** – Data is useless unless it is correct. Use of the network to communicate and store data must not change the data or allow the data to be changed without authorisation. Imagine the seriousness of an error on your health records or in a manufacturing control system.

**Availability** – A network is useless if data cannot be accessed when it is needed. Complex systems are likely to fail at some time (e.g. a piece of hardware might stop working and have to be replaced, or program code might become corrupted), but it is also important that protection is put

# Communication and the internet

in place to prevent failures caused by criminals. Virus or **denial of service (DoS)** attacks can, for example:

- slow down network performance or stop it working altogether;
- delete data;
- allow data to be stolen or eavesdropped on;
- alter data or program code.

## Network security importance

Here are some more specific examples of the importance of network security. The data stored on the network could be:

- **required for the running of the organisation** – The business might have details of its customers, stock and outstanding orders saved on the network. If the data were lost and the business failed to fulfil any outstanding orders, this could mean losing the trust of customers who then go elsewhere. This could lead to the business going bankrupt. This has happened to a number of businesses, some of them very large.

  Even a school would struggle to run effectively without its network and the data stored on it. Data, such as contact details, registers, timetables, medical conditions, handouts for learners, presentations to be shown by tutors, are stored on the network and could become inaccessible if the network fails for some reason.

- **private and confidential** – There are many types of private and confidential data that people or businesses wouldn't want to make public. For example, a hospital stores patient details on its network, including medical conditions and what drugs have been prescribed. There is a legal requirement to keep personal data secure. If the network isn't secure and the confidential data is leaked, then the hospital could be sued. Many potential patients would be put off using the hospital due to a lack of trust in the ability of the hospital to maintain patient confidentiality, which could result in the hospital being closed down.

- **financially valuable** – Many types of data stored on business networks might be financially valuable. For example, imagine a business was planning a huge sale to increase its revenue and attract new customers. If a competitor managed to get hold of the details of the planned price reductions before the sale started, it could launch its own sale beforehand, undercutting the business. This tactic would reduce the chance of the sale increasing revenue or attracting new customers.

## Authentication and validation

Authentication is the process of checking the identity of a user of a computer system or network. This is often done by validating a username and password against details stored on a central server, but other systems of authentication exist, such as using a PIN (personal identification number) or fingerprint recognition. If the details you provide match those on record, then you are allowed access to the network and its resources:

### Extend your knowledge

Passwords have many weaknesses, for example people write them down or use guessable passwords (like a pet's name). Programs exist that repetitively try guessing passwords. To improve the security that passwords provide, an additional check, such as having to type in the code from a portable hardware device called a 'secure token' or from an SMS message sent to your mobile phone, is being introduced by some businesses. This is called two-factor authentication. How does this enhance security? Try researching some different two-factor authentication systems and think about which ones are likely to be the most secure.

### Activity 7

Think about how you would write a program so that only approved users who enter their password correctly can get beyond the log-in screen.

1   Write the pseudo-code for the username and password checking part of the program.

2   Write your program.

3   Discuss how secure you think your implementation is. How could it be improved?

## Other ways to secure a network

There are many different ways to help secure a network, authentication alone is not enough. Three others you need to know about are: access control, firewalls and physical security.

### *Access control*

Once a user has been authenticated they gain access to the network; however, you wouldn't want every user on a network to have access to every file.

**Access control** is the method that controls whether a particular user will gain access to a particular file. Access control also decides if that user gets:

* read-only access – in this case the user can open the file and read its contents, but not modify the contents or delete the file;

* read and write access (modify access) – in this case the user can read the file, alter the contents and then save the changes.

### Key term

**Access control**: this determines which users have access to which data, and what they are allowed to do with it.

# Communication and the internet

In some network systems you might need further permission if you want to delete a file – this is sometimes referred to as full control of the file.

Controlling the level of access a user has to a file is useful for many reasons. For example, you might want employees of a shop to be able to open a price list, but not accidentally or deliberately modify any prices.

Access controls are set up by an organisation's system administrators according to the management's requirements.

## Firewall

A firewall is a network security system that monitors and controls data that is moving from one network to another. Often one of these networks is the internet, in which case the firewall sits between the local internal network and the internet.

A firewall inspects incoming and outgoing data and uses a set of rules (often known as a firewall policy) to decide whether to allow or disallow the data to move from one network to another. The rules in a firewall are designed to secure the internal network from a range of potential threats. The organisation that owns the firewall can customise the rules so that the firewall is suitable for their particular circumstances. Some examples of what the rules can do are:

- Stop certain protocols from being used (for example FTP) to stop the organisation's data from being potentially copied to an external server.

- Block data coming from or going to certain network addresses. The blocked addresses could be of particular computers, servers or websites, or even a range of network addresses that belong to particular countries or organisations.

- Stop attempts at **hacking** the internal network's servers by disallowing data that matches the pattern an attacker would use.

Firewalls can be software or hardware based. Individual computers (such as your home computer or laptop) are likely to have a software firewall installed with some default rules to protect your computer from common threats. A business with a LAN and internet connection is likely to have a hardware-based firewall because these have much more flexibility in terms of the rules that can be applied and allow faster throughput of data.

## Physical security

**Physical security** ensures that critical parts of the network can only be physically accessed by authorised people, such as the network technicians or a systems administrator. It also includes protecting against theft of equipment and might involve installing a burglar alarm, security tagging and physically locking down equipment, etc.

The starting point for physically securing a network is having the servers located in a locked room, normally referred to as the server room. Electronic lock systems have many advantages over traditional lock-and-key systems as entry/exit times can be recorded and individual cards/fobs can be deactivated if lost or if an employee leaves the company.

Physical security is very important because anyone with physical access to the server can more easily bypass the security provided by the authentication system or access control system. Having done so they could copy, modify or delete any data on the network, or install **malware** that would allow them to gain remote access whenever they wanted.

**Key term**

**Malware**: short for 'malicious software'. It is used as a generic term for any kind of software that is designed to disrupt the use of a computer system.

### Activity 8 ?

A business has a network comprising 50 computers, several printers and an internet connection. The business

- employs two technicians to manage the network;

- has several departments, including sales, accounts and human resources;

- is run by a managing director, with a manager in charge of each department and around 60 other employees.

1 Create a poster explaining to the employees what authentication is and what makes a secure password.

2 Where should the servers in this business be located? Justify your answer and explain who should be able to get physical access to the servers.

## Cloud storage and security

The concept of the 'cloud' is discussed in Chapter 4, section 4.2 on page 151. This section covers the security issues associated with cloud storage.

Many of the advantages to cloud storage relate to securing the availability of data.

- The cloud storage provider is responsible for the hardware your data is stored on. They will need to ensure that the data is accessible and that they maintain the hardware and software needed to make the data available.

- The amount of storage available to an organisation can easily be changed as and when required – the cloud storage provider can normally make extra storage available in minutes. Doing this physically would mean ordering more hard drives and employing technicians to install them and set them up. This would take considerably longer than a few minutes.

- Having data stored off-site (not on the organisation's premises) means that it is protected from loss due to fire, theft of computers/servers, electrical failure, and so on. As the data is still available the business may be carried on from elsewhere. This could be the difference between staying in business or going bankrupt.

- Many cloud storage systems also manage the back-up of your data. They may take hourly or daily snapshots of your data and be able to restore from these in the case of hardware failure or accidental deletion of files.

However, cloud storage also has a number of security disadvantages.

- You are relying on a third-party storage provider to keep your organisation running. What happens if the cloud storage provider goes bankrupt, has a catastrophic failure or has its servers stolen? In any of these cases it is likely you would be unable to access your data, at least temporarily, but possibly permanently.

- Data stored anywhere accessible via the internet carries the risk of other people gaining access to it. This might happen through a deliberate attack by hackers, or as a result of an accidental configuration error that results in the data becoming publicly accessible. Also the internet isn't a particularly secure network and data may be accessed as it is being sent to/from the cloud storage provider. The loss of data, particularly of a confidential nature, could be devastating for an organisation.

- Users of cloud storage have to assume that the people providing the service are trustworthy and that their data is being held safely and securely.

- The cloud storage provider might have its servers located in a different country (or countries) to your organisation. Some types of data can only legally be stored in countries that have similar data protection laws to our own.

- Access to cloud storage is dependent on having a reliable, high-speed internet connection available. How will a business operate if the internet becomes unavailable for some reason?

The decision to use cloud storage involves carefully weighing up the advantages against the disadvantages. Many of the disadvantages present risks to the operations of an organisation, but the impact of some of these risks can be reduced. For example:

- Many cloud storage providers will store your data at multiple locations so that fire, flood, hardware or electrical failure should have no major impact on accessing your data.

- You can encrypt your data so that it is much more difficult to read while it is either being transferred to/from the cloud storage provider or stored on the provider's servers.

## Contemporary storage and security

The types of storage systems available are constantly evolving. One recently developed storage system is network-attached storage (NAS).

NAS is a hardware device that is connected to a network to provide file storage for any device connected to that network. A typical NAS device designed for home use could consist of a single hard drive and associated network hardware, whereas an organisation's NAS device might consist of many hard drives and the associated network hardware.

**Activity 9** **?**

Discuss with a classmate the advantages and disadvantages of moving your school's files/data to cloud storage. Focus on the security and privacy issue that the school will need to address.

NAS devices often include a wide range of additional features, such as allowing access over the internet, and specialist apps to allow smartphones and tablets to access the files stored on the NAS easily.

Often NAS devices are designed for ease of use rather than being secure. Once a NAS is connected to the internet it becomes possible for it to be hacked remotely. Home users often make mistakes such as:

- Not changing a device's default password, thus giving access to the stored files to anyone who looks up the default password on the internet.

- Not updating the software running on the NAS. Manufacturers tend to release updated software to fix security weaknesses as they are found. If the software isn't kept up to date, these weaknesses might be used to gain access to the stored data. The security weaknesses are often published on the internet for criminals to read.

There are ways to minimise the security risk to data when using a NAS or similar device. Firstly, decide if the data does indeed have to be accessible over the internet and if NAS is the correct storage device for the data. If the data needs to be available over the internet, then ensure you use a complex password, remove any default passwords and ensure that all software patches (updates) are applied.

Another widely used storage device is the **USB** flash drive. USB flash drives are easy to transport, relatively cheap for the amount of storage available and very convenient to use.

> **Key term**
>
> **USB**: Universal Serial Bus sockets found on most modern computer systems.

The downside is that people can carry large amounts of possibly sensitive information around with them on a small drive that is easily lost. Anyone can find a lost flash drive and access the information. To overcome this, encrypted USB flash drives are available. These are unreadable until a password or numeric code is entered on to a very small keypad on the body of the drive itself. (See Chapter 3, section 3.4, page 125 for more on encryption.)

USB storage devices also present an ideal opportunity for an employee to steal data, perhaps to sell to somebody else.

> **Activity 10** ?
>
> Many providers offer cloud storage aimed at individuals.
>
> 1 Create a table to compare what three of these providers offer. Headings for the table should include: Amount of free storage space, Cost for more storage, Security measures.
> 2 Research and write a brief report that explains what commitments these providers make to keep your data secure. Relate this to the security measures you found out about in step 1 of this activity.

# Communication and the internet

## Key terms

**Cyberattack**: any kind of malicious attack on a network-connected device.

**Social engineering**: any kind of attack on a computer system or network that exploits how people behave and respond to certain situations.

**Phishing**: attempting to get confidential information by sending a user a message that appears to come from a trustworthy person or organisation.

**Shoulder surfing**: gaining access to information by watching someone enter it into a computer system.

## Cyberattacks

A **cyberattack** is any kind of electronic attack on a computer system, server, network or other IT device. These attacks might be designed to:

- gain access to data contained within the system;
- delete or modify information;
- make the system unavailable for use;
- physically damage a device connected to the network (usually by overriding safety limits).

## Types of cyberattack

There are many different forms of cyberattack and these are constantly changing as technology evolves. Most cyberattacks can be classed as exploiting either human behaviour or technical weaknesses.

### Social engineering

Attacks that rely on exploiting human behaviour are often referred to as **social engineering** because the attacker will 'engineer' a situation where the target person (or group of people) gives away confidential information or gives access to the confidential information.

Two common forms of social engineering are **phishing** and **shoulder surfing**.

### Phishing

A phishing attack is an attempt to get sensitive, confidential information from the user of a computer system or service. Often the information the phishing attack is targeting is usernames and passwords or financial details such as bank account or credit card details.

There are various forms of phishing. The most common types are through email or fake websites that look legitimate, but phishing can also happen via phone calls or instant messaging.

A typical phishing attack might start with an email that asks the user to update details at a bank, online payment system, online auction website or social network. Sometimes the bogus reason given for this request is that there has been a fraud attempt on the user's account.

Once the user clicks on a link within the email, a website that looks and acts like the real website will open, but when the user enters his or her login details they are passed to the attacker, who will use them for financial gain.

Phishing takes advantage of people trusting the contents of emails to be genuine. Many people don't bother to look at the web address they have been taken to or think about whether their bank is really going to email them to request a security update.

### Shoulder surfing

Shoulder surfing means gaining access to confidential information by directly observing a user, possibly literally looking over their shoulder, as they complete a task. Often shoulder surfing is used to get a person's username/password or PIN.

Often shoulder surfing happens in busy places where the target is concentrating on completing a task quickly. A classic example is at a cash machine on a street, where the shoulder surfer stands near the cash machine and sees the user enter his or her PIN on the keypad. Once the PIN has been seen the card is stolen. The card and PIN can then be used to withdraw cash.

---

### Activity 11 ?

1 Research recent cyberattacks. What kinds of organisations are targeted? How successful were the attacks? What information was taken?

2 Some organisations have been known to deny that a cyberattack successfully happened or downplay the effects of a cyberattack. Why might they do this? What are the risks to a business of lying about cyberattacks?

---

## Technical weaknesses

Other forms of cyberattack rely on technical weaknesses (vulnerabilities) in the system being attacked. Some common examples are described below.

### Unpatched software

Software is very complicated and usually security issues are found as it is used in the real world. The maker of the software will normally provide updates (referred to as patches) to fix security issues as they are found.

Often these security issues are discussed on the internet and some people will use this knowledge to attack **unpatched software** to gain unauthorised access to information.

The patches to fix the security issues often have to be manually installed by a technician. Sometimes these patches get forgotten about or the organisation doesn't have any technicians to install the patch, so the software remains vulnerable.

> **Key term**
>
> **Unpatched software**: software that hasn't had the latest security updates applied to it, making it vulnerable to attack.

### USB devices

You read earlier about the weaknesses associated with USB flash drives, but any USB device can potentially be a security threat because it might contain malware that could be transferred to your system or copy data to the attacker via the internet.

### Eavesdropping

One form of attack mentioned earlier is an eavesdropping attack. In computer security terminology, eavesdropping means intercepting data being sent to/from another computer system. In a similar way that a person can eavesdrop on a conversation without the speakers knowing about it, eavesdropping on a network is simply reading data without actually copying or stealing it. The owner of the data might not know that the data has been read until it is used by the criminal.

Security weaknesses such as unpatched software or a USB device might allow malware to be installed on the network that allows an eavesdropping attack to be carried out, but specialised hardware might also be used.

## Protecting against security weaknesses

There are many ways to strengthen computer systems and networks from attacks, starting from when software is designed and written, to deciding on what kind of operating system should be used and how network security provision will be implemented.

### Design and implementation of software

Security must be considered at the system and software design stage if a piece of software is to be as resistant as possible to cyberattack. It should not be an afterthought when the system has been implemented.

The software and system designers will need to consider the following, for example:

- What kind of authentication is needed?
- Do different users need different levels of access to the information stored within the system?
- Should warnings be issued before allowing users to carry out potentially risky operations such as copying or deleting large amounts of information?
- Does stored data need to be encrypted?
- What threats will the software face? Will the software be run on computers that are connected to the internet? How do they guard against phishing, malware and other hacking attempts?

Once the designers have considered security, they need to look at the implementation (writing the code) phase.

One major issue at this point is guarding against bad programming practice. Usually a software project will have many different programmers working on the code. Some programmers write poor quality code and don't consider how safe or secure their code is, and sometimes time pressure might make even a good programmer take shortcuts to meet deadlines.

Another major issue is that some methods used in programming might lead to **code vulnerabilities**. A code vulnerability is when the code does the task intended, but has been written in such a way that it creates a potential security issue.

More details about the kinds of issues and their impact that need to be considered when creating software can be found in Chapter 6 page 216.

Issues like these can be minimised by having regular code reviews. There are two main types of code review.

- Review by another programmer, usually someone who is more senior and has more experience of writing secure code. The reviewer will look at the code produced, checking to see if any bad programming practices have been used or if any code vulnerabilities are present. This is fairly labour intensive and therefore expensive.

> ### Key term
>
> **Code vulnerability**: a computer program (the code) that has been written in such a way that it creates a security issue that may be taken advantage of to gain access to the computer system or data within it.

- An automated review. Here, a specialist piece of software is used to examine the code. The software will highlight potential issues such as common vulnerabilities in the programming language or obvious bad programming practice. This software can't find every issue and is also fairly expensive.

Sometimes a combination of both types will be used. If issues are found, then the original programmer will be asked to improve the code and another code review will be scheduled.

**Modular testing** is important to security because if small problems remain they might be used by hackers to gain access to the system or the data it contains. For example, failing to validate input correctly could lead to a hacker being able to crash the program and then gain access to the underlying system, which could allow valuable data to be accessed.

## Other security measures to protect from cyberattacks

Here are some other methods to reduce the chance of cyberattacks succeeding.

- Use an **audit trail**. An audit trail is a record of activities that have taken place on a computer system, and which cannot be changed. The audit trail is automatically generated and likely to be in chronological order. Ordinary users of a system shouldn't be able to read an audit trail. The amount of detail in an audit trail varies but is likely to contain date and time of change, what change happened, who or what (as in a user or other software that is part of the system) made the change. Audit trails allow technicians to figure out what happened during a cyberattack, if the attack was successful, what sections of the system were accessed and if data was copied or modified.

- Use secure operating systems. Different operating systems are designed for different purposes. Some are designed with security in mind and these are likely to be much harder to attack successfully due to the way they have been written and the features they offer. When implementing a computer system that will contain sensitive or confidential data the choice of operating system must be considered carefully.

- Provide effective network security. To keep a network secure requires effective management, monitoring and training of its users. Well-educated technical staff, with up-to-date training, are needed to keep software patched correctly, implement policies that reduce the chance of an attack being successful, train users in best practice in terms of security and monitor the systems to ensure there is no unauthorised access.

## Identifying vulnerabilities

Ethical hacking is the branch of computer science that relates to cybersecurity and preventing cyberattacks from being successful. Ethical hacking is essentially 'good' hacking – it is looking for weaknesses in software and systems so that they can be improved – whereas hacking is seen as 'bad' – trying to gain access to a system to steal data or cause damage.

There are many ways that vulnerabilities can be identified and some of these are explained below. Once a vulnerability has been found, steps to remove or reduce its impact can be taken.

### Key terms

**Modular testing**: testing each block of code as it is completed to ensure the code works as expected.

**Audit trail**: a record of activities that have taken place on a computer system. This record is generated automatically and will record what has happened and who or what made the change.

### Activity 12

A patch has become available for a major web browser. Research the risks that the user faces by not updating his/her software and add details of the potential risks to your revision notes.

### Penetration testing

Penetration testing (often shortened to 'pen testing') is where the IT systems of an organisation are deliberately attacked to find any weaknesses. These attacks are authorised by the organisation and are therefore legal. The attacks might be run by employees of the organisation or by a business that has been contracted to run the tests.

The pen tester(s) is likely to try to gain access to all systems that the organisation has and the attacks will often include looking for technical weaknesses and trying social engineering methods.

Once the pen testing has been completed, a report is usually presented to a senior manager within the organisation explaining what issues were found and the likely impact of them.

### Commercial analysis tools

It is possible to use software tools to scan a system for vulnerabilities. These commercial analysis tools or vulnerability scanners can be either purchased or hired. The tools look for common issues and alert the user to them.

These tools can only identify already-known vulnerabilities and must be kept up to date to be effective. They can be used to scan the network from within (internally) or from outside (externally). Both of these scans can be valuable. An internal scan can show up issues that could be exploited by a rogue employee or a hacker who managed to physically get into the building or gain access to the network in some other way. The external scan might show vulnerabilities that a hacker could exploit from outside the company network.

One negative aspect is that these analysis tools aren't really restricted in terms of who can purchase them, so they could be used by a potential hacker to find security vulnerabilities.

### Reviews of network and user policies

All networks should have written policies that document:

- who is authorised to carry out various activities on the network;

- how and when patches to software should be applied;

- access controls;

- password requirements, including how complex passwords should be and how often they should be changed;

- how security is set up and maintained on the network;

- what data audit trails should collect and how long they should be kept for;

- anything else relevant to the security and maintenance of the network.

Before an employee is given access to the network they should be given a copy of the network user policy to read and sign to show they accept the organisation's rules on the use of the network.

This user policy is likely to contain details of:

- what is acceptable and unacceptable use of the network;
- what will happen to the user if they do something unacceptable (depending on the severity of what they do wrong, this could include losing their job);
- how to report faults, problems and security issues;
- security information, such as good practice when choosing and using passwords.

Over time the hardware, software and usage of a network are likely to change. Any policies relating to the network should be regularly reviewed to ensure that they are up to date and suitable to help maintain network security.

### Activity 13

Find your school's Network User Policy (you might need to ask your tutor for a copy).

1 Review the policy. Has it been updated recently? Is it easy to understand? Is it detailed enough?

2 Using your school's policy and any others you can find on the internet, try to redraft the policy to make it easy to understand for non-specialist users of IT.

### Exam-style question

Describe how an email phishing attack targeting bank customers might work. **(4 marks)**

### Exam tip

- This question tests your understanding of what a phishing attack is and how one might work.
- A good answer should state the chain of events that might lead to someone entering their bank logon details into a fake bank website.

### Summary

- Authentication is the process of checking the identity of someone trying to use a computer system.
- Cloud storage is storing data using a third party, usually in a system connected to the internet.
- A cyberattack is any kind of electronic attack on a computer system, server, network or other IT device.
- There are many different types of cyberattack; most exploit technical weaknesses or human behaviour.
- Many different measures need to be taken to prevent cyberattacks from being successful. These start at the design stage of the system and include keeping systems up to date, training staff and proactively testing the security of the network regularly.

### Checkpoint

#### Strengthen

**S1** What is the most common authentication method in use?

**S2** What is access control?

**S3** What is social engineering?

#### Challenge

**C1** In your own words, summarise the different types of cyberattack.

**C2** The number of cyberattacks happening is increasing each year. Why do you think this is the case?

How confident do you feel about your answers to these questions? If you're not sure you answered them well, try writing a list of questions then work through this section adding relevant points as you find them.

## 5.3 The internet and the World Wide Web

### The internet

The word internet is a shortened form of the words 'inter' and 'network', which together means interconnected networks. It's a good idea to think of the internet as a network of networks (i.e. the biggest WAN of all). Your school, many organisations and many people's homes all have a network that is a part of the internet.

The reach of the internet is global – all countries have multiple cables, fibre-optic links and satellites that connect it to other countries. These links plus others within each country can be thought of as the internet backbone – the connections that link all the networks together.

### How the internet works

Your computer or network is likely to be connected to the internet using an **Internet Service Provider (ISP)**. An ISP is an organisation that provides internet connections. This connection to the internet can be provided in a number of ways, but the most common is through telephone lines.

The internet uses the TCP/IP protocol stack to allow communication between all the different networks. More detail about protocols can be found in section 5.1, page 185.

The Internet Protocol (IP) part of the stack provides the technical rules on addressing; that is, it provides each device or network connected to the internet with a unique address to send data to/from.

As discussed in section 5.1, two versions of IP, Internet Protocol version 4 (IPv4) and Internet Protocol version 6 (IPv6), are currently in use.

The networks that are a part of the internet are linked together using routers. A **router** is a piece of networking hardware that forwards packets between networks. A router has a routing table that is essentially a list of rules stating where to send packets for different destinations. When a router receives a packet it looks in the packet header for the destination address and then uses the rules within the routing table to decide where to send it. It is likely that a packet will need to be forwarded between several routers before it reaches its destination.

When an internet-connected computer wants to send data to another whose IP address it already knows the following happens.

> **Key terms**
>
> **Internet Service Provider (ISP)**: an organisation that provides its customers with a connection to the internet.
>
> **Router**: a piece of networking hardware used to forward packets of data from one network to another.

1   The sending computer splits the data into packets.

Each packet has a header that contains the sender's address, the destination address, the current packet number and the total number of packets that make up the data.

2   Each packet is sent to your ISP.

3   Your ISP will have a router. This router will inspect the packet header, and decide where to send the packet depending on its destination IP address.

4   The packet is likely to end up at another router, which will again look at the destination IP address and forward it on. This can happen many times before the packet reaches its destination network and intended recipient.

5   Once a packet reaches its destination, the receiving computer will reassemble the data from the packets. Depending on the protocol being used, the packets might arrive in the wrong order and have to be put back in order using the information in the packet header.

The internet, like any network, has many different services running on top of it. Email and the World Wide Web are two of the most commonly used services to which the internet provides access.

## The World Wide Web

The World Wide Web (often shortened to WWW or 'the Web') is a service that runs on the internet. It provides access to web pages (a type of document), which are linked together using a hypertext system. Hypertext is simply text that contains links (hyperlinks) that can be selected to go to another document/web page. These documents can contain text, graphics and multimedia.

### Accessing the World Wide Web

You access the World Wide Web using a program called a web browser. There are many different web browsers to choose from but they all use the same protocols and use the internet to transfer information. The web browser's job is to convert the data received from a web server (see page 186) to a human-readable format. When a user accesses a website using the client–server system mentioned on page 174 in section 5.1, the web browser is the client and the web server provides the service to the web browser.

### How the World Wide Web works

The World Wide Web uses the internet to transfer data from one computer system to another. The computer being used to access the World Wide Web connects to the internet using an ISP and will be running a web browser.

Getting a web page or other file using the World Wide Web involves a large number of steps that use different protocols and standards.

### Activity 14   ?

Find out what services other than the World Wide Web and email use the internet. Create a list with a brief definition of each service, what protocols it uses and how it uses the internet.

### Did you know?

The World Wide Web was invented in 1989 by a British scientist called Tim Berners-Lee. Can you find out when the internet was invented?

# Communication and the internet

1 The user of a computer enters the web address of the information he or she wants to look at. A web address is also known as a URL (Uniform Resource Locator). A URL may be for a web page or an individual file, for example a URL could be just for a particular picture file rather than a web page.

2 The computer uses a system called the Domain Name Service (DNS) to find the IP address of the required web server.

3 The web browser connects to the web server using the IP address and requests the relevant web page or other object (picture, sound or video file).

4 A web page is transferred from one computer (normally a web server) to another using HTTP or HTTPS, which were covered in 'Network protocols' in section 5.1.

5 Data sent from a web server to a web browser is in **HyperText Markup Language (HTML)** format. The web browser displays the web page as described by the HTML.

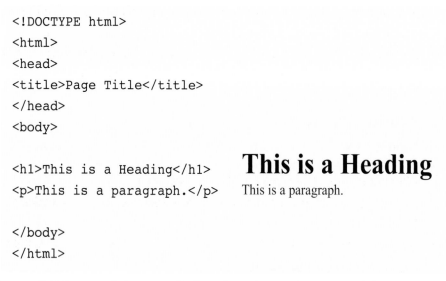

**Figure 5.7** How a web browser display of a web page is generated from HTML

If the user selects a hyperlink, then the URL that the link points to will be loaded using the method outlined above. The URL might point to a web page on the same web server or on a different web server. This is where the 'web' part of World Wide Web comes from – different pages and web servers are linked together in a complex pattern.

## Exam-style question

Explain the difference between the internet and the World Wide Web.
**(2 marks)**

## Activity 15

1   Draw an annotated diagram that shows how a packet gets from one computer to another through a number of routers on the internet.

2   The internet is capable of continuing to work even when some parts of the physical network fail. Research and discuss how the internet deals with faults of this kind.

## Exam tip

*   This question tests your understanding of how the internet and World Wide Web are related.

*   A good answer should state what the internet and WWW are and how the WWW uses the internet.

## Summary

*   The internet is a global network of networks. It is used to transfer data between different computer systems.
*   The internet has many different services running on top of it. Two common services are the World Wide Web and email.
*   The World Wide Web runs on top of the internet. Although people often mix the two terms up, they are not the same and as a learner studying Computer Science you need to use the terminology correctly.

## Checkpoint

### Strengthen

**S1**  Write your own definition of what the internet is.

**S2**  Write a definition of what the World Wide Web is and add an explanation of how it is different from the internet.

**S3**  Describe what happens when you enter a web address into a web browser.

### Challenge

**C1**  Explain in your own words the role of all the protocols used when requesting a web page from a web server.

**C2**  Explain why you think the internet and World Wide Web are so embedded in modern life.

How confident do you feel about your answers to these questions? If you're not sure you answered them well, try finding some online videos that explain the concepts visually.

# Chapter 6

The bigger picture

# 6.1 Computing and the environment

It's hard to imagine what life would be like without the internet, social media, search engines and e-commerce. Global demand for smartphones, tablets and other forms of **computing technology**, including embedded processors, web servers, sensors and hard drives, is growing rapidly year on year. At the same time, the pace of new product releases and consumers' desire to own the latest model is shortening the lifespan of these devices. The average life expectancy of a smartphone, for example, is estimated to be less than two years. The more computing technology we buy, the more we throw away.

Not surprisingly, the manufacture, use and disposal of computing technology have a significant impact on the environment, using up dwindling resources of non-renewable materials, creating massive piles of potentially harmful **e-waste**, consuming vast quantities of energy and damaging people's health.

## Manufacture

Manufacturing a smartphone, a PC or any other piece of computing technology is a complex process, starting with the extraction of raw materials and ending with the finished item being shipped to the customer, with lots of stages in between. This makes it difficult to determine accurately the overall environmental impact, although there's no doubt that it's considerable.

### Raw material extraction

A number of non-renewable natural resources are used in the manufacture of computer products. They include sand (to make glass for screens), oil (used to make plastics) and various metals used in wiring and circuit boards. Some of the metals used, such as silver, gold, copper and palladium, are precious and in short supply. Others, such as arsenic, cadmium and chromium, are hazardous and pose a serious health risk. Radioactive metals used in computer products, such as uranium and thorium, can contaminate air, soil and groundwater, and are toxic to human health.

In some regions of the world, mining of raw materials is poorly regulated. Excavation causes extensive damage to the local environment, scarring the landscape with unsightly holes and waste heaps, contaminating water

# The bigger picture

## Extend your knowledge

China is the world's largest producer of rare earth metals – a group of 17 chemical elements that, due to their unique magnetic, luminescent and electrochemical properties, help improve the performance of computing technology and make it more energy efficient.

## Extend your knowledge

The United Nations University has estimated that the manufacture of a computer and monitor weighing 24 kilograms requires ten times the amount of fossil fuels (240 kilograms), approximately the same weight of chemicals and around 1,500 litres of water.

supplies and endangering wildlife habitats. Poorly equipped miners working in dangerous conditions run the risk of being seriously injured and are also susceptible to long-term respiratory illnesses, such as silicosis, bronchitis or lung cancer.

## Production

Once extracted, the raw materials are shipped to factories – often thousands of miles away – to be manufactured into components, such as circuit boards, chips, screens, disk drives and cases.

In turn, the components are dispatched onwards for assembly into finished products.

The manufacture of computing technology is energy intensive. Large amounts of non-renewable fossil fuels, such as coal and oil, are used during the process. Burning fossil fuels produces carbon dioxide ($CO_2$) and contributes to global warming.

Semiconductors are present in every piece of computing technology. Manufacturing semiconductors is highly water intensive. For example, a factory producing 40,000 semiconductors a month uses around 20 million litres of water a day – on a par with the consumption of a city with a population of 60,000. This can result in water shortages in areas where semiconductor factories are located, and untreated wastewater discharge can cause environmental pollution.

This table lists six of the most hazardous materials used in the manufacture of computing technology.

| Material | Examples of use |
| --- | --- |
| Cadmium | A metal used in the manufacture of rechargeable batteries, printer inks and toners. |
| Lead | A metal used in the manufacture of circuit boards and cable sheathing. |
| Mercury | A metal used in the manufacture of LCD screens. |
| Hexavalent chromium | A chemical compound used to make casings. |
| Polychlorinated biphenyls (PCBs) | Toxic compounds added to plastics, circuit boards, and connectors to make them more fire retardant. |
| Polybrominated diphenyl ethers | |

Research indicates that exposure to these materials is harmful to human health, causing both physical and neurological damage. Furthermore, chemical emissions and wastewater from manufacturing plants put people living in the vicinity at risk.

There is growing recognition of the need to address this problem.

The EU Restriction of Hazardous Substances (RoHS) Directive was transposed into UK law in 2013. It restricts the use of all six of the materials listed in the table above, forcing manufacturers of computing technology to replace them with safer materials.

At the same time, governments are imposing tough recycling targets designed to ensure that more reusable material is recovered from redundant computing technology, and reused so that fewer raw materials are needed and reserves of scarce resources are protected.

Growing public awareness is putting pressure on manufacturers to improve working conditions in their plants and impose stricter requirements on their component suppliers.

## Usage

The amount of energy consumed in the manufacturing process pales into insignificance when compared with the energy required to keep mobile phones, computers, networks, telecommunication links, etc. up and running day after day. Even though each individual device doesn't require a huge amount of electricity, close to two billion connected PCs and laptops and more than six billion mobile devices collectively do.

In recent years considerable efforts have been made to improve the energy efficiency of computing devices. However, the amount of energy they actually consume depends on how they are used and what they are used for. The task that a computer is performing and the software being used are key determinants of the actual energy usage. High-end applications, complex calculations, 3-D modelling and video games are particularly power hungry.

Cloud computing (see section 4.2, page 151) and data centres in particular are major energy guzzlers. Vast amounts of electricity are needed to power and cool all the computer equipment that is needed, putting them ahead of the aviation industry in terms of the energy they consume. The worst culprits are the small, inefficient data centres hosted by private organisations and government departments, which tend to be far less efficient than the large facilities operated by cloud providers such as Google® and Apple.

Energy efficiency measures and the use of renewable energy can significantly reduce the **carbon footprint** of data centres. Facebook, for example, has built a huge data centre in northern Sweden, just 100 km south of the Arctic Circle. Its location was selected because of its access to renewable hydroelectricity and the cold climate that helps to keep the servers cool.

> **Did you know?**
>
> A lot of energy is wasted while a computer or printer sits idle. Using the 'sleep mode' when a device is not in use can reduce consumption by more than 50 per cent.

> **Activity 1** ?
>
> Research why using a laptop rather than a desktop is more energy efficient.

> **Key term**
>
> **Carbon footprint**: the amount of carbon dioxide an individual or organisation produces as a result of the energy they consume.

> **Activity 2** ?
>
> Data centres consume large amounts of energy.
> 1 Research what this energy is used for.
> 2 Identify four measures that can be taken to make data centres more environmentally friendly.

## Disposal

The disposal of redundant computing technology represents another serious threat to the environment. The quantity of e-waste is growing at a tremendous pace. According to the UN's StEP Initiative, e-waste will soon weigh as much as eleven of the great Egyptian pyramids.

Although great efforts are now being made to recycle more e-waste, large amounts are still shipped overseas to developing countries where they are dumped in landfill sites. This can have serious consequences for the environment and public health. The problem is compounded by the fact that the developing nations themselves are generating more and more waste of their own.

E-waste that is not recycled properly can be a serious health and environmental issue. As you know, computer products contain a whole host of dangerous materials. Once a computer is dumped in a landfill site, the likelihood is that some, if not all, of these toxic substances will leak out into the ground, contaminating water supplies, infiltrating the food chain and polluting the air.

For every one million mobile phones, 24 kg of gold, 250 kg of silver and nine tonnes of copper can be recovered. The presence of these valuable metals in old computing technology is a powerful incentive for local people living near the landfill sites, many of whom are desperately poor, to try to recover them. However, dismantling old computer equipment without protective clothing and specialist training is extremely dangerous. People who do so risk exposure to hazardous materials such as mercury and lead and are in danger of inhaling toxic fumes.

### Did you know?

Electronic waste is expected to top 60 million tonnes globally by 2017 – an increase of a third in five years.

### Activity 3 ?

'One person's cast-off is another person's treasured possession.'
Research, then briefly describe two initiatives that aim to prolong the life of pre-owned computing technology.

The Waste Electrical and Electronic Equipment (WEEE) Regulations (2013) set targets for the collection, recycling and recovery of computing technology and other electronic items. They apply to businesses but not to individuals.

The aim of responsible recycling is to recover valuable metals and reusable components such as plastic, glass and metal, and to dispose of dangerous substances safely.

Major manufacturers of computing technology now have recycling programmes. In developing countries there are some promising initiatives to create state-of-the-art recycling plants that can turn e-waste into an e-opportunity.

## Preserving the environment

The picture is not entirely bleak. Computing technology is at the heart of efforts to combat climate change, provide disaster warnings, protect endangered species and habitats, and reduce energy consumption.

### Climate change

NASA is analysing satellite data and measuring sea surface temperatures to learn more about how and why sea levels are rising.

Networks of wireless sensor probes are used to gather information about glaciers. The probes are placed under the surface of the ice and measure temperature, pressure, stress, weather and sub-glacial movement. A base station collects the data from them. The system is helping scientists to understand more about the speed at which glaciers are melting.

Researchers at the University of Oxford are using spare home computer time to establish if global warming is to blame for heavy flooding in the UK in recent years.

### Early warning

Tsunami early warning systems use sensor networks to detect approaching tsunamis and a communications infrastructure to issue timely warnings so that coastal areas at risk can be evacuated.

### Conservation

Information from GPS and satellites is being used to track Malaysian elephants. The results are analysed by computer to help improve conservation strategies and assess the effectiveness of the Malaysian Government's elephant conservation programme.

Miniature transponders fitted to bees allow scientists to study the effects of disease and pesticides.

Mobile phones are being used to listen out for illegal logging activities in the rainforest and provide rangers with real-time alerts.

### Energy

Engineers at Manchester Metropolitan University are working on a project to make buildings more energy efficient. Sensors in each room monitor light levels, temperature, how many people are present and electricity consumption. Real-time analysis of the room data enables automatic adjustment of electricity usage.

A lioness with a tracking device. GPS collars help to monitor and conserve wildlife.

# The bigger picture

The latest generation of giant solar energy farms uses sensors to track the movement of the sun and computer-controlled motors to adjust the position of the solar panels to optimise power generation. Developments in battery storage allows surplus electricity to be stored.

## Exam tip

Make sure you give real positive and negative examples of how computing technology affects the environment.

## Exam-style question

Discuss the impact of computing technology on the environment.
**(6 marks)**

## Summary

- Some of the materials used in the manufacture of computer components are non-renewable and in short supply. Others are dangerous and pose a risk to human health.
- The Restriction of Hazardous Substances (RoHS) Directive restricts the use of hazardous materials in computing technology, forcing producers to find more environmentally friendly alternatives.
- Computing technology consumes huge amounts of energy. Data centres are one of the worst culprits.
- Energy efficiency measures and use of renewable energy can significantly reduce the carbon footprint of computing technology.
- There is a possible health risk, especially for children, from exposure to the electromagnetic fields generated by wireless devices, such as smartwatches and smart clothing.
- Unregulated disposal of e-waste in landfill sites poses a significant threat to the environment.
- The Waste Electrical and Electronic Equipment (WEEE) regulations set targets for responsible recycling of e-waste.
- Computing technology is helping to preserve the environment in a number of ways, including monitoring and modelling climate change, conservation and smart energy.

## Checkpoint

### Strengthen

**S1** Identify two hazardous substances used in the manufacture of computing technology.

**S2** Which UK law restricts the use of hazardous substances in the manufacture of computing technology?

**S3** Why is dumping e-waste in landfill sites harmful to the environment?

**S4** List two ways of reducing the environmental damage caused by data centres.

**S5** List two ways in which computing technology is helping to preserve the environment.

### Challenge

**C1** Summarise the health risks associated with the manufacture and disposal of computing technology.

**C2** Describe three ways in which computing technology can help to reduce energy consumption.

How confident do you feel about your answers to these questions? If you're not sure you answered them well, reread this section and have another go at the activities.

# 6.2 Privacy

Now that you know about the damaging environmental impact that computing technology has, does it make you have second thoughts about swapping your smartphone for the latest model? Might you decide that your concern for the environment outweighs your desire for a new phone? If so, you are making an ethical decision. **Ethics** relate to what is right and wrong and govern a person's behaviour.

An action might be legal, but not necessarily ethical. For example, it's perfectly legal to leave your old desktop computer gathering dust in the attic, but if you know that someone in a developing country would benefit enormously from having it, the right thing to do might be to dust it down and pass it on to them.

Computing technology confers a wide range of social and economic benefits, but it also creates a host of challenging ethical issues. **Privacy** and security are two of them.

While most people would agree that computing technology has helped to create a much more open society, some would argue that it comes at too high a cost. The amount of personally identifiable information that is gathered, stored and analysed represents a massive invasion of privacy.

## Personal data

Every time you post an update on social media, sign up for an online account, use a web-based email service or a search engine you are adding, knowingly or unknowingly, to an enormous hoard of **personal data** that is held about you – where you live, what you look like, who your friends are, your likes and dislikes, your bank account details, products you're interested in buying, the route you take to school each morning.

This personal data is stored on servers that belong to online services, such as Facebook and Google®, not to you.

Every organisation you come into contact with, not just the online companies, is likely to collect information about you. Your school, for example, stores your attendance record, your end-of-year exam results, which books you've borrowed from the library, the after-school activities you take part in and much more besides. Does this worry you?

# The bigger picture

Some people are very concerned about the amount of personal information that is collected, often without their consent and over which they believe they have little or no control. They are worried about who has access to it, what they are using it for, how secure it is and how accurate it is.

Weak security could result in personal information falling into the wrong hands, making people vulnerable to phishing attacks, scams, **identity theft** and fraud.

Sometimes the information is inaccurate, but getting it changed or removed is extremely difficult, if not impossible. It's not unheard of for inaccurate information about a person to follow them throughout their entire life, affecting how they are seen and treated by others.

> **Key term**
>
> **Identity theft**: the stealing of another person's personal details, such as their bank account number, sort code or passport number, for the purpose of making purchases and running up debts in their name.

> **Did you know?**
>
> The UK Data Protection Act (1998) controls how organisations and the government can use personal data. It specifies the following principles.
>
> - Data must be processed fairly and lawfully.
> - Data must be obtained and used only for the specific and lawful purposes for which it was collected.
> - Data must be adequate, relevant and not excessive.
> - Data must be accurate and up to date.
> - Data must be kept for no longer than necessary.
> - Data must be kept secure.
> - Data must **not** be transferred to regions not bound by similar principles of the Act.

> **Activity 5**
>
> 1  What information can you find out about yourself by typing your name into a search engine? Is it accurate? What sort of impression of you does it portray?
> 2  Research the Safe Harbor Decision privacy principle. Why has the EU declared it invalid?

One reason why so many people voluntarily give away information about themselves is that it enables an organisation to understand their needs better and provide them with a more personalised service. For example, setting up an account with an online supplier makes it faster and more convenient to purchase from them.

But do these benefits outweigh the drawbacks?

You might not mind that an online retailer knows who your favourite band is if it means you get to hear quickly when their next album is released, but is it right to target a financially vulnerable person with adverts for products they will want but can't afford?

## Did you know?

Cookies are small data files that keep a record of your web browsing history. They record which websites you visit and how often, which products or services you buy or show an interest in. Cookies enable online stores to learn a lot about you.

The Privacy and Electronic Communications Regulations (2011) gives consumers the right to opt out of having data about their browsing habits collected in this way.

Unlike a cookie, spyware is a computer program stored on your hard drive (usually without you realising it's there) that collects information about you and transmits it to a third party. It represents another serious threat to privacy.

## Big data

Data analysts are able to learn more and more about us and gain insights into our behaviour by analysing huge volumes of personal data gathered from various sources.

Analysis of so-called 'big data' can benefit society. For example, by helping to identify adverse side effects of drugs that might otherwise go unnoticed, optimising energy use in cities and providing insights into the spread of disease.

But is the price we pay too high? Where do we draw the line? Big data comprises large amounts of information, each piece of which on its own could be seen as being harmless, for example your phone number, what music you download, your hobbies, etc. However, when collated together these individual bits of information produce a very accurate, detailed profile of an individual, revealing far more about them than they might have willingly disclosed. This might lead to the individual becoming a victim of identity theft or an intruder illegally accessing personal information through social engineering. (See 'Personal data' on page 213.)

## Surveillance

Have you any idea how often you've been watched on CCTV today? Could a drone have been hovering overhead taking aerial photographs of you on your walk to school? If you've driven anywhere by car, travelled by public transport or been in a shop, the chances are you've been recorded by some form of **surveillance technology**.

Most people are willing to allow the security forces to use surveillance technology to track people's movements and tap their phones if it enables them to uncover terrorist plots. But what if it were used by companies to monitor your shopping habits or by criminals noting the time you leave the house each morning? It's not unheard of for employers to use hidden cameras to check up on their staff. Is this acceptable?

Some people believe that use of surveillance technology goes too far. In 2013 Edward Snowden, a so-called '**whistle-blower**', raised awareness of the extent to which governments worldwide are now monitoring and spying on their citizens.

---

## Activity 6 ?

Find two examples of how society is benefiting from big data analysis.

---

## Key terms

**Surveillance technology**: CCTV, drones, number plate recognition, bugging and tracking devices used to monitor and record people's activities, often without their knowledge.

**Whistle-blower**: someone who draws attention to the activities of an organisation or person believed to be acting illegally or unethically.

215

# The bigger picture

## Activity 7   ?

The right to privacy must be balanced against the needs of society. Describe two situations in which you believe an invasion of privacy is justified. Explain your reasoning.

## Key term

**Location-based services**: services that enable people to access and share real-time location information online.

## Activity 8   ?

Describe three ways in which location-based services can benefit a user and three risks associated with their use.

## Did you know?

UK police track vehicle movements in real time using automatic number plate recognition and CCTV. Records can be kept for two years to be analysed for intelligence.

CCTV combined with facial recognition software enables the police to identify and track specific individuals.

## Location-based services

With the help of **location-based services** and Wi-Fi, people can share their current location, arrange to meet up with friends nearby, check in to a venue, find their way to a particular location and much more. A drawback is that location-based services also allow other people to track your movements, find out where you live and what you are doing. This can be dangerous and represents a huge invasion of privacy.

## Privacy-enhancing tools

Privacy-enhancing tools, while not 100 per cent effective, do give some protection against privacy invasion. This table lists some of the most popular of these tools.

| Tool | Purpose |
|---|---|
| Encryption | Prevents unauthorised people from reading your data. |
| Cookie cleaners, anti-spyware and ad blockers | Software that detects and removes cookies, spyware and adware installed on your computer. |
| Identity management services | A trusted third party holds evidence of your identity and issues you with an identifier that enables you to conduct transactions with other parties without revealing any personal information about yourself. |
| Password managers | Stores all your website login information in an encrypted password database with a master password, which is the only one you have to remember. |

## Cyber-security

As you learnt in Chapter 5 (see page 192), hacking represents a serious security threat.

The Computer Misuse Act (1990) makes hacking a crime. It identifies three types of illegal activity.

- Unauthorised access to computer material, either a program or data.
- Unauthorised access with intent to commit further offences (e.g. accessing personal data about a person so as to steal their identity).
- Intentional and unauthorised destruction of software or data (e.g. by installing malware).

A 2015 amendment to the Act grants immunity from prosecution to the security services, enabling them to hack data on laptops and mobile phones, and in databases belonging to suspected criminals.

## Activity 9 ?

Research the 'Carphone Warehouse Data Breach' of 2015. How many customer records were thought to have been stolen? What are the implications of this breach for both the customers and the company?

## Summary

- Computing technology enables organisations to gather, store and analyse vast quantities of personal information about the people they come into contact with.
- Individuals give away all sorts of personal information about themselves online.
- Collecting and analysing information about the people they come into contact with enables organisations to provide a more personalised service.
- Big data analysis benefits society at the expense of many individuals' privacy.
- Surveillance technology helps keep us secure, but encroaches on our privacy. It is difficult to determine what level of surveillance is acceptable.
- The Computer Misuse Act (1990) makes hacking illegal.

## Checkpoint

### Strengthen

**S1** Describe two ways in which an individual's personal data could end up stored in databases owned by a third party.

**S2** What might happen if personal information falls into the wrong hands?

**S3** List two privacy-enhancing tools and describe what they do.

**S4** List the activities that the Computer Misuse Act (1990) makes illegal.

### Challenge

**C1** Why do some people decide that the benefits of revealing personal information about themselves outweigh the drawbacks?

**C2** Describe a situation where the right to privacy is less important than the needs of society.

How confident do you feel about your answers to these questions? If you're not sure you answered them well, reread this section and have another go at the activities.

# The bigger picture

## 6.3 Digital inclusion

### Learning outcomes

By the end of this section you should be able to:

* explain how people benefit from being 'technology-empowered' and the disadvantages of being 'technology-excluded'.
* describe measures that are being taken to promote digital inclusion.

### Key terms

**Digital inclusion**: ensuring that everyone has affordable access to computing technology and the necessary skills to take advantage of it.

**Digital divide**: the gap between people who are technology-empowered and those who are technology-excluded.

Computing technology is a great enabler, giving many people access to news, information, products and services at any time wherever they are. But those people who neither have the opportunity nor knowledge to use this technology are excluded from the advantages it provides. Is this fair?

**Digital inclusion** is about providing everyone with affordable access to computing technology and the skills to use it.

The gap between those who are 'technology-empowered' and those who are 'technology-excluded' is known as the **digital divide**.

There is a digital divide between industrialised and developing countries and also between people who live in the same country.

### Impact

There are many reasons why technology exclusion is not a good idea.

| Information and services | The internet is becoming the default option for accessing information, public services and entertainment. |
|---|---|
| Employment | Having poor digital literacy skills makes it harder to find a job and limits employment opportunities, relegating individuals to poorly paid work with little prospect of progression. |
| Democracy | The internet gives people a voice and lets them express their views to a worldwide audience. This is particularly important where citizens have limited freedom of expression. |
| Economic growth | Businesses that are able to exploit computing technology to the full have a competitive advantage over those that can't. |
| Saving money | Paying bills and shopping online often saves consumers money and gives them better protection. |
| Social isolation | Having access to the internet helps people to keep in touch with friends and relatives. |

### Towards digital inclusion

Data from the Office for National Statistics suggest that the UK is making good progress towards achieving digital inclusion for its citizens. Figures for 2015 for England, Scotland and Wales show that:

* the internet was accessed every day by 78 per cent of adults (39.3 million), compared with 35 per cent (16.2 million) in 2006;

218

- 96 per cent of adults aged 16 to 24 accessed the internet 'on the go', compared with only 29 per cent of those aged 65 years and over;
- 61 per cent of adults used social networking and, of those, 79 per cent did so every day or almost every day;
- 76 per cent of adults bought goods or services online;
- 86 per cent of households (22.5 million) had internet access, up from 57 per cent in 2006.

Other industrialised nations in North America, Europe and Northern Asia are also doing well.

The same can't be said for other parts of the world. According to the United Nations' *State of Broadband* report (2015), billions of people living in the developing world are still without broadband internet, including 90 per cent of those living in the poorest nations.

Age, disability, disinterest, poverty and cultural norms all play a part in digital exclusion, but lack of connectivity is one of the major causes.

The good news is that, according to the World Bank, 77 per cent of the world's population already live within range of a mobile phone network. In areas with a limited or non-existent landline infrastructure, mobile phone technology can fill the gap. Even though the number of phones per 100 people in poor countries is much lower than in the developed world, they are having a huge impact.

## Did you know?

Facebook plans to use drones and satellites to bring the internet to Africa. They have also developed an app, called Free Basics, which provides free basic access to services.

## Activity 10 ?

Use the internet to find some actual examples of how mobile phones are being used in Africa or elsewhere to promote digital inclusion. Write a brief report summarising your findings.

Efforts to bridge the digital divide require more than simply giving people internet access. The UK's digital inclusion strategy sets out the actions that the government and its partners are taking to reduce digital exclusion.

## Activity 11 ?

Identify five actions a government can take to reduce digital exclusion.

Ambitious digital literacy programs are under way in India, Kenya, Colombia and elsewhere to ensure that people have the know-how and skills they need to exploit digital technology to the full

# The bigger picture

## Summary

- Digital inclusion means that everyone has affordable access to computing technology as well as the skills to use it.

- A number of factors contribute to the digital divide – lack of or poor connectivity is one of the main ones.

- Someone who is 'technology-excluded' misses out on all the opportunities computing technology offers.

## Checkpoint

### Strengthen

**S1** What is meant by the terms 'technology-empowered' and 'technology-excluded'?

**S2** List three drawbacks of being 'technology-excluded'.

**S3** List four factors that contribute to the digital divide.

**S4** Describe two ways of providing access to the internet in areas with a poor landline infrastructure.

### Challenge

**C1** Access to the internet is a key factor in reducing the digital divide. Describe two further measures that governments can take to promote digital inclusion.

How confident do you feel about your answers to these questions? If you're not sure you answered them well, reread this section and have another go at the activities.

# 6.4 Professionalism

Computer scientists write software to make computers do new things or accomplish tasks more efficiently, create mobile apps, design and build embedded systems, devise security policies, invent new products and much more besides.

Some work for big multinational computing companies, such as Microsoft® and Apple, others for small start-ups; some are self-employed, some are employed in the IT departments of organisations such as hospitals, universities and companies.

Wherever they work they are expected to behave ethically and demonstrate **professionalism**.

The British Computer Society (BCS) is the Chartered Institute for IT. The BCS Code of Conduct sets out the professional standards its members are expected to uphold. Among many other matters, it specifies that computer scientists must:

- respect the privacy, security and wellbeing of others and the environment;
- avoid injuring others, their property, reputation, or employment;
- develop their professional knowledge, skills and competence on a continuing basis;
- be familiar and comply with relevant legislation;
- **not** disclose confidential information;
- **not** misrepresent or withhold information on the performance of products, systems or services.

## Key term

**Professionalism**: the skill and competence expected of a person in a professional setting.

## Did you know?

Most computer scientists pay an annual membership fee to belong to a professional association. This gives them access to specialist technical conferences, training and publications. It also provides them with an opportunity to interact and share knowledge and expertise with each other. Having membership of a professional association on their Curriculum Vitae (CV) sometimes carries weight when a computer scientist is applying for a new job.

The three main professional bodies for computer scientists in the UK are:

- The British Computer Society (BCS)
- The Institute of Electrical and Electronics Engineers (IEEE)
- The Association for Computing Machinery (ACM).

## Exam-style question

Airtest produces exhaust emissions testing software. A programmer discovers that there is a bug in the software that produces inaccurate results under particular circumstances.

State what course of action the programmer should take and explain why. **(3 marks)**

## Exam tip

This is a scenario-based question, so make sure you relate your answer to the scenario – don't mention what you personally would do, but what the Airtest programmer should do. Don't forget to refer back to the code of conduct.

# The bigger picture

## Summary

- Computer scientists must abide by the law.
- They should behave ethically by adhering to a professional code of conduct.
- It is important that programmers demonstrate professionalism as the work they do could put the lives of other people at risk.

## Checkpoint

### Strengthen

**S1** What does the BCS Code of Conduct say a computer scientist should do?

### Challenge

**C1** What does 'professionalism' mean for a computer scientist?

How confident do you feel about your answers to these questions? If you're not sure you answered them well, reread this section and have another go at the activities.

# 6.5 The legal impact

## Intellectual property

Intellectual property (IP) – not to be confused with an IP address – is a unique creative product of a human mind. A piece of software, a computer game, a design for a new processor, a digital image, a piece of music and a literary work are all examples of IP. Each of them was created by somebody, is unique and has a commercial value.

## Copyright and patents

The Copyright, Designs and Patents Act (1988) makes it illegal to copy, modify or distribute intellectual property without permission.

That said, there are a multitude of peer-to-peer networks, torrent sharing websites and forums on the internet that allow people to download copyrighted software without paying for it. Not only is this illegal, it is also unethical, since it means that the programmer who wrote the code doesn't get the money that is due to them.

Copyright only protects the expression of an idea, not the idea itself. So if you were to develop an original piece of software, its source code would be protected, but there's nothing to stop someone else from copying the idea and writing a program that essentially performs the same task. You would have to prove that the similarities between the two programs are more than just coincidence and can only be explained by copying.

The © symbol indicates that a piece of software, a movie or some other type of artefact is protected by copyright.

**Did you know?**

In 1994, Apple agreed to license parts of its GUI (see section 4.4, page 162) to Microsoft® for use in the first version of Microsoft® Windows®. When Microsoft® released Windows® 2.0, it used the overlapping windows feature of the Macintosh OS, which was not included in the original licence agreement. Consequently, Apple sued Microsoft® for copyright infringement.

A **patent** offers more protection than copyright. It protects the idea or design of an invention, rather than just a particular form of it. In order to get a patent you have to be able to demonstrate that what you have invented is distinct from anything else that already exists. A patent holder has the exclusive right for 20 years to make, use and sell their invention.

**Key terms**

**Intellectual property (IP)**: a creation of the human mind that is unique and has a commercial value.

**Patent**: an exclusive right granted to an inventor to make, use and sell an invention for a fixed period of time.

**Did you know?**

The creators of the illegal software sharing website, The Pirate Bay, received a prison sentence and were fined over US$4,000,000 for hosting hyperlinks to illegally obtained software and media.

**Top tip**

Make sure you know which laws affect the use of computing technology, including the Data Protection Act (1998), the Computer Misuse Act (1990), the Copyright, Design and Patents Act (1988) and the Regulation of Investigatory Powers Act (2000).

Keep an eye out for any amendments to these laws or for relevant new government legislation.

# The bigger picture

## Did you know?

For years, various smartphone manufacturers including Apple and Samsung have been battling in the courts over patent infringements. Apple alleged that Samsung had stolen the 'look and feel' of its iPhone and used it in the Galaxy smartphone.

There is a real concern that the inventiveness that patents are designed to encourage will suffer as a consequence of these so-called 'patent wars', with manufacturers spending their money on lawsuits rather than on new inventions. This would be very bad news for consumers.

## Activity 13

1   Get into groups of three. Each person in the group should describe how they would feel if an app they have created was made available for free on the internet, without their permission.

2   Create a podcast for software developers, explaining how software can be protected as intellectual copyright.

## Key terms

**Creative Commons**: an organisation that allows people to set copyright terms for their intellectual property. One use of a Creative Commons licence is to allow people to copy material as long as it is not used commercially.

**Open-source software**: software that is free to edit and redistribute.

## Exam-style question

Assess the extent to which the patent system is a barrier to technological innovation. **(4 marks)**

## Exam tip

The command word here is 'assess', which means you should consider both sides of the argument and come to a conclusion.

## Licensing

Every piece of software, even if it is free, has a licence. Even though the user purchases a piece of software, the licence states that they don't actually own it. The licence allows the buyer to use the software subject to the licence terms, but the manufacturer retains ownership. Before you can install the software you have to agree to the terms of its licence. These specify:

- how many copies of the software you are allowed to use;
- whether you can install the software on more than one computer;
- what type of organisation can use the software – some licences are for charities, students or home users only;
- how long the software can be used for – perpetual software licences last forever, but some licence agreements expire unless you renew them.

You are usually not allowed to resell the software. Paid-for software is often supplied with a unique licence key, which certifies that the software is genuine and prevents illegal copying.

If a computer scientist wants to permit other people to use their code without charge, they can use an open-source licence to specify what restrictions (if any) there are.

A **Creative Commons** licence provides a way for the creator of a piece of music, a photograph or other form of intellectual property - including software - to allow other people to use it providing they abide by the conditions specified in the licence.

## Open-source and proprietary software

**Open-source software** is freely available on the internet. Anyone is permitted to edit the code and pass it on to others, providing they don't charge a fee.

The advantages and disadvantages of open-source software are shown in this table.

| Advantages | Disadvantages |
|---|---|
| • It is free to use. <br> • It can be modified. <br> • It can be used to demonstrate programming concepts. | • It might not be particularly 'user friendly' and might look unprofessional. <br> • There might be little or no technical support available. <br> • Criminals may be able to identify and exploit vulnerabilities in the code. |

**Proprietary software** is the opposite of open source – it is closed source. This means its source code is protected and users are not allowed to modify it.

On the plus side, proprietary software is extensively tested prior to release, any bugs that do come to light thereafter are quickly fixed and there is plenty of user support. The drawback is that if the software doesn't exactly do what you want it to, you're not allowed to change it.

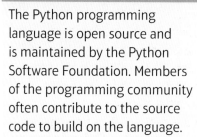

**Did you know?**

The Python programming language is open source and is maintained by the Python Software Foundation. Members of the programming community often contribute to the source code to build on the language.

**Key term**

**Proprietary software**: software that belongs to an individual or a company. Its licence specifies that users are not allowed to modify the source code and places restrictions on its use.

**Did you know?**

Microsoft® Windows® 10, iTunes, Adobe Photoshop and Mac OSX are all examples of proprietary software.

**Activity 14    ?**

Create a table that summarises the differences between open-source and proprietary software.

## Summary

- A programmer loses out financially if their software is downloaded illegally.
- The Copyright, Designs and Patents Act (1988) makes it illegal to copy, modify or distribute intellectual property without permission.
- Copyright protects the expression of an idea, not the idea itself.
- A patent offers more protection than copyright. It protects the idea of an invention rather than just a particular form of it.
- A software licence specifies how a piece of software can be used.
- Open-source software is freely available and can be edited and shared.
- The source code of proprietary software is protected and users are not allowed to modify it.

## Checkpoint

### Strengthen

**S1** Describe the purpose of a software licence.

**S2** What are the main differences between open-source and proprietary software?

### Challenge

**C1** Explain how a patent would protect you as an inventor of a product.

**C2** Identify relevant legislation that computer scientists should be familiar with.

How confident do you feel about your answers to these questions? If you're not sure you answered them well, reread this section to enhance your knowledge.

# Preparing for your exam

This section of the book will help you to prepare for the external assessment. GCSE (9–1) Computer Science has two written examination papers and a project. You must carry out the project in the final year of your course and sit both examinations in your final term.

## Paper 1 – Principles of Computer Science

This paper is worth 40 per cent of your GCSE Computer Science qualification and is 1 hour and 40 minutes in length. It is designed to test your knowledge and understanding of the principles of computer science, and covers aspects of all six topics listed in the specification.

The number of questions in the paper can vary, but you must try to answer all of them. Most questions have some straightforward parts and some more challenging ones; even if you can't answer all of a question you should be able to tackle at least parts of it.

## Understanding the questions

Each question begins with a short introduction. Don't be tempted to skip these as they give guidance as to the sort of answer expected. You could miss out on marks by giving generic responses when a contextualised answer is required.

It's important to pay attention to the command words at the start of questions. These indicate what sort of answer is needed and how much depth you should go into. The meaning of some frequently used command words is described below.

**State, give, name, identify, list.** Recalling facts. For example: 'State what is meant by the term overflow.' or 'Give **one** reason why programmers use subprograms.' A simple statement will usually suffice as an answer.

**Describe.** Giving a description of something. For example: 'Describe how binary digits are used to represent bitmap images.' Use the number of marks allocated as a guide to how many distinct points you should make.

**Explain.** Providing points that are linked to a justification. For example: 'Explain why increasing the size of the cache will improve a computer's performance.' This requires you to describe the purpose of the cache and then go on to explain why its size makes a difference.

**Calculate.** Carrying out a calculation. For example: 'Calculate the file size in bytes of a 24-bit colour image that has a width of 600 pixels and a height of 400 pixels.' Remember that you are not allowed to use calculators. Instead you should show the relevant stages involved in carrying out the calculation.

**Compare.** Observing similarities and differences between two or more alternatives. For example: 'Rosie is developing a program to control a smart lighting system. Compare using an interpreter with using a compiler to translate the program into executable code.' In this instance it's advisable to take account of the context in your answer.

**Evaluate.** Making critical judgements by considering relevant information. For example: 'Evaluate the use of a "divide and conquer" strategy for sorting and searching data.'

**Discuss.** Exploring an issue, situation or problem. For example: 'Discuss the ways in which computing technology can make a positive contribution to household energy consumption.' You must structure your response and use appropriate evidence to support your conclusions.

**Show.** Show the sequence of steps involved in applying a bubble sort algorithm to this list of names: "William", "Rhys", "Maddie", "Greta", "Edward", "Daani", "Anja".'

There will be at least one six-mark extended writing question in this paper. Make sure you allow enough time to plan your answer and try to use correct terminology where appropriate.

Write your answers in the spaces provided on the paper. Try not to use more space than is provided and if you do write your answer somewhere else make sure it is clearly labelled.

# Sample answers with comments

Here is a sample answer to a Paper 1 style question.

Smarts Leisure owns a chain of fitness centres throughout the north-west. Its head office is in Stockport. Each fitness centre has its own wireless LAN. All the fitness centres are connected to head office via a WAN.

1(a) (i) Identify **two** ways in which a LAN differs from a WAN. (2 marks)

1 LAN on one site.
2 WAN covers a wider geographic area.

(ii) Explain how devices are connected on a wireless network. (3 marks)

Radio waves are used to connect devices on a wireless network. Each device has a wireless network adapter that sends and receives radio signals. A router broadcasts a wireless signal that devices can detect and 'tune' into.

1(b) Files are divided up into packets before transmission. Two fields in a network packet are source and destination.

Give **two** additional fields found in a network packet. (2 marks)

1 Sender
2 Sequence Number

1(c) Members of a fitness centre can log on to Smarts Leisure's website to view details of their training.

Explain the server-side processing that takes place when a member views their training online. (3 marks)

The server receives the request from the client computer and retrieves training data from the database. It sends data to the client computer.

1(d) Smarts Leisure is concerned about cyber-security.

Discuss what measures Smarts Leisure should take to reduce the security risks from social engineering. (6 marks)

Social engineering involves tricking people into revealing confidential information. Hackers use a variety of methods to get people to give away confidential information.

An attacker could call the Smarts Leisure help desk pretending to be an employee who has forgotten their password. Staff might be fooled into helping them to log on remotely and reset their password.

Smarts Leisure must make sure that all their employees are aware of this kind of attack and know that they should always verify a caller's identity before giving them access to the network or parting with sensitive information over the phone.

Emails that tempt users to click on a weblink are another risk. Staff might be fooled into filling in a web form that asks for personal information. Or without realising it they might allow Trojan software to be secretly installed on their computer, which will capture sensitive information and email it to an attacker.

Smarts Leisure must ensure that all their employees are aware that they must never reveal personal or sensitive information in response to an email, no matter who appears to have sent it. Hackers sometimes visit a company posing as a bogus employee or visitor. If they are allowed in, they can look for information lying on desks, listen in to conversations, plant a key logger or connect a laptop to the network.

Smarts Leisure has a lot of people going in and out of their fitness centres. This makes it more difficult to prevent unauthorised access. They should issue their employees with passes and restrict access to the office area to people with passes. Confidential information should never be left on desks and screen locks should be activated on all computers when not in use.

Smarts Leisure should consider employing someone to carry out penetration testing to identify which of its employees are vulnerable to social engineering. These employees can then be given training to help them spot an attack and respond appropriately.

*(Total for Question 1 = 16 marks)*

## Verdict

1(a) (i) The student has only given one difference between a LAN and a WAN, not the two that were required. Each answer should compare a LAN with a WAN.

> **Exam tip**
>
> They could have said that a LAN is relatively inexpensive to set up and run, whereas a WAN requires costly hardware and dedicated leased lines. Using 'whereas' is a good way of making sure you compare one thing with another.

1(a) (ii) The candidate has made three distinct points, demonstrating sound understanding.

1(b) There are lots of possible answers to this question, but you would get no marks for giving source or destination as an answer, since these are provided in the question. 'Sender' is just another name for 'source' so in this case the candidate only identified one additional field.

1(c) This question is worth three marks, suggesting that the examiner is expecting three distinct points to be made. The student has only given two points so loses out on a mark. They omitted to say that the server constructs a web page to display results of a search.

They have, however, related their answer to the scenario, which is a sensible thing to do.

> **Exam tip**
>
> Your answers should take account of the context of the question. You could miss out on marks by giving generic responses.

1(d) This question requires an extended answer.
The student has selected relevant knowledge and demonstrated good understanding of key concepts. They have produced a well-structured, coherent response, identifying risks and suggesting appropriate measures. Their answer takes account of the context, giving advice directed at Smarts Leisure.

## Paper 2 – Application of Computational Thinking

This paper is worth 40 per cent of your GCSE Computer Science qualification. It focuses on topics 1 and 2 of the subject content of the specification and assesses your computational thinking and problem-solving skills. It is 2 hours in length, which means you have plenty of reading and thinking time, as well as a chance to check your answers, especially the algorithms. (It's easy to overlook logic errors and to use the wrong comparison operator in an expression.)

Calculators are not allowed but you can use a stencil to help you draw flowchart symbols.

## Pseudo-code

Some of the questions will use pseudo-code. It's a good idea to familiarise yourself with the Edexcel pseudo-code before the exam.  But don't worry if you don't remember all the commands. You will have a clean copy of the pseudo-code booklet to refer to in the exam. You don't have to use the Edexcel pseudo-code in any of your answers. Any version is acceptable providing it is unambiguous and easy to follow.

## Understanding the questions

You should familiarise yourself with the scenario that appears at the start of the paper. It sets the context for the whole paper. Further information is given at the start of each question. Read this carefully. In some cases, you won't be able to answer the question without referring to it.

All the questions are compulsory. They are split into a number of parts, some more straightforward than others.

Here are some of the command words you might encounter in this paper.

**Amend.** Making changes. For example, amending an algorithm so that it performs differently or in order to correct an error.

**Assess.** Judging or deciding the value, or appropriateness, of something. For example, assessing the appropriateness of a particular data structure.

**Complete, fill in.** Filling in gaps. For example, completing a flowchart or a table.

**Construct, draw.** Creating something. For example, constructing a flowchart, an expression or a validation test.

**Write.** For example, a line of pseudo-code or an algorithm.

Longer answers in this paper are likely to involve creating an algorithm expressed either in pseudo-code or as a flowchart.

---

### Exam tip

Calculators aren't allowed in this exam. If you're no good at mental arithmetic, then you can at least show how the answer would be worked out.

### Exam tip

Look at the number of marks allocated to the question for an indication of how many separate points you need to give.

---

# Sample answers with comments

Here are sample answers to Paper 2 style questions.

1   The Riverside is a large, out-of-town shopping mall with shops, restaurants and leisure facilities.

(a) The rent that retailers pay depends on the area of their unit (in square metres) and the number of years they have been there.

The rental charge is £100 per square metre, with a discount of 1 per cent for each year of occupancy. Construct a general expression showing the rent that a retailer will have to pay.                                                        (2 marks)

rent = unitSize * (100 – years)

(b) The Riverside wants to limit the discount it gives to no more than 10 per cent.

Write an algorithm expressed in pseudo-code to calculate the rent for each retailer, taking into account the maximum discount.                              (2 marks)

IF years >= 10 THEN
    rent = unitSize * 90
ELSE
    rent = unitSize * (100 – years)
IFEND

2   The Riverside produces visitor statistics. Data about the number of people who visit the shopping mall each day is collected and analysed.

Complete the table to show an input, process and output.                     (2 marks)

| INPUT | PROCESS | OUTPUT |
|---|---|---|
| Number of visitors on each day for one year | Calculate overall total number of visitors in a year | Sum of visitor numbers for the year |
| Number of visitors on each day for one year | Calculate overall total number of visitors in each month. Sort month totals to find month with the highest number of visitors | Month with the highest number of visitors |

3   The number of security and medical staff required each day depends on how many visitors are expected.

The pseudo-code for a subprogram that calculates the number of security and medical staff required is shown.

| 1 | PROCEDURE staff_required |
|---|---|
| 2 | |
| 3 | SET days TO [80000, 30000, 30000, 50000, 55000, 60000, 100000] |
| 4 | SET useAgain TO 'no' |
| 5 | WHILE useAgain = 'yes' DO |
| 6 |     SEND 'Enter day number (Sunday = 0)' TO DISPLAY |
| 7 |     RECEIVE dayNumber FROM (INTEGER) KEYBOARD |
| 8 |     SET visitors TO days[dayNumber] |
| 10 |     SET security TO visitors DIV 1000 |
| 11 |     SET medical TO visitors DIV 20000 |
| 12 | |
| 13 |     SEND 'Do you want to enter another day (yes or no)?' TO DISPLAY |
| 14 |     RECEIVE useAgain FROM (STRING) KEYBOARD |
| 15 | END WHILE |
| 16 | END staff_required |

(a) There is a logic error in the algorithm.

Identify the error and explain how it can be corrected. (2 marks)

The variable useAgain is initialised to 'no' before the start of the while loop, so the loop never executes. The error can be corrected by amending the statement in line 4.

(b) Explain why the operator DIV is used in lines 10 and 11 rather than the divide (/) operator. (2 marks)

Only whole people are needed.

(c) Complete line 12 so that a sentence is displayed on the monitor stating:

'The number of security staff required is *** and the number of medical staff is ***.' (2 marks)

SEND 'The number of security staff required is' + security + 'and the number of medical staff is' + medical TO DISPLAY

(d) Using the algorithm, calculate the numbers of security and medical staff needed on a Thursday. (2 marks)

| Number of security staff needed: | 55 |
|---|---|
| Number of medical staff needed: | 2 |

(e) Explain the benefits of using subprograms when writing algorithms. (3 marks)

Makes main program clearer and easier to understand and shorter. No repeated blocks of code – can be reused from anywhere in the program – easier to test – can be reused in other programs.

4   The Riverside issues customers with a loyalty card, which they can use to get a discount in any of the shops. The discount varies according to how much they have already spent in the current year. If they have spent between £250 and £500 the discount is 5 per cent. If they have spent £500 or more it is 10 per cent.

Complete the flowchart to show how the discount is calculated.

(6 marks)

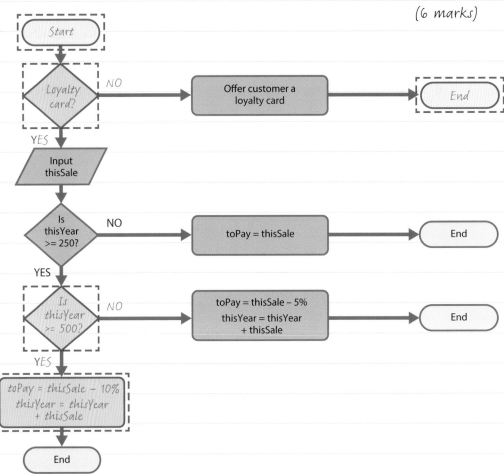

5   Riverside tries to keep the temperature constant at 20°C and the humidity at 50 per cent by opening air vents if it is too warm or too humid and closing them and using heaters when it is too cold.

Temperature and humidity sensors are located at various positions within the shopping mall. The external temperature is also monitored.

The air vents are operated by electric motors, which rotate a bar clockwise to open them and anticlockwise to close them.

If the temperature falls below 20°C the air vents are closed and the heaters are switched on. If the external temperature is 26°C or above and the air vents are open, then the air vents are closed and the air conditioning units are switched on.

(a) Complete the table to give the inputs and outputs of this system.          (6 marks)

| Inputs | Outputs |
| --- | --- |
| Internal temperature | Air vent motors |
| Humidity | Heaters |
| External temperature | Air conditioning unit |

(b) Write an algorithm to control the temperature and humidity. Use pseudo-code.          (9 marks)

```
SET heatersOn TO False #initialises variables
SET airVentsOpen TO False
SET airConOn TO False
SET riversideOpen TO True
WHILE riversideOpen = True DO #loops while shopping mall is open
      RECEIVE intTemp FROM (REAL) SENSOR
      RECEIVE humidity FROM (REAL) SENSOR
      RECEIVE extTemp FROM (REAL) SENSOR

      IF intTemp > 20 OR humidity > 50 THEN
            IF heatersOn = True THEN
                  SEND 'switch off signal' TO HEATERS
                  SET heatersOn TO False
            END IF
            SEND 'clockwise signal' TO AVMOTORS #opens air vents
            SET airVentsOpen TO True
      END IF
      IF intTemperature < 20 THEN
            IF airVentsOpen = TRUE THEN
                  SEND 'anticlockwise signal' TO AVMOTORS #closes air vents
                  SET airVentsOpen to False
            END IF
            SEND 'switch on signal' TO HEATERS
            SET heatersOn TO True
      END IF
      IF extTemp >= 26 AND airVentsOpen = True THEN
            SEND 'anticlockwise signal' TO AVMOTORS #closes air vents
            SET airVentsOpen to False
            SEND 'switch on signal' TO AIRCON
            SET airConOn TO True
      END IF
      SET riversideOpen TO check__if__open()
END WHILE
```

## Verdict

1(a) Order of precedence is key here. The student has used brackets so that the subtraction is done before the multiplication. Remember BIDMAS! This answer was awarded two marks.

1(b) In this question there was one mark for getting the condition in the IF statement correct – 'years > 10' would also have been correct. The second mark was for correctly calculating the rent in both cases.

2   One mark is awarded for each empty cell correctly filled in with the correct information.

The candidate has given a full description of the process needed to identify the month with the highest number of visitors.

3(a) The student has clearly identified the error and has indicated how it can be fixed but they haven't spelled it out. They should have given the correct code, i.e. SET useAgain TO 'yes'.

3(b) This explanation is far too vague. The candidate probably knew that the DIV operator returns the total number of times that one number divides into another without a remainder but should have spelled it out to be sure of getting two marks.

3(c) One mark for using the append operator (ampersand) and one mark for using the correct variables in the output statement.

3(d) Both calculations are correct.

3(e) The student has jotted down a list of separate benefits without any justification. A better answer would have been:

The use of subprograms makes code clearer and easier to understand (1) because the main program is shorter and doesn't contain any repeated blocks of code (1) and because by putting a name to a block of code it is easier to see at a glance what it does. (1)

4 The student has done a great job of completing the flowchart. Three marks are awarded for functionality. In other words, a solution that works. The other three marks are for correct notation.

5 There's a lot of text at the start of this question, but don't be tempted to skip it. Read it carefully and underline key words, these are references to values that need to be stored and processed.

5(a) The student achieved all six available marks for this question.

5(b) The student has written very clear, readable code and has earned all nine marks - three for the functionality of the algorithm, three for the accuracy of the pseudo-code and three for the efficiency of the solution.

This is a well thought-out response that includes keeping track of whether the heaters and air con units are on or off and whether the air vents are open or closed.

A few more explanatory comments would have been helpful, including an explanation of the subprogram check_if_open.

## Non-examined assessment – the project

The non-examined assessment component is worth 20 per cent of your GCSE Computer Science qualification. It is a project set by Edexcel that involves analysing a problem and then developing a computer program in a high-level language to solve it. You will have 20 hours to work on the project in the final year of your course.

You must complete the project under controlled conditions. This means that you are not allowed to seek help from anyone else and must only work on the project when supervised by your teacher. Use of the internet is not permitted. But you are allowed access to a clean copy of the pseudo-code booklet, a syntax guide for the programming language you are using and a flowchart stencil.

There are four stages to the project: analysis, design, implementation, and testing, refining and evaluation.

At the end of the project you must submit the program you have written, along with a report showing the development process and including an evaluation.

Your work will be assessed by your teacher and moderated by Edexcel.

## Sample project with comments

Here is a sample project that will give you an idea of what to expect.

## How well are we doing?

A train company runs rail services between Buxton and Manchester. It collects data about each of the services it runs. The starting point, day and departure time of each service, along with the number of passengers carried and the delay (in minutes) are recorded and stored in a text file. All the data for a week for services starting from Buxton is stored in one text file. A second file holds the data for services starting from Manchester.

An extract from a file is shown below.

Services from Buxton – week beginning 30 November 2015

| Day | Time | Passengers | Delay (mins) |
|-----|------|------------|--------------|
| Monday | 05.59 | 150 | 0 |
| Monday | 06.18 | 350 | 0 |
| Monday | 06.48 | 525 | 2 |
| Monday | 07.19 | 814 | 0 |
| Monday | 07.44 | 902 | 4 |
| Monday | 08.21 | 870 | 5 |
| Monday | 09.21 | 522 | 11 |
| Tuesday | 05.59 | 158 | 1 |
| Tuesday | 06.18 | 409 | 0 |
| Tuesday | 06.48 | 590 | 0 |
| Tuesday | 07.19 | 832 | 2 |

Train company managers want to use the data that is collected each week to find out the average number of passengers per day, the average service delay time and the average number of passengers travelling on a particular service, e.g. the 06.48 train.

Your task is to analyse this problem and design, implement, test and evaluate a solution.

## Stage 1 Analysis (6 marks)

### Requirements

**Exam tip**

Begin by summarising the problem and listing each of the requirements.

The program must:

- Ask the user which data file they want to use, i.e. which week and which station starting point.
- Read in the service data from a text file.
- Offer users a menu of options to choose from.
- Calculate and output the average number of passengers per day.
- Calculate and output the average service delay.
- Calculate and output the average number of passengers for a particular service.

### Sub-problems

Decompose the problem into a set of sub-problems. Briefly describe each sub-problem. Write a short explanation of why you have decomposed the problem in this way.

I have decomposed the problem into a set of sub-problems that cover all of the specified requirements.

**Data import:** The data from the text file must be read in and stored in an appropriate data structure. In the course of a year 104 text files will be created. The user will need to specify which one they want to use. Currently there is no requirement to compare data for different weeks.

**Menu:** The program must provide the user with three menu choices –

(1) calculate daily average passenger numbers,

(2) calculate average delay, and

(3) calculate average passenger numbers for a specified service.

It must also give the user the option of exiting the program. User input must be validated so that inappropriate data entry does not cause the program to crash.

**Average number of passengers:** The program must compute the average number of passengers per day. To do this it needs to calculate the number of passengers who travelled each day and divide by the number of services on that day. The results should be displayed as a table with two columns – Day and Average number of passengers.

**Average delay:** The program must calculate the average service delay. To do this it needs to compute the total amount of time taken up by delays in a given week and divide by the total number of services in that week.

**Service average:** The program must prompt the user to select a particular service and compute the average number of passengers who travelled on that service in the given week.

Each of the three menu options requires an average to be calculated. I plan to write a subprogram that returns the average of a set of values that is passed to it. This will avoid code duplication and maximise the efficiency of the solution.

I have broken the problem down in this way so that each sub-problem focuses on a specific requirement. For example, the sub-problem 'Average number of passengers' deals with the requirement to calculate and display the average number of passengers per day.

When I move on to design my solution I will write a subprogram to solve each sub-problem.

# Stage 2 Design (18 marks)

## The algorithm (12 marks)

Now it is time to design your solution. You can use pseudo-code or a flowchart or a combination of both to express your algorithm.

Aim to design a subprogram to solve each of the sub-problems you identified in the analysis stage. Make sure you show how the subprograms link together.

Study the data in the text file carefully and devise a suitable data structure to accommodate it.

Don't forget to select meaningful identifier names for variables, data structures and subprograms.

Here is part of the algorithm for the service analysis program.

```
READ service_data151130.txt Records

PROCEDURE Menu()
BEGIN PROCEDURE
    SEND 'Please select one of the following options:' TO DISPLAY
    SEND '1: Calculate average number of passengers' TO DISPLAY
    SEND '2: Calculate average delay:' TO DISPLAY
    SEND '3: Calculate the total number of passenger within a time period:' TO
    DISPLAY
    SEND '4: Exit'
    RECEIVE Choice FROM (Integer) KEYBOARD
    IF Choice >= 1 AND Choice <=4 THEN
        IF Choice = 1 THEN
            avgPassengers()
        END IF
        IF Choice = 2 THEN
            avgDelay()
        END IF
        IF Choice = 3 THEN
            avgService()
        END IF
        IF Choice = 4 THEN
            exitProgram
    ELSE
        SEND "Please select a valid option" TO DISPLAY
        Menu()
    END IF
END PROCEDURE
...
```

### Activity 1  ?

Complete the design for the service analysis program.

## Test strategy and initial test plan (6 marks)

As part of the design stage you must devise a strategy for testing your finished program. Your aim is to ensure that the program works and meets all the requirements.

### Exam tip

Don't fall into the trap of only testing that your program works when valid data is entered. You should use normal, boundary and erroneous test data to ensure that your program runs correctly in all circumstances. Don't forget you'll need to test that the subprograms interact as intended.

Try to make your test plan as comprehensive as possible. It might help to 'walk through' your solution mentally, jotting down anything that needs testing as you go along. Pose 'what if' questions as key points.

It's not sufficient to have a strategy in your head. You need to summarise what your tactics are and explain why you think this approach will work.

Here is a partially completed test plan.

| Test no | Purpose of the test | Test data | Expected result | Actual Result | Action needed/ comments |
|---|---|---|---|---|---|
| 1 | To ensure that only valid menu choices are accepted | 1 | avgPassengers subprogram called | | |
| | | 2 | avgDelay subprogram called | | |
| | | 3 | avgService subprogram called | | |
| | | 4 | exitProgram subprogram called | | |
| | | 0, 'a', 99 | Invalid choice message displayed and user asked to re-enter their choice | | |
| 2 | To ensure that the average number of passengers per day is correctly calculated | The test file service_data151130. txt | | | |
| ... | ... | ... | ... | ... | ... |

### Activity 2 ?

Copy and complete the test plan. Ensure the tests cover all aspects of the planned program.

## Stage 3 Implementation (24 marks)

If you've made a good job of the design, implementation should be easy.

### Activity 3 ?

Implement the solution you designed in the high-level programming language you are studying. Add comments to your program so that it's easy for other people to understand how it works.

### Exam tip

Your aim is to produce a fully functioning, error-free solution that addresses all the requirements of the problem. Your program should be fully decomposed into subprograms and the code should be clear and easy to understand.

## Stage 4 Testing, refining and evaluation (12 marks)

Time to put your test strategy into action and run the tests. Don't be afraid to add extra rows to the table if you think of other tests you need to do.

### Activity 4 ?

Carry out your planned test strategy, filling in the remaining columns of the test plan as you do so.

The final step is to evaluate your solution against each of the requirements that you identified in the analysis stage of the project.

### Exam tip

Make testing an integral part of the development process and don't leave it to the end. It's important to log any tests, outcomes and fixes that you carry out.

If you come across any errors whilst testing remember to test again once you've finished correcting them, just to make sure that you haven't introduced any new ones.

For full marks it's not enough simply to carry out the tests, you need to record the outcome in your test plan.

If you do identify any errors you must show that you corrected the program to overcome them.

### Activity 5 ?

Write an evaluation of your solution. Critically assess how successfully it meets the specified requirements.

### Exam tip

Write a critical evaluation of how the program code meets the requirements of the task, rather than just a commentary.

### The report

You will need to gather evidence of the work you have done during the project and submit it as a report. This is what should be included.

| Stage 1 – Analysis | • A brief summary of the problem<br>• A list of the requirements of the problem<br>• A list of the sub-problems you have identified, together with a brief description of each one<br>• A short explanation of your rationale for breaking down the problem in the way you have |
|---|---|
| Stage 2 – Design | • Your algorithms<br>• A brief description of your test strategy<br>• Your initial test plan with the first four columns filled in |
| Stage 3 – Implementation | • A copy of your program code<br>• A couple of screenshots showing debugging in action |
| Stage 4 – Testing, refining and evaluation | • The completed test plan with all six columns filled in and extra lines added if required<br>• The evaluation of your program |

# Glossary

**Abstraction**: the process of removing or hiding unnecessary detail so that only the important points remain.

**Access control**: this determines which users have access to which data, and what they are allowed to do with it.

**Algorithm**: a precise method for solving a problem. It consists of a sequence of step-by-step instructions.

**Analogue**: using signals or information represented by a quantity (e.g. an electric voltage or current) that is continuously variable. Changes in the information being represented are indicated by changes in voltage.

This method requires very accurate sending and receiving mechanisms.

**Application software**: software that performs a task that would otherwise be done by hand, perhaps with pen and paper.

**Arithmetic/logic unit (ALU)**: the part of the CPU that performs calculations and logic operations.

**Arithmetic operator**: an operator that performs a calculation on two numbers.

**Arithmetic shift**: used for signed binary numbers. When performing a right shift the bits at the left are replaced by copies of the most significant bit.

**Array**: an organised collection of related values that share a single identifier.

**Ascending order**: this is arranging items from smallest to largest (e.g. 1, 2, 3, 4, 5, 6 or a, b, c, d, e, f).

**Assembly language**: a low-level language written using mnemonics.

**Assignment statement**: the SET…TO command is used to initialise variables in pseudo-code, for example:

```
SET anotherGo TO 0
SET correct TO False
```

**Attribute**: an item of data stored about an entity.

**Audit trail**: a record of activities that have taken place on a computer system. This record is generated automatically and will record what has happened and who or what made the change.

**Authentication**: the process of proving to a computer system who you are (e.g. using a username and password).

**Back-up**: a copy of files in another location so that they are still available if the original copy is damaged or lost. Backing up is the process of making a back-up copy.

**Bandwidth**: the amount of data that can be carried on a network in a given period of time.

**Binary**: information represented by only two values (e.g. a voltage or no voltage, on or off).

There are no communication errors or misunderstandings because there are no small differences.

**Binary digit or bit**: the smallest unit of data that is represented in a computer. It has a single binary value, either 1 or 0.

**Binary prefix**: multiplies a unit by powers of 2.

**Binary shift**: an operation done on all the bits of a binary value in which they are moved by a specific number of places to either the left or right.

**Bit depth**: the number of bits used to encode the information from each sample. Increasing the number of bits used increases the amount of detail contained in each sample.

**Boolean**: something that can take only the values True or False; named after English mathematician George Boole.

**Brute force**: an algorithm design that does not include any techniques to improve performance, but instead relies on sheer computing power to try all possibilities until the solution to a problem is found.

**Built-in functions**: functions that are provided in most high-level programming languages to perform common tasks.

**Bus**: a group of connections between devices in a computer.

**Bus width**: the number of wires that make up a bus – this determines the range of binary numbers that can be transmitted.

**Byte**: the basic combination of bits used to represent an item of information. A byte typically consists of 8 bits.

**Cache**: memory used to make up for the difference in speed between two internal components.

**Carbon footprint**: the amount of carbon dioxide an individual or organisation produces as a result of the energy they consume.

**Central processing unit (CPU)**: hardware device that carries out the processing in a computer.

**Character set**: the defined list of characters recognised by a computer's hardware and software.

**Checksum**: an error detection technique. A mathematical formula is applied to the data and the resulting numerical value is transmitted with the data. The recipient computer applies the same formula to the received data and then compares the checksum sent with the data to the calculated checksum. If the checksums don't match the data is likely to have been corrupted and the recipient computer requests the data again.

**Client–server network**: a network that has at least one server to provide services to the client computers.

**Clock**: an electronic device inside a CPU that 'ticks' at regular intervals and is used to synchronise the actions of the other parts of the CPU.

**Cloud storage**: secondary storage, often belonging to a third party, that is accessed via a network, usually the internet, and so is not in the same physical place as the machine's RAM/ROM. Files stored 'in the cloud' can be accessed from anywhere via an internet connection.

**Code vulnerability**: a computer program (the code) that has been written in such a way that it creates a security issue that may be taken advantage of to gain access to the computer system or data within it.

**Colour depth**: the number of bits used to encode the colour of each pixel.

**Communication media**: the means by which data is transmitted between devices on a network. Coaxial cable, fibre-optic cable and microwaves are all forms of communication media.

**Compiler**: a translator that converts high-level language source code into object code, often machine code. The source code is translated all at once and saved to be executed later.

**Compound key**: a key that consists of two or more fields used to identify a record uniquely.

**Compression**: changing the format of a data file so that the size of the file becomes smaller.

**Computational thinking**: the thought processes involved in formulating problems and their solutions so that the solutions are represented in a form that can be effectively carried out by a computer.

**Computing technology**: an all-encompassing term referring to the hardware, software and infrastructure that underpin current and emerging computer systems.

**Concatenation**: the linking together of two or more items of information.

**Concurrent**: processes that run apparently at the same time are described as being concurrent.

**Constant**: a 'container' that holds a value that never changes. Like variables, constants have unique identifiers.

**Construct**: a component from which something is built. Letters and numbers (i.e. a to z and 0 to 9) are the constructs we use to build our language and convey meaning. Bricks and cement are the basic constructs of a building.

**Control unit**: the part of the CPU that organises the actions of the other parts of the CPU.

**Creative Commons**: an organisation that allows people to set copyright terms for their intellectual property. One use of a Creative Commons licence is to allow people to copy material as long as it is not used commercially.

**Cyberattack**: any kind of malicious attack on a network-connected device.

**Data structure**: an organised collection of related elements. Arrays and records are two common data structures used in programming.

**Data type**: specifies what kind of data it can hold. Common data types are integer, real, Boolean and character. The data type of a value determines the operations that can be performed upon it.

**Database**: an organised store of data.

**Decimal prefix**: multiplies a unit by powers of 10.

**Decomposition**: breaking a problem down into smaller, more manageable parts, which are then easier to solve.

**Definite iteration**: this is used when the number of iterations, or turns of the loop, is known in advance. It can be set to as many turns as you want. This sort of loop is said to be count controlled.

**Defragmenter**: a utility that moves file clusters on a disk so they are closer to each other in order to speed up disk access.

**Denial of service (DoS)**: an attack on a network that attempts to prevent legitimate users from accessing its services.

**Descending order**: this is arranging items from largest to smallest (e.g. 6, 5, 4, 3, 2, 1 or f, e, d, c, b, a).

# Glossary

**Digital**: information represented by certain fixed values (e.g. high, medium or low). Any signal between these values would be meaningless and not used.

Sending and receiving mechanisms do not have to be as accurate as for analogue communication.

**Digital divide**: the gap between people who are technology-empowered and those who are technology-excluded.

**Digital inclusion**: ensuring that everyone has affordable access to computing technology and the necessary skills to take advantage of it.

**Divide and conquer**: an algorithm design that works by dividing a problem into smaller and smaller sub-problems, until they are easy to solve. The solutions to these are then combined to give a solution to the complete problem.

**e-waste**: any form of discarded electronic equipment, including computing technology.

**Eavesdrop**: having unauthorised sight of data being sent from one computer to another over a network.

**Encryption**: the process of encoding a message into a form that only the intended recipient can decode, or decrypt, and read. The message is encoded using an agreed method or algorithm. This is called the key. The encrypted message is called a cipher.

**Entity**: something that is recognised as being capable of an independent existence, is uniquely identified and about which data is stored.

It is usually a physical object (e.g. a car, a person or a book), but it can be a concept (e.g. a customer transaction where details of the items that were purchased are stored).

**Ethics**: a set of moral principles that govern a person's behaviour.

**Execution**: the process by which a computer carries out the instructions of a computer program.

**Fetch-decode-execute cycle**: sequence of steps carried out repeatedly by a CPU.

**Field**: an individual element in a record.

**File**: all of the records in a table or a group of linked tables.

**Firewall**: a utility that controls program access to the network, both incoming and outgoing.

**Flowchart**: a graphical representation of an algorithm. Each step in the algorithm is represented by a symbol. Symbols are linked together with arrows showing the order in which steps are executed.

**Foreign key**: a field in one table that uniquely identifies records in another table (i.e. it is a primary key in another table).

**Function**: a function is a subprogram that performs a specific task and can be used at any point in the program. High-level programming languages have a number of useful built-in functions. You can also create your own or use functions available in online libraries.

**Global variable**: a variable that can be accessed from anywhere in the program, including inside subprograms.

**Hacking**: the act of gaining unauthorised access to a computer system and the data it contains.

**Heuristic**: a type of algorithm capable of finding a solution to a problem quickly and easily, by using a combination of trial and error and educated guesswork to cut corners and eliminate less likely alternatives.

**Hexadecimal**: a base-16 number system. There are 16 digits and the place values increase in powers of 16.

**High-level programming language**: a programming language that resembles natural human language.

**HyperText Markup Language (HTML)**: essentially a text document that contains any text to be displayed along with:

- details of how the text should be formatted (e.g. font size, colour etc.);
- details of any hyperlinks and where they link to using a URL;
- details of any objects such as pictures or videos that should be shown within the web page when it is displayed.

**Identifier**: a unique name given to a variable or a constant. Using descriptive names for variables makes code much easier to read.

**Identity theft**: the stealing of another person's personal details, such as their bank account number, sort code or passport number, for the purpose of making purchases and running up debts in their name.

**IF…THEN…ELSE statement**: the IF…THEN…ELSE statement allows a choice to be made between two alternatives based on whether or not a condition is met (e.g. IF it is cold THEN wear a jumper ELSE wear a T-shirt).

**Indefinite iteration**: this is used when the number of iterations is not known before the loop is started. The iterations stop when a specified condition is met. This sort of loop is said to be condition controlled.

**Infinite loop**: a loop that is never-ending since the condition required to terminate the loop is never reached.

**Initialisation**: the process of assigning an initial value to a variable.

**Input**: to enter data into a computer.

**Instruction set**: the list of all possible commands a particular CPU knows how to carry out.

**Integer**: a whole number (e.g. 3, 6, 9).

**Integrated Development Environment (IDE)**: a package that helps programmers to develop program code. It has a number of useful tools, including a source code editor and a debugger. One of the most useful features of an IDE is the debugger. One of its tasks is to flag up syntax errors in the code and issue helpful error messages.

**Intellectual property (IP)**: a creation of the human mind that is unique and has a commercial value.

**Internet**: a worldwide system of interconnected networks that enables information to be exchanged and shared.

**Internet Service Provider (ISP)**: an organisation that provides its customers with a connection to the internet.

**Interpreter**: a translator that converts high-level language source code into object code, often machine code. The source code is translated and executed one line at a time.

**Iteration**: a construct that means the repetition of a process. An action is repeated until there is a desired outcome or a condition is met. It is often referred to as a loop.

**Local area network (LAN)**: a network that covers a relatively small geographical area, often a single site.

**Local variable**: a variable that is accessed only from within the subprogram in which it is created.

**Location-based services**: services that enable people to access and share real-time location information online.

**Logic circuit**: an electronic circuit that has inputs and outputs that follow one of the Boolean operators.

**Logic error**: an error in an algorithm that results in incorrect or unexpected behaviour.

**Logical operator**: a Boolean operator using AND, OR and NOT.

**Lossless compression**: compressing a file in such a way that it can be decompressed without any loss of data.

**Lossy compression**: compression where some of the data is removed; the original file cannot be restored when the lossy file is decompressed.

**Low-level programming language**: a programming language that is closely related to the CPU's machine code.

**Machine code**: the binary codes representing each of the instructions in the instruction set.

**Magnetic storage**: secondary storage that works by magnetising parts of a substance as north and south poles to represent binary 1s and 0s.

**Main memory/random-access memory (ROM)**: a temporary store for data and instructions (programs).

**Malware**: short for 'malicious software'. It is used as a generic term for any kind of software that is designed to disrupt the use of a computer system.

**Median**: the middle number when the numbers are put in ascending or descending order (e.g. if there are 13 numbers, then the 7th number is the median). If there are an even number of items in an ascending list, choose the item to the right of the middle (e.g. if there are 10 numbers, then choose the 6th as the median).

**Memory address**: a number that uniquely identifies a (memory) storage location.

**Mnemonic**: a short, simple, acronym that represents each of the instructions in a CPU's instruction set, e.g. LDR (load register), STR (store) and CMP (compare).

**Modular testing**: testing each block of code as it is completed to ensure the code works as expected.

**Monte Carlo methods**: carrying out a statistical analysis of a number of random samples in order to obtain approximate solutions to a problem. The larger the number of samples used, the more accurate the result is likely to be.

**Most significant bit (MSB)**: the bit with the highest value in a multiple-bit binary number.

# Glossary

**Nested IF statement**: a nested IF statement consists of one or more IF statements placed inside each other. A nested IF is used where there are more than two possible courses of action.

**Nested loop**: a loop that runs inside another loop. The inner one executes all of its instructions for each turn of the outer loop.

**Network**: an arrangement of computers and other devices connected together to share resources and data.

**Network security**: activities designed to protect a network and its data from threats such as viruses, hacker attacks, denial of service attacks, data interception and theft, and equipment failure.

**Network topology**: describes how the devices on a network are connected together.

**Neural networks**: processing information in a similar way to human brains and learning and adapting over time. This makes them useful tools for solving pattern recognition problems, such as facial recognition, medical diagnosis and quality control, which computers are normally not very good at.

**Non-volatile**: memory that is not lost when the power is turned off.

**Object code**: the translated source code. Often this will be machine code, but might also be an intermediate code, which has to be further translated before it can be executed.

**Open-source software**: software that is free to obtain, edit and redistribute.

**Operating system**: software designed for particular hardware and which manages other programs' access to the hardware.

**Operator precedence**: the order in which you apply the operators (including logical operators) in a mathematical equation.

**Optical storage**: secondary storage that works using differences in light reflection from a material.

**Output**: to display or output data that has been processed (or has been stored).

**Packet**: a small quantity of data being sent through a network. The packet is labelled with the sender's address (source), the recipient's address (destination), how many packets are being transmitted and the position of this packet in the complete message.

**Paging**: the algorithm the OS uses to move programs from RAM to disk and back again when needed once main memory is full.

**Parameters**: values that are passed into a subprogram when it is called.

**Patent**: an exclusive right granted to an inventor to make, use and sell an invention for a fixed period of time.

**Peer-to-peer network**: a network that doesn't have any centralised servers. Each computer in the network can act as client and server.

**Personal data**: information that is personal and unique to an individual.

**Phishing**: attempting to get confidential information by sending a user a message that appears to come from a trustworthy person or organisation.

**Physical security**: controlling access to critical parts of a network using physical methods (such as locked doors) rather than software.

**Pixel**: short for 'picture element', the smallest single point of colour in a graphic image.

**Primary key**: a unique identifier for each record in the table. It is usually a field that is guaranteed to hold unique information for each record.

**Privacy**: the right to be left alone and free from unwanted scrutiny and intrusion.

**Procedure**: a subprogram containing a set of statements that are executed when the procedure is called. Unlike a function, a procedure does not return a value to the main program.

**Process**: to change the meaning or format of some data.

**Professionalism**: the skill and competence expected of a person in a professional setting.

**Proprietary software**: software that belongs to an individual or a company. Its licence specifies that users are not allowed to modify the source code and places restrictions on its use.

**Protocol**: a set of rules that govern how communications on a network should be formatted and what data they should include.

**Pseudo-code**: a structured, code-like language that can be used to describe an algorithm.

**Random number**: a number within a given range of numbers that is generated in such a way that each number in the range has an equal chance of occurring.

There are many devices for generating random numbers. A die is used in games to get a random number from 1 to 6. Computer programming languages have a function for generating random numbers across variable ranges. In the Edexcel pseudo-code there is a useful built-in RANDOM command.

```
RANDOM(upperLimit)
```

For example, number = RANDOM(6) would generate a random number from the numbers 1 to 6.

**Read-only memory (ROM)**: memory that cannot be altered and is not lost when the power is turned off.

**Reading**: when the CPU retrieves the data stored at a given address.

**Record**: a data structure that stores a set of related values of different data types.

**Recursion**: a process that is repeated. For example, a document can be checked and edited, checked and edited and so on until it is perfect.

**Register**: a storage location inside the CPU used to hold an instruction, an address or other single item of data.

**Relational database**: a database that allows data elements in one table to be related to any piece of data in another table as long as both tables contain a common element.

**Relational operator**: an operator that compares two values.

**Resolution**: the number of pixels per inch when the image is displayed (for example, on a monitor or on paper).

**Router**: a piece of networking hardware used to forward packets of data from one network to another.

**Runtime error**: an error that occurs while the program is running – the operation the computer is asked to do is impossible to execute.

**Sampling**: taking measurements of the sound wave at regular but distinct intervals of time (e.g. 44,100 samples per second).

**Scheduling**: the algorithm that the OS uses to allow each running process to use the CPU.

**Scope**: the region of code within which a variable is visible.

**Secondary storage**: any kind of permanent storage to which the contents of ROM/RAM are copied (usually a hard disk, optical or solid-state device).

**Selection**: a construct that allows a choice to be made between different alternatives.

**Sequence**: an ordered set of instructions.

**Shoulder surfing**: gaining access to information by watching someone enter it into a computer system.

**Simulation**: a representation of a real-world process or system.

**Social engineering**: any kind of attack on a computer system or network that exploits how people behave and respond to certain situations.

**Software**: the set of programs run by a computer system.

**Solid-state storage**: secondary storage that works by storing charge (electrons).

**Source code**: the text of the program that a programmer writes.

**Spyware**: software, possibly a virus, that is designed to be installed secretly on a computer and record private information as the user enters it.

**String**: a sequence of characters. They can be letters, numbers, symbols, punctuation marks or spaces.

**String traversal**: using a loop to cycle through each character in a string.

**Subprogram**: a self-contained module of code that performs a specific task. It can be 'called' by the main program when it is needed.

**Surveillance technology**: CCTV, drones, number plate recognition, bugging and tracking devices used to monitor and record people's activities, often without their knowledge.

**Syntax error**: an error that occurs when a rule of the programming language is broken.

**Table**: a collection of cells organised in rows and columns used to store data in a structured and organised manner.

**Text file**: a sequence of lines, each of which consists of a sequence of characters.

**Trace table**: a technique used to identify any logic errors in algorithms. Each column represents a variable or output and each row a value of that variable.

# Glossary

**Translator**: a program that converts source code into machine code.

**Traversal**: travel across or through something. An array can be traversed by moving from the first to the last element in order to examine the data stored at each index position.

**Truth table**: a table showing all possible combinations of the inputs and outputs of an operator.

**Two-dimensional array**: a matrix of rows and columns resembling a table. Two indices are used, one to reference the rows and the other the columns. All the elements of a two-dimensional array share the same data type.

**Type coercion**: the process of converting the value stored in a variable from one data type to another.

**Unambiguous**: this means that the instructions cannot be misunderstood. Simply saying 'turn' would be ambiguous because you could turn left or right. All instructions given to a computer must be unambiguous or it won't know what to do.

**Unpatched software**: software that hasn't had the latest security updates applied to it, making it vulnerable to attack.

**USB**: Universal Serial Bus sockets found on most modern computer systems.

**User interface**: the way the user interacts with the operating system

**Utility software**: software that does a useful job for the user that is not essential to the operating system and not the reason for using a computer in the first place.

**Validation**: to check that the data entered by a user or from a file meets specified requirements.

**Variable**: a 'container' used to store data. The data stored in a variable is referred to as a value. The value stored in a variable is not fixed. The same variable can store different values during the course of a program and each time a program is run.

**Virtualisation**: any process that hides the true physical nature of a computing resource, making it look different, usually to simplify the way it is accessed.

**Virus**: software that is designed to make and distribute copies of itself, usually for a malicious purpose.

**Volatile**: memory that is erased when the power is turned off.

**von Neumann architecture**: computer system design in which the program is stored in memory with the data.

**Web server**: powerful computer systems that store web pages and any multimedia that the pages might contain.

**'What if?' question**: running a computer model with a given set of inputs to see what the model produces as an output or prediction.

**Whistle-blower**: someone who draws attention to the activities of an organisation or person believed to be acting illegally or unethically.

**Wide area network (WAN)**: a network that covers a large geographical area. It connects together two or more LANs and is usually under collective ownership. The largest wide area network is the internet.

**Wireless local area network (WLAN)**: a local area network in which connected devices use high frequency radio waves to communicate.

**Writing**: when the CPU sends data to memory to be stored at a given address.

# Index

Page numbers in **bold** indicate where definitions of key terms can be found

# Index

# Index

# Index